KEYNESIAN ECONOMICS

KEYNESIAN ECONOMICS

By

MABEL F. TIMLIN

Associate Professor of Economics
The University of Saskatchewan

THE UNIVERSITY OF TORONTO PRESS
TORONTO, CANADA
1948

University of Toronto Press
London: Geoffrey Cumberlege
Oxford University Press
Printed in Canada

First printed, 1942
Reprinted, 1948
Reprinted in 2018

SCHOLARLY REPRINT SERIES
ISBN 0-8020-7044-2
ISBN 978-1-4875-7340-9 (paper)
LC A43-2023

PREFACE

THIS book is based upon the analysis of the *General Theory of Employment, Interest and Money*. In the three years since actual writing was begun, certain differences between the analysis presented here and the analysis of the *General Theory* have developed. In the technical apparatus of this study, the long-term rate of interest, typically used as "the" rate for Keynesian analysis, has been abandoned in favour of the short-term rate, interpreted as a margin of substitution binding many markets together; the internal structure of the interest-rate complex has taken on practically equal importance with the average level of interest-rates; and the "liquidity-preference" theory of the rate of interest, so important in the *General Theory*, is represented as only one aspect of the determination of rates. Because under the methods used it is possible to connect the operations of the individual firms of an economic society straightway to the margins of substitution of the system, Mr. Keynes' Aggregate Functions have been omitted.

The book developed from a doctoral dissertation written at Seattle, Washington, during the year 1939-40 and accepted in July, 1940, by the University of Washington. During the two years since that time the study has been shortened by the excision of practically all institutional material; the whole has been rewritten, some sections many times; and new material has been introduced. Chapters III and XIV are, for example, completely new; Chapter XIII consists almost altogether of new material; and Chapter VI has been considerably extended. The long general bibliography of the original has been omitted with the expectation that the numerous bibliographical foot-notes, related to specific subjects, will prove more useful.

I am indebted to the staff in Economics of the University of Washington for the training in advanced economics which made this study possible. In the preparation of the dissertation my greatest obligation was to Professor R. F. Mikesell. Dean H. H. Preston and Professor Joseph Demmery also gave valuable advice and encouragement. A number of other favours, too numerous to be detailed here, were conferred on me by Dean Preston and the University of Washington during my sojourn in Seattle.

The 1940 draft was read by Dr. Oscar Lange of the University of Chicago and by Professor A. F. W. Plumptre of the University of Toronto, and a number of suggestions made by them have had influence upon the revision. I have also to thank them and Dr. Mikesell for their kindness in reading and criticizing Chapter III in its final stages, and Dr. Lange and Dr. Mikesell for similar services with respect to Chapter VI.

The final draft has been written mainly at the University of Toronto during the spring and summer of 1942. Professor H. A. Innis extended the hospitality of the University of Toronto during that period, and in the previous summer. Professor V. W. Bladen kindly assisted in making the business arrangements for publication and gave useful editorial advice. Professor H. S. M. Coxeter of the Department of Mathematics of the University of Toronto redrew my charts and his fine draughtsmanship has added greatly to the appearance of the book. He also made suggestions for the clarification of figures and sections of the text in Chapters VIII and IX. My colleague, Dr. J.-O. Clerc of the University of Saskatchewan, and Miss E. M. Rosengren of the University of Toronto assisted in the reading of proof. Mrs. Hewitt and her staff in the Editorial Department of the University of Toronto Press gave valuable assistance in seeing the manuscript through the Press; the compositors of the Press by careful workmanship lightened the work of proof-reading and have beautified the finished book. To all of these I am greatly indebted.

The book contains extended quotations from *The General Theory of Employment, Interest and Money* (Macmillan and Company, Ltd.), Professor Hicks' *Value and Capital* (Oxford University Press), Professor Ohlin's article, "Some Notes on the Stockholm Theory of Savings and Investment," published in the *Economic Journal*, and Mr. Lerner's note on "Savings and Investment: Definitions, Assumptions, Objectives," from the *Quarterly Journal of Economics*. Permission to make these quotations has been received from the respective publishers and editors and is hereby acknowledged.

I must also express my gratitude to the members of the Canadian Social Science Research Council for the generous assistance by which publication of the book was made possible, and to President J. S. Thomson, Dr. W. W. Swanson, and the Board of Governors of the University of Saskatchewan for the conditions under which leaves of absence were freely granted.

Those who are familiar with the field of monetary theory will have no difficulty in seeing, in addition to the influence of Lord

Keynes, how strong have been the influences upon my thought of Dr. Oscar Lange, Professor J. R. Hicks, Mr. A. P. Lerner, Dr. P. N. Rosenstein-Rodan, Professor D. H. Robertson, and Professor Bertil Ohlin. The faults of analysis and exposition are all mine. The light is all theirs.

MABEL F. TIMLIN

The University of Saskatchewan,
October, 1942.

PREFACE TO SECOND PRINTING

THIS book is being reprinted with only minor corrections. Had more extensive changes been possible, I should have undertaken some rewriting, in particular of Chapters IX and XIII. However, since under present conditions a complete revision was not feasible, the publishers and I felt that, in view of continuing demand for the book, this reprint should not be postponed.

An error in logic, called to my attention by Professor Carl Shoup, has been corrected on page 23. On page 112, I have made certain alterations to allow for the possibility that the propensity to consume may be a linear function. Minor changes have been made on pages 49, 80, 123, 126, 139, and 144.

M. F. T.

CONTENTS

CHAPTER I

INTRODUCTION

IT is the intention in this study to explore the system of economic analysis set out in its original form in Mr. John Maynard Keynes' *The General Theory of Employment, Interest and Money*[1] in order to consider first its internal consistency and second its application to the world we know. No attempt will be made to restate Mr. Keynes' own analysis directly. Mrs. Robinson[2] and Mr. Lerner[3] have already done this. It is expected rather to synthesize with the work as it stands in Mr. Keynes' own publications such ideas of other authors as appear relevant to the content of the system and useful in making its properties apparent. Beyond this, since it appears to the writer that the system constitutes a vital expansion of the *corpus* of economic doctrine developed in Britain and elsewhere in the one hundred and sixty-six years since the publication of *The Wealth of Nations*, the right is expressly reserved to expand and to qualify the analysis of the system in the directions and to the degrees which appear to be required by logic and by the statistical studies which have succeeded the presentation of the system in Mr. Keynes' *General Theory*.

In this chapter the specific analysis of the system is prefaced by a very general discussion of the place of Keynesian thought in the development of economic philosophy since the beginning of the Industrial Revolution.

The development of economic equilibrium theory followed the philosophical development of the eighteenth to the twentieth centuries. Newtonian concepts were succeeded by Darwinian, and Darwinian by Bergsonian. Under the first, an "invisible hand" had set a great mechanism into operation and man's part was to allow the machinery to function in accordance with the beneficent intention. A *laissez-faire* philosophy was conceived to agree with the purposes of God and the best interests of men. The Darwinian

[1]London, 1936.

[2]Joan Robinson, *Introduction to the Theory of Employment* (London, 1937).

[3]A. P. Lerner, "Mr. Keynes' *General Theory of Employment, Interest and Money*," *International Labour Review*, XXXIV (1936), pp. 435-54.

theory was less optimistic, but in its turn it justified the same conclusion by what appeared to be a more rational approach. If men restrained themselves from interference with the biological struggle for survival, the fit would survive the battle and progress would be inevitable. When the emerging social history of the nineteenth century made it very plain that all forms of competition were not beneficial and that monopolistic combination was quite as natural a form of human organization as the old realist, Adam Smith, had maintained it to be, the doctrine of individualism was modified by degrees into the paradox which Dr. Viner so aptly terms "compulsory individualism." It came to be thought that the business of men in the regulation of economic life was to maintain the conditions of the struggle for existence upon bases of fairness analogous to those of the playing field. In the minds of many of the older economists of Western countries the development of the organon of economic thought still rests at that stage.

Parallel with these developments came others. In every decade some persons clung, consciously or unconsciously, to the Christian ethic as the ideal for social as well as for individual morality. The growth of behaviourist psychology furnished an additional basis for the inclusion of altruism as a constructive rather than a destructive force in the evolution of economic society. With the Bergsonian idea of creative evolution, the consciousness of man became one of the variables through which the creative energies of the universe manifested themselves. Social forces no longer, in the absence of positive interventions, were conceived to carry economic society inevitably forward under the guidance either of an "invisible hand" or of a biological struggle, seemingly cruel but actually beneficent. As a corollary to this new idea, failure to define ends and to design means to achieve them might now under the new viewpoint mean regress instead of progress. It was now only by taking thought that man might create the world anew after the image of his desire.

It is not to be implied that the developments of economic philosophy swept with force along a single, noble stream. We may quite reasonably see the development fitting together as a dialectic process does. In this the forms taken by individualistic or liberal doctrines may be labelled as the *theses*, and doctrines which relegate the individual personality to a position of subservience to some sort of variously conceived over-soul—class, nation, or race—as *antitheses*, while attempts to reconcile the institutions guaranteeing freedom to the human personality with policies directed to achieving the general good may be called the *syntheses*.

The resemblance to the dialectic process persists. Among the economic philosophies of today the three types still appear in more fully developed forms. With the *theses* may be identified the ultra-liberalism of such economists as Dr. Hayek, Dr. von Mises, Professor Lionel Robbins, and many economists of the United States. The chief representatives of the *antitheses* are to be found in the order of their appearance in Russia, Italy, and Germany. In Russia, the metamorphosis of liberalism into its opposite passed through Marxism and Leninism into Stalinism. In Italy, the general equilibrium economics of Pareto had issue in the theory of the corporative state. In Germany, the philosophies of Carlyle, Nietzsche, and William Houston Chamberlain, and the economics of Knapp, Spann, and others have been merged through the "illumination" of Hitler into the central concepts of Nazism. The chief examples of *synthesis* are perhaps to be found in the economic philosophies on the one hand of the Stockholm School and on the other of Mr. Keynes.

It is not strange that one of these syntheses should have been achieved at Cambridge. The concept of welfare in economic theory has had a considerable history there. Nevertheless even there it remained a qualifying and conditioning element upon the theoretical structure rather than an integral part of it. Dr. Marshall qualified the principles of his value theory so carefully as to restrict valid applications of these to the value of an individual good, while Professor Pigou works in his economic-equilibrium theory almost entirely in "real" terms.[4] Even in a modern model of the "classical" system running in terms of money and presented as "typical" by Professor Hicks there is an assumption of an "unchanged money income" which would rule out the complications arising from changes in the level of money income which will be the chief matter for study in this analysis.[5]

But parallel though unintegrated there grew up another structural element for a theory of economics less static in its implications.

[4]Thus in *The Theory of Unemployment* (London, 1933), it is not until page 100 that the problem of "The Elasticity of Demand in Terms of Money for Labour as a Whole" is approached. In *The Economics of Stationary States* (London, 1935) less than ten pages are devoted to the subject of money.

[5]J. R. Hicks, "Mr. Keynes and the 'Classics': A Suggested Interpretation," *Econometrica*, V (1937), pp. 147-50. See also Gottfried von Haberler, *Prosperity and Depression* (1st ed., League of Nations, 1937), pp. 203-4, 204n., 253n., for another statement to the effect that in general equilibrium analysis static theory usually relies for its conclusions upon an assumption that MV remains constant.

The cash-balance theory of money, whose principal evolvers[6] were Dr. Marshall, Professor A. C. Pigou, Professor D. H. Robertson, and Mr. J. M. Keynes, gave a basis for the use of a triple margin of substitution in the choices of income-receivers rather than the double margin represented in "orthodox" equilibrium theory. The choice for the individual was no longer between consumption and investment, but between consumption, money-saving, and investment.

The consequences of this innovation in the theory of money for trade-cycle theory were quickly perceived; yet so solidly established was the concept of a self-equilibrating economic universe, the "automatic" repercussions of which tended toward a mathematically determined norm, that terms were borrowed from the vocabulary of religion to describe the attitude of economists toward this tenet of their philosophies. Those who subscribed to the dogma were "orthodox." Any man who challenged the doctrine could be almost as effectively damned before his fellow economists by being called a "heretic" as any dissenter from the dogmas of the medieval church could be. Whole generations could pass a large part of their working lives in states of chronic unemployment linked with downward trends of prices, and yet these trends could continue to be regarded as resulting from "frictions" in a self-equilibrating universe. Economic theory continued to be analysed into separate economic, monetary, and cyclic categories without attempt to bring these back into the synthesis required by logic. Judgments with respect to social policy continued to be made upon the basis of the findings of one body of theory or the other in accordance with whatever appeared to be the particular requirements of the case. No attempt was made for a long time to correlate the findings of the three fields so that inconsistencies might be removed and decisions made from the basis of a broader picture of reality.

Meanwhile on the Continent the problem of the establishment of the principles for the determination of value for the individual good received somewhat less attention, and the problems of the general equilibrium of the whole system received somewhat more, than at Cambridge. The Austrians worked out the conditions of equilibrium for the stationary state according to their own type of

[6]The principal developments by the four men named are as follows: Alfred Marshall, "Remedies for Fluctuations in General Prices," *Contemporary Review*, LI (1887), pp. 355-75; A. C. Pigou, "The Value of Money," *Quarterly Journal of Economics*, XXXII (1917-18), pp. 38-65; D. H. Robertson, *Banking Policy and the Price Level* (London, 1926); J. M. Keynes, *Monetary Reform* (New York, 1924).

reasoning. Walras and Pareto set up mathematical models of general systems and analysed the conditions necessary for equilibrium. These models were handled in terms of money but the theories remained static.[7] The dynamic problems were assumed away in the general systems even where they were recognized by the same writers in their works on applied economics. The conditions of the ideal equilibrium were set up, but in a world in which negative quantities cannot have an objective existence, human institutions were not examined to see whether or not they were in all cases compatible with the establishment of the ideal equilibrium. Nevertheless the use of systems of simultaneous equations to represent the general equilibrium contributed a great deal, since it gave a method of expression for the relations of the economic universe which escaped in an elegant manner the concept of linear causation almost inevitably inhering in attempts to handle the total situation in terms of language.

The first really important attempt to link the theory of economic equilibrium with the theory of the determination of the system of money prices under conditions of change came with Dr. Knut Wicksell's division of the rate of interest into the "natural" and the "money" rate.[8] The two rates were conceived to be indirectly connected through a link of money-prices for commodities, though this link was described as "elastic, just like the spiral springs often fitted between the body of a coach and its axle."[9] But the Wicksellian construction still depended upon a static concept of equilibrium[10] and the success of the union depended upon the possibility of isolating a "normal" element in entrepreneur returns. The difficulties involved in such a union became apparent when Mr. Keynes in his turn attempted to make it the basis of his construction in his *Treatise on Money*.[11]

The problem has been handled with more success by two alternative but consistent ways. The first of these lies in the methods of process analysis used by Professor D. H. Robertson and by Professor Ohlin and others of the Stockholm School. The second is the type of analysis undertaken by Mr. Keynes in the *General Theory*. Both

[7]C. Bresciani-Turroni, "The Theory of Saving," *Economica*, III n.s. (1936), pp. 3-6; P. N. Rosenstein-Rodan, "The Coördination of the General Theories of Money and Price," *Economica*, III n.s. (1936), pp. 269-78.

[8]*Lectures on Political Economy* (2 vols., New York, 1935). For definition and discussion of the natural and money rates, see II, pp. 185 ff.

[9]*Ibid.*, II, p. 206.

[10]Rosenstein-Rodan, "The Co-ordination of the General Theories," p. 276.

[11]Vols. I and II, New York, 1930.

have become the bases of attempts to direct and to evaluate policies of social control aimed at the combination of high levels of employment and output with maximum freedom for the individual personality under the hereditary institutions of liberalism. Hence we have called them *syntheses* in the dialectic parallel set out in the preceding pages.

The *General Theory* substitutes for Dr. Wicksell's division of the rate of interest into the "natural" and "money" rates a parallel division into the return *anticipated* by the entrepreneur upon his investments and the amount which must be *paid* to the lender to induce him to part with the possession of sums of money. On the basis of this division, the triple margin of the cash-balance theory is built into a mechanism which applies the method of equilibrium analysis to conditions where portions of the supplies of factors are unemployed as well as to conditions of full employment. Moreover it examines the ideal conditions of equilibrium with respect to their compatibility with the nature of human institutions.

It is not free of limitations upon its own account. In its pure form it is limited to temporary equilibrium conditions. It requires both expansions and adjustments before it can give us more than a very narrow view of the world in which we live. But because it lies nearer to this world than does the older model of orthodox analysis, it is well worth studying. As a beginning for that study we turn in the next chapter to a general outline of method.

CHAPTER II

THE CHARACTER OF THE KEYNESIAN SYSTEM AND ITS UNITS

THERE are three tasks to be accomplished in this chapter: in the first section, we shall describe the main outlines of the system and the general limitations upon the analysis; in the second, we shall define the units on which the system is based and, in connection with these definitions, we shall describe the general characteristics of the models with which we shall work; in the third section, we shall demonstrate the equality between the levels of saving and investment which will be a necessary corollary of the system if it is to have a unique solution.

(1) THE CHARACTER OF THE KEYNESIAN SYSTEM

The Outline of the System. The main development of the system of the shifting equilibrium which lies at the heart of Keynesian theory is based upon three sets of functions which may shift their positions between defined units of time. The set to be studied first in our analysis deals with the nature of the demand for money and its relation to the money rate of interest; in this the individual functions are called the Liquidity Functions. The second deals with the nature of the division of individual incomes between consumption and saving, and the functions are called the propensities to consume or, alternatively, the Multiplier Functions. The third set forms the basis of an analysis of the factors determining the rate of investment for a unit of time, and its individual functions are called the Investment Functions.[1]

The economic magnitudes of this highly simplified system will be the quantity of Money (M), the levels (or rates) of Consumption (C), Investment (I), Saving (S), and Income (Y), and the rate of interest (i). (What we mean by "the rate of interest" in this system is a matter which will be amplified at a later stage of the argument.) The Liquidity, Multiplier, and Investment Functions will be represented by the symbols L, ϕ, and F respectively. It will be our busi-

[1]See the *General Theory*, pp. 245-7, for the positions Mr. Keynes gives these functions in his general system.

ness in this study to define these symbols further, to show the relations of the magnitudes to each other, and to a more limited extent to analyse the relation of the system to the so-called orthodox theory of economics. Throughout the analysis there will be implications to be derived concerning the adequacy of social policies and in the final chapter an attempt will be made to bring these together so far as this may be done without detailed descriptions of specific institutional structures.

Because it will be necessary to take a great deal of time and care in the analysis of each set of functions forming a part of the system, it is desirable at this stage to give the skeleton structure of the development. The most important of the objects in setting it out at this stage is to make clear the interdependent character of its elements. We shall adopt as the basis of the explanation (with some minor changes) the set of simultaneous equations used by Dr. Oscar Lange to explain his own "general system."[2] The equations of this system are as follows:

$$i = L(M, Y) \quad (1)$$
$$C = \phi(Y, i) \quad (2)$$
$$I = F(i, C) \quad (3)$$
$$Y = I + C \quad (4)$$

Since we shall define investment and saving in such a way as to make these always equal to each other without time-lag, the final equation may be written alternatively, $Y = S + C$.

[2]Oscar Lange, "The Rate of Interest and the Optimum Propensity to Consume," *Economica*, V n.s. (1938), pp. 12-14. The above version differs from Dr. Lange's system in that in the first equation Dr. Lange's system reads $M = L(i, Y)$ and the fourth, $Y \equiv I + C$. The changes made above were suggested to me for mathematical reasons by Professor A. F. W. Plumptre. It is to be noticed that on page 245, *General Theory*, Mr. Keynes describes the rate of interest as one of the independent variables of the system. On page 246, however, he describes the rate of interest as *dependent* "partly on the state of liquidity-preference (i.e., on the liquidity function) and partly on the quantity of money measured in terms of wage-units." Equation (1) above conforms to this description. It is to be noted that Mr. Keynes' own formulation puts the quantity of money in the position of the dependent variable, just as Dr. Lange's does. See *General Theory*, p. 199.

In this study, the Keynes-Lange system is handled in a somewhat different way from that which Dr. Lange uses in the above article, since it is here related to a defined unit of time. Shapes and positions of the functions will also be studied in more detail.

With reference to Mr. Keynes' approval of Dr. Lange's "general system" as an analysis of his own, see "On Mr. Keynes and 'Finance' " (Comment on), *Economic Journal*, XLVIII (1938), p. 321n.

If we set these relations out in words, they would read somewhat as follows: per unit of time, the rate of interest depends upon the quantity of money and the level of income; the level of consumption depends upon the level of income and the rate of interest; the rate of investment depends upon the rate of interest and the level of consumption; and the level of income is equal to the sum of investment and consumption, or, alternatively, of saving and consumption. It follows that, as we set up the system, the rate of saving must also be equal to the rate of investment. At this stage, the latter statement is based upon an assumption with respect to the character of the system rather than a necessary consequence of its naturé, and we shall return to the definitions which make this equality logical at a later place.

The General Assumptions of the System. If we set out the characteristics of our system according to its mathematical nature, a given set of functional relationships for the functions L, ϕ, and F will hold for a given unit of time, whose assumptions will later be defined. The shapes of the functions will be the result of the whole psychological-institutional complex,[3] given by the supplies of the physical factors of production, by the character of existing institutions interpreted as including social habits and attitudes, and by the history of the system—and especially by the history of the very recent past. Between any two units of time, the existing set of relations may be modified in its character by changes in any of the functional relationships and in its results by a change in the effective quantity of money. If the time-unit is defined and the functions and the effective quantity of money are given, the solution of the system of equations for that time-unit will be determinate.

[3]Mr. Keynes himself tends to attach the term "psychological" to the three sets of functional relationships (see *General Theory*, pp. 246-7). Some persons have impugned Mr. Keynes' analysis because they interpret his use of the term "psychological" as implying a condition stable over time or only slowly modified. (Note this assumption in Mrs. E. W. Gilboy's article, "The Propensity to Consume," *Quarterly Journal of Economics*, LIII (1938-9), pp. 120-40, and Mr. Keynes' reply in a letter included by her in another note in the same volume, pp. 633ff.) In this study, the term "psychological-institutional complex" is used to describe the totality of the effects determining the shapes of these functions per unit of time in order that we may escape such imputations of meaning. Between units of time, changes in the shapes of the functions and in their positions will be imputed to changes in this complex. It is hoped also that the method used here of holding the functions stable for defined units of time and describing by degrees the effects of various forms of change will have the virtue of making meanings clearer.

Limitations Set on the Analysis. It has been stated in the preceding paragraphs that the Keynes-Lange system is determinate if "the effective quantity of money" is given. What we mean by the "effective" quantity of money can be plain only after we have defined the units of the system. We wish in this place, however, to enter the *caveat* that we shall not in this study undertake the analysis of the whole system of economic relations. The specific problems involved in the determination of specific prices (and hence of specific sectional price levels) will in general be ignored.[4] The institutional arrangements which serve to determine the elasticity of the supply of money are likewise ordinarily passed over. We omit these important areas in order to explore more thoroughly the partial system we have set out above. We shall make it determinate under the assumption that the effective quantity of money is given.

In the next section, we proceed to define the money-unit, the wage-unit, and the time-unit. In connection with the latter we shall explore the concept of temporary equilibrium and describe the models with which we shall work.

(2) THE UNITS AND MODELS OF THE SYSTEM

The Money-Unit. One unit for the measurement of our system will obviously be the money-unit, understood as the standard unit for the bank-deposit. Since we shall carry out this analysis fundamentally in terms of a closed system, there are no practical complications in the understanding of the meaning of this unit. But since the effects of current or anticipated changes in the quantity of money will constitute one of our chief problems for analysis, it is necessary to find a second unit of measurement which will have none of the characteristics of money. We shall adopt for this purpose the unit which Mr. Keynes has devised, namely the wage-unit.[5]

The Wage-Unit. For purposes of defining the wage-unit, an hour's employment of common labour is taken as basic and is called the labour-unit. The remuneration for the labour-unit is the wage-unit. Thus if common labour receives fifty cents an hour, fifty cents is the wage-unit. Other types of labour are reduced to a common denominator with common labour upon the bases of their relative remunerations. If plasterers are receiving three dollars an hour when the wage-unit is fifty cents, one hour of plasterer's labour is rated as six labour-units. A sum of three dollars will be equal to

[4]For the theory of price formation, see Book V of the *General Theory.*

[5]See *General Theory*, pp. 41-5.

six wage-units if we are measuring sums of money in wage-units on this basis.

The expectation will be that rises in wages will be relatively the same. If the wage of common labour rises to seventy-five cents an hour, it will be expected that plasterers will be earning four dollars and fifty cents an hour. If this happens, the wage-unit will be seventy-five cents, and four dollars and fifty cents will be equal to six wage-units as three dollars was before. If, in fact, the condition with respect to the stability of the relative remunerations is not fulfilled, this situation is to be regarded as "a rapid liability to change in the supply of labour and the shape of the aggregate supply function."[6]

A further qualification of the definition requires to be made. It is clearly understood that employers, so far as they can, will tend to employ the most able workmen first, and that the last labourers coming into employment at the same rate of pay are likely to differ in efficiency from the earlier ones, who secure more stable employment as a reward for their superior efficiency. Of this we dispose in our definition by subsuming the decline under the decline in the efficiency of the equipment due to the operation of the principle of diminishing returns.[7]

The wage-unit is a much less objective concept than is the concept of the money-unit, but I think at least one advantage may be urged for its use. This is the one set out by Mr. Hugh Townshend in a note entitled "Liquidity Premium and the Theory of Value."[8] Mr. Townshend points out that "labour carries no liquidity premium";[9] that is, since labour cannot be used as a store of value, it cannot be used as a substitute for money as a store of value: therefore there can be no varying premium as a price for giving up possession of a stock held to satisfy a desire for certainty. Since the wage-unit shares none of the functions of money, the two units are logically independent of each other.

The value of this independence in our unit will be much more apparent when we have considered some of the problems which

[6] *Ibid.*, p. 43.

[7] *Ibid.*, p. 42.

[8] *Economic Journal*, XLVII (1937), pp. 157-69. This article treats the store-of-value or liquidity-preference attributes of durable assets and money-claims much more extensively than we shall do here and is an important article in this literature.

[9] *Ibid.*, p. 166. Mr. Townshend also adds (p. 165) "the enormous resistance to either rises or falls in money-wages" as a reason for making the assumption of wage stability the best basis for a convention of price stability.

arise out of a change in the quantity of money in terms of money-units. Speculation in many commodities as stores of value is a familiar phenomenon of cyclical change in the world we know. Where other goods in an exchange system can be used as stores of value to varying degrees ("have liquidity-preference schedules"), the system is imperfectly monetized and the money in use is not a "perfect money" but shares at least one of its functions with other goods in the system. A change in the attitude toward money as a store of value ("a change in the liquidity-preference schedule for money") will be accompanied by a change in the attitude toward goods able to perform the same function and may result in a pervasive change throughout the value system.[10] Therefore when we wish to measure quantities of money, employment, consumption, and investment in a very limited field of relations over periods of time, the use of a unit which entirely escapes liquidity-preference changes will enable us better to account for change and will relieve us of a very baffling complication of the whole problem, at least temporarily.

We have now established two units for our system, namely the money-unit and the wage-unit. Since changes in the wage-unit will tend to be relatively discontinuous, the periodic revaluation of the wage-unit in terms of money will not present a great problem. The wage-unit will be the fundamental unit we use in presenting the system. In our system of equations set out in the previous section, all symbols will be referred to measurements in wage-units unless otherwise stated. Thus for us, within the system of the equations, "the effective quantity of money" will be the quantity measured in wage-units.

Through the use of the wage-unit and the money-unit we may set up parameters for the system of functions, but the limits of use

[10] P. N. Rosenstein-Rodan, "The Co-ordination of the General Theories of Money and Price," *Economica*, III n.s. (1936), pp. 257-69. Mr. Keynes thinks that an ideal cost-unit which would be found by taking "a weighted average of the rewards of factors entering into marginal prime-costs" might be a better unit than the wage-unit (*General Theory*, pp. 302-3). I have some reservations on this matter. Such a unit would perhaps bring this parameter of our system into closer unity with changes in the national dividend; but there is to be urged against it the fact that the concept of *user* cost which Mr. Keynes includes among prime costs has very definite subjective elements based upon the state of expectation with respect to future changes in prices, interest rates, quantities salable, and upon the probabilities of events (war, peace, weather, etc.) occurring to affect these. The unit would therefore appear to have less independence of the situation which it is presumed to measure than does the wage-unit.

for a given system of functional relations will not, however, be apparent until we have defined our unit of time.

The Unit of Time and the Fundamental Model. We seek to establish our unit of time in such a way that we may assume the functions L, ϕ, and F to be stable for a given time-unit. For the flowing rivers of change in the real world we must therefore substitute some type of convention which will give us moments of rest in which we may study the system of economic relationships to see how they determine each other and how they are in turn affected by changes in the psychological-institutional complex.

To do this, we shall set up three model worlds. The first we shall call our "Fundamental Model" and to this model we shall give practically all our attention. In this model we shall study the world in terms of a series of temporary equilibria, a convention which is implicit in the *General Theory*[11] itself and which has been made explicit and expanded by both Mr. Lerner[12] and Professor Hicks.[13] Like the latter we shall call our time-unit the Week. The other two model worlds, to be called the First and Second Supplementary Models, will be characterized by time-lags to be described in their place.

Many of the attributes of the Fundamental Model are inherent in the nature of the concept of the Week. Because Professor Hicks' description fits very conveniently into this model, though perhaps it is more precisely developed than we require (since we shall be dealing with quite macroscopic qualities of the economic system), we can perhaps set out the qualities of this time-unit no better than by quoting very extensively from Professor Hicks' own description of it:[14]

> . . . I shall define a week as that period of time during which variations in prices can be neglected. For theoretical purposes this means that prices will be supposed to change, not continuously, but at short intervals. The calendar length of the week is of course quite arbitrary; by taking it to be

[11]Page 90.

[12]A. P. Lerner, "Saving and Investment: Definitions, Assumptions, Objectives" (Note), *Quarterly Journal of Economics*, LIII (1938-9), pp. 611-19.

[13]J. R. Hicks, *Value and Capital* (Oxford, 1939), chap. IX. Professor Hicks devises his concept for the purposes of his own analysis but owns that the "latter half of this book [*Value and Capital*] would have been very different if I had not had the *General Theory* at my disposal when writing. The final chapters of Part IV, in particular, are very Keynesian" (p. 4). It is for this reason probably that the Hicksian concept of the time-unit, which we shall take over wholly for our Fundamental Model and modify only a little for the Supplementary Models, suits our purposes so well.

[14]Abridged from pages 122-4 inclusive of *Value and Capital.*

very short, our theoretical scheme can be fitted as closely as we like to that ceaseless oscillation which is a characteristic of prices in certain markets. I think we shall find, however, that when the week is supposed to be very short our theory becomes rather uninformative; I believe that it is better to think of it as fairly long[16] though that means we have to be content with a fairly loose approximation to reality.

A convenient way of visualizing this assumption of constant prices during the week is to suppose that there is only one day in the week (say Monday) when markets are open, so that it is only on Mondays that contracts are made. Contracts can, indeed, be carried out during the week (goods can be delivered, and so on); but no new contracts can be made until Monday week. Monday's prices will therefore rule during the week, and they will govern the disposition of resources during the week.

Now it is not hard to see that prices will remain constant during the week, when the markets are not open, and when there is therefore no opportunity for prices to change. But we need also to try and bring ourselves to suppose that price-changes are negligible during the market hours on the Monday, when the market is open and dealers have to fix market prices by higgling and bargaining, trial and error. This implies that the market (indeed, all markets) proceeds quickly and smoothly to a position of temporary equilibrium—in Marshall's sense . . . . For the present, I must ask the reader to accept the assumption of an easy passage to temporary equilibrium as one kind of "perfection" which we may assume into market conditions; just as we shall assume perfect contemporaneous knowledge—that everyone knows the current prices in all those markets which concern him. As far as I can see, these simplifications do not make very much difference to the sort of results which we may expect to obtain by our analysis.

A second property of the week follows from this first, or rather follows from the way we have interpreted the first property. We assume that the week is the planning interval—that is to say, all decisions about the disposition of resources for the future are made on Mondays. Since almost any new decision will involve the making of new contracts, and new contracts can only be made on Mondays, we can very reasonably assume that Mondays are the planning dates too.

It is fundamentally important to realize that the decisions of entrepreneurs to buy and sell (and to some extent also the similar decisions of private persons) nearly always form part of a system of decisions which is not bounded by the present, but has some reference to future events. The current activities of a firm are part of a plan, which includes not only the decision to make immediate purchases and sales, but also the intention to make sales (at any rate, and usually purchases as well) in the more or less distant future. . . .

. . . We shall assume that every firm more or less reconsiders the whole situation every Monday; though this means that we shall tend to impute to the system a higher degree of efficiency than it is in fact likely to possess.

[16]As Mr. Lerner points out ("Saving and Investment," p. 617), the period assumed must be long enough for consumption and saving to be considered stable functions of income or "some very strange results appear." We shall take this matter up further when we come to discuss the Multiplier Functions.

But I do not think this much matters, for it is fairly easy to make allowances for inertia at a late stage in the argument.

Let us then assume that firms (and private persons) draw up or revise their plans on Mondays in the light of the market situation which is disclosing itself; and that any minor adjustments made during the week can be neglected. This means, in combination with our other assumptions, that when markets close on Monday evenings, they have reached the fullest equilibrium which is possible on that date; not only have prices settled down, but every one has made the purchases and sales which seem advantageous to him at those prices. The making of these purchases and sales indicates that plans have been adjusted to these prices—or, if we prefer to allow for inefficiency, that they are as well adjusted as is consistent with the imperfect efficiency of the planners.

Thus we reach a concept within the terms of which we may assume a single set of values for our functions L, ϕ, and F, for a period of time. Within this time-unit of the Week, the entrepreneur aims to maximize his profits. This maximization, as Professor Hicks points out above, will not ordinarily mean that the individual seeks the largest possible realized profit for one Week. The plan for the Week, as Professor Hicks states, exists within a larger plan which may reach over many Weeks. The length of the series may differ with circumstances. If the enterprise is in the control of one individual, the shape of the income stream which is desired may be different and perhaps shorter than the desired shape of the stream where the enterprise is owned by many shareholders and where the object of the management may be conservation and progressive increase of income. It is sufficient to see that the plan for the Week will have reference to and be modified by some longer plan.

From the above discussion, it appears clearly that the world in which we are moving in the Fundamental Model is not to be identified with the world we know. It is almost infinitely closer to that world, however, than is the world of orthodox equilibrium analysis—as we shall find as we move through it.

The Supplementary Models. In the worlds of the Supplementary Models, we get a little closer to the real world. In the First, we make substantially the same assumptions as above, except that we assume that while contracts for the services of the factors of production are still made on Mondays, *the entrepreneur contracts for the sale of consumption goods and services and of new securities are made on Tuesdays.* Thus when entrepreneurs make their plans for production for the Week, they may either under-estimate or over-estimate demands on the succeeding Tuesday.

In the Second Supplementary Model, reverse assumptions are made. In this model, contracts for the sale of consumption goods and new securities are made on Monday, while contracts for the factors which produce the goods and services will not be concluded until Tuesday.

The Supplementary Models therefore permit conditions of limited disequilibrium. While it will be a characteristic of the Fundamental Model that prices will always be based upon marginal products of value because of the degree of market perfection assumed, in the Supplementary Models prices may be either more or less than the ideal short-period prices. Two general types of adjustment to error may be made on Tuesdays: one involves a money and the other an investment adjustment. Under the First Supplementary Model, if entrepreneurs find on Tuesday that in letting their contracts the day before they have either over- or underestimated demand, they may lower or raise prices in order to adjust production to sales. Adjustment between marginal cost and price will therefore be imperfect. Alternatively, they may hold prices at the level expected on Monday and make suitable adjustments in their inventories. Under these conditions, they will have either unplanned investment or unplanned dis-investment for the Week. Under the conditions of the Second Supplementary Model, if entrepreneurs find on Tuesday that the rates of remuneration for factors of production differ from the expected rates under which contracts for output were made on Mondays, they have a similar opportunity to adjust to the new situation either by pocketing money gains or losses or by adjusting inventory holdings. It is obvious that these methods of adjustment are not exclusive. Entrepreneurs may make their adjustments partly by one method and partly by the other in each case.[16] It is equally obvious that

[16]There are marked resemblances between our Supplementary Models and the models of the process analysts such as Professor D. H. Robertson and Professor Bertil Ohlin. It is to be noted that whereas in the Fundamental Model, within the short-period, *ex post* and *ex ante* magnitudes will be equal, in the Supplementary Models these may differ. There will be other similarities which may be found by inspection as we work the relations out.

For Professor Robertson's outline of his own apparatus, see "Saving and Hoarding," *Economic Journal*, XLIII (1933), pp. 399-413, and in particular pp. 401-10. For his comments on the system of the *General Theory*, see: "Some Notes on Mr. Keynes' General Theory of Employment," *Quarterly Journal of Economics*, LI (1936-7), pp. 168-91; "Alternative Theories of the Rate of Interest: Three Rejoinders," *Economic Journal*, XLVII (1937), pp. 428-36; "Mr. Keynes and 'Finance': A Note," *Economic Journal*, XLVIII (1938), pp. 314-18.

Professor Ohlin gives the outline of his own system in "Some Notes on the Stockholm Theory of Savings and Investment," *Economic Journal*, XLVII (1937), I, pp. 53-69; II, pp. 221-40. For his comments on the Keynesian system,

where goods are perishable price adjustments are the only ones possible.

The Models and the Real World. The worlds of the Supplementary Models are very evidently much more complicated than the world of the Fundamental Model. We shall not use the Supplementary Models very extensively, but we shall find comparisons between these models and the Fundamental Model useful from time to time, since such comparisons will give us some opportunity to make judgments as to the differences in character between the world of the Fundamental Model and the world in which we live. The latter is really a combination of all three models: business units offering personal services operate rather frequently under the conditions of the Fundamental Model; business units producing goods directly for the consumer's market operate mostly under the conditions of the First Supplementary Model; and business units in the "heavy" industries, which ordinarily make current commitments for labour, etc., only after orders have been received, operate typically under the conditions of the Second Supplementary Model. Yet we should find ourselves hopelessly involved in complications should we try, at least at this stage, to work in terms of a model which exhibited in one section or another characteristics of all three of the foregoing models.

We have not sketched the full properties of our system until we have demonstrated that under the definitions we are using saving and investment must always be equal. In the following section we turn to that task.

(3) "SAVING EQUALS INVESTMENT"[17]

The Definitions of Saving and Investment in the Treatise on Money. The inequality between the rates of saving and investment, which

see "Alternative Theories of the Rate of Interest: Three Rejoinders," *Economic Journal*, XLVII (1937), pp. 423-7.

For three outstanding demonstrations of the internal consistencies of the systems of Mr. Keynes, Professor Ohlin, and Professor Robertson, see the following: Hicks, *Value and Capital*, pp. 153-62; A. P. Lerner, "Alternative Formulations of the Theory of Interest," *Economic Journal*, XLVIII (1938), pp. 211-30; Oscar Lange, "Savings in Process Analysis," *Quarterly Journal of Economics*, LIII (1938-9), pp. 620-2.

[17]For an extended discussion of this subject, see A. P. Lerner, "Saving Equals Investment," *Quarterly Journal of Economics*, LII (1937-8), pp. 297-309. For a contrast between the structures of the *Treatise on Money* (2 vols., New York, 1930) and the *General Theory* with respect to the handling of these entities in their respective systems, see *Treatise*, I, pp. 123-6; *General Theory*, pp. 61-5 and chap. VII.

was basic to the Fundamental Equations of the *Treatise on Money* and which depended upon the natures of the definitions of terms set out in these volumes, disappears in the system of the *General Theory*. In the structure of the *Treatise*, the receipts of the entrepreneur over and above the payments to be made to labour and capital and the allowances for regular monopoly gains, rents, and the like were divided theoretically into two portions. The first portion was the "normal remuneration" of the entrepreneur, which was classed as an income-item; the second portion was a profit or windfall (positive or negative) which was excluded from effects upon the magnitudes of both income and saving.[18]

Under these definitions, the value of new investment could exceed saving by the item which represented the net windfall gains of entrepreneurs, or it could fail to reach the aggregate of the money saving of the period by the net sum of their losses. If entrepreneurs spent their windfall gains from one set of transactions upon another set, such actions would merely increase their money profits as explained under the parable of the widow's cruse;[19] if they attempted to recoup their losses by extra saving, they would be unsuccessful in filling in the gap between investment and saving for the reasons set out in the celebrated parable of the banana plantation.[20]

It is to be pointed out that in this construction the inequality between saving and investment as defined is "simply another name for the windfall gains or losses or for the differences between prices and costs of output."[21] The conceptual difficulties of the structure become obvious when we consider that an entrepreneur may under the definitions presented save from one portion of his entrepreneur receipts but not from another, though both may serve equally to increase his cash balances! The new definitions of the *General Theory* rid us of such inconsistencies.

The Definitions of Income, Investment, and Saving in This Study. Before we examine the structure of the system of the *General Theory* with respect to the equality between investment and saving, we should set out a little more closely the definitions of the latter with respect to the concepts of gross and net income for the entrepreneur and the community. The *gross* income of the entrepreneur for one of our Weeks under the new structure is interpreted to be "the excess

[18]See the *Treatise*, I, pp. 137-40, 156, 172-3 for further analysis of the profits concept.

[19]*Ibid.*, I, p. 139.

[20]*Ibid.*, I, pp. 176-8.

[21]R. G. Hawtrey, *The Art of Central Banking* (New York, 1932), p. 336.

of the value of his finished output sold during the period over his prime cost."[22] The prime cost, in turn, consists of the amounts paid directly to the factors of production, called his "factor cost," and in addition an item to cover the voluntary sacrifice of value involved in using his equipment to produce the output of the Week, called the "user cost."[23] Since the output of the remainder of the community will be equal to the entrepreneurs' aggregated factor costs, the *gross* income for the community including the entrepreneur income will be equal to their sales proceeds *minus* user cost.[24]

In order to get the *net* income of the community for a Week, we must of course deduct a further amount to cover "supplementary costs" or cost due to losses which "whilst they are unavoidable, are—broadly speaking—not unexpected; such as losses through the lapse of time irrespective of use, and also 'normal' obsolescence."[25]

The symbol Y we shall identify with *net* income. It is made up, as said before, of the sum of consumption and investment. Investment for us will mean the *net* additions for the Week to the community's stocks of working, liquid, and fixed capital.[26]

In the category of windfalls which was so inclusive in the *Treatise*, there remains now only "the change in the value of the equipment, due to unforeseen changes in market values, exceptional obsolescence or destruction by catastrophe, which is both involuntary and—in a broad sense—unforeseen."[27] These windfalls enter into none of the values of our equations. They merely affect the quantum of capital inherited by one of our Weeks from the preceding

[22]*General Theory*, p. 53. The only change made here from Mr. Keynes' treatment of these concepts is our explicit application of the income-terms to our own time-concept of the Week. The material is much abbreviated here and we shall return to this subject in chapter x in which we discuss the Investment Functions.

[23]*Ibid.*

[24]*Ibid.*, p. 54. Gross Income of the whole community = Income of the entrepreneurs + Income of the remainder of the community = [Sales proceeds − (Factor Cost + User Cost)] + Factor Cost = Sales proceeds − User Cost.

[25]*Ibid.*, p. 56.

[26]Mr. Keynes works more largely than we shall with the concepts of *current investment* and *gross income*. See *General Theory*, pp. 62-3, for his definition of current investment. Similarly Mr. Keynes distinguishes between saving and *net* saving. By our symbol S we shall always mean *net* saving. I have made these changes because I wish to give more explicit treatment to depreciation funds and dis-saving and dis-investment than has been undertaken in the *General Theory*. The use of net income, net investment, and net saving concepts in the structure will also facilitate relating the theory set out to orthodox equilibrium theory.

[27]*Ibid.*, p. 57.

Week. If necessary, we can think of such an adjustment in the value of the capital inheritance as taking place "over the Week-end."

The Demonstration of the Equality between Investment and Saving. We come at last to the demonstration of the equality between investment and saving as defined. Let us recapitulate a little. The income concept (Y) is to be defined as the sum of consumption (C) and investment (I) for the Week. Investment means the ***net*** addition to the value of the capital equipment of the community and consists of additions to the stock of fixed, working, and liquid capital. Saving (S) is to be defined as ***the excess of income over consumption.***[28] We have to demonstrate that $C + I = C + S$ and therefore that $I = S$.

We can probably demonstrate our proposition most clearly by shortening our Week indefinitely until it contains only a single transaction. Since the equality between saving and investment really rests upon the fact that every transaction has two sides, this equality is continuously maintained and we shall not run into the "very strange results" which would beset us if, for example, we shortened the Week to the same extent for the study of the Multiplier Functions. We shall therefore consider the nature of this equality for three different Weeks, each containing a single income transaction, representing in the first an investment, in the second a consumption, and in the third a maintenance transaction.[29] Subscripts 1, 2, and 3 will be added to the symbols of our equations to represent each of the three individual Weeks.

1. ***The Week contains only an investment transaction; consumption and maintenance transactions are zero:***

The entrepreneur pays out in costs for services in production the sum of a. Depreciation is assumed to be zero and the sum a is fully represented by an addition to the capital stock of the community during the Week.

$$I_1 = a \qquad C_1 = 0 \qquad Y_1 = C_1 + I_1 = a + 0 = a$$

Since consumption is zero, the income-receiver added the whole sum a to his cash balances. Saving is *defined* as the "excess of

[28] *Ibid.*, p. 62. In Mr. Keynes' terminology, our Saving is the excess of ***net*** income over consumption.

[29] For any given Week, the sum of investment ***plus*** consumption ***plus*** maintenance items gives the aggregate of ***gross*** income, or sales proceeds ***minus*** user cost. These items will be matched by entrepreneur input. If investment and maintenance items are zero, entrepreneur input is equal to consumption. If maintenance items are less than supplementary costs, investment is negative.

income over consumption." The whole of a is saving therefore, since

$$Y_1 - C_1 = a - 0 = a. \qquad I_1 = S_1 = a.$$

2. *The Week contains only a consumption transaction; investment and maintenance transactions are zero:*

The entrepreneur pays out the sum b to cover current production and receives the sum b from purchasers of consumption goods. (In the market sense, goods are consumed as soon as they pass by purchase to the consumer.) Consumption or $C_2 = b$. Depreciation is assumed to be zero Therefore

$$Y_2 = b + 0 = b.$$

Income exceeds consumption by $Y_2 - C_2 = b - b = 0$, which by definition is saving.

$$I_2 = S_2 = 0.$$

3. *The Week contains only a maintenance transaction: consumption and investment transactions are zero:*

The entrepreneur pays labour for doing work which just maintains the value of the entrepreneur's capital (covers supplementary cost).

$C_3 = 0$ and $I_3 = 0$. Therefore $Y_3 = 0$, and since S_3 by definition is equal to the excess of Y_3 over C_3, it also must be zero.

The cash balance of the entrepreneur will be drawn down by the exact amount by which the cash balance of labour is built up. The economic system will enter Week 4 with a stock of liquid capital, working capital, and fixed equipment just equal in value to that with which it entered Week 3. Without the sacrifice of cash by the entrepreneur there would have been a decrement of capital, due to the passage of time and its effects, and investment would have been negative.

For a Week containing a number of transactions, we may set up an equation of this type for each transaction and summate these algebraically to get the aggregates for the community for the Week. Thus we might consider that all three of the foregoing transactions took place within a single Week, in which case the aggregates for the various magnitudes would be shown as below:

$$\text{Income} = Y_1 + Y_2 + Y_3 = Y = a + b + 0 = a + b.$$
$$\text{Consumption} = C_1 + C_2 + C_3 = C = 0 + b + 0 = b.$$
$$\text{Investment} = I_1 + I_2 + I_3 = I = a + 0 + 0 = a.$$
$$\text{Saving} = S_1 + S_2 + S_3 = S = a + 0 + 0 = a.$$
$$\text{Investment} = \text{Saving} = a.$$

It is obvious that we are dealing with truisms. If we defined our aggregates differently, our equations would be different. The only excuse for dealing with these at such great length arises out of the fact that so much bickering and confusion have existed with reference to the nature of the change in terminology between the *Treatise* and the *General Theory*.

Nevertheless though this change is a change in form and not in substance, it indicates a far-reaching change in the character of the conceptual system. It is fundamental to an understanding of the structure of the *General Theory* to see that the abandonment of the division of the entrepreneur share into normal and windfall items means an abandonment of the implication of a "normal" trend or equilibrium level to which the economic system has an inherent tendency to conform. We may follow the variables of the new system through conditions of under-equilibrium and study the position of the system for each Week *as it stands* without being required to define the elements of any conceptually established "normal equilibrium" or to refer the elements of the shifting equilibrium to these definitions before they have any meaning for us. In the *Treatise*, on the other hand, it was necessary to define our *norm* before we were in position to make any estimate concerning the values of the system. Lack of identity of monetary equilibrium with the concept of general economic equilibrium made the task practically impossible. Under the new theory the position which is established as normal by general equilibrium theory is rather regarded as the optimum position which the variables of the system set up in our set of equations may occupy under particularly favourable circumstances. It is this change in Mr. Keynes' technique between the structure of the *Treatise* and the structure of the *General Theory* which more than anything else perhaps makes possible the wider uses of the latter.

The Place of the Saving-Investment Equality in the Fundamental and Supplementary Models. Before we close this chapter it is perhaps well that we should inspect our three model systems to see what place the saving-investment equality holds in each. In the Fundamental Model, the relationship is simple. Because of the degree of market perfection assumed (and because of the perfect matching of marginal costs to marginal revenues implicit in this assumption), plans of savers and investors will be consistent with the realized levels of saving and investment. In Professor Bertil

Ohlin's terms,[30] not only will *ex post* saving and investment be equal to each other, but *ex ante* saving will be equal to *ex post* saving and *ex ante* investment to *ex post* investment.

With the Supplementary Models, the case is as usual more complicated. In the First, entrepreneurs undertake contracts with factors on Monday on the basis of imagined demands of income-receivers on Tuesday. If their expectations are correct, planned and realized saving and investment magnitudes will all four be equal to each other as in the Fundamental Model. If expectations are incorrect, entrepreneurs must, as explained before, make adjustments either through inventory changes or through price changes. If on Tuesday, for example, demands for goods, services, and new securities are lower than entrepreneurs had expected them to be on Monday, entrepreneurs may use part of the factors already contracted for to manufacture goods for inventories, and thus investment will be raised for the Week to match saving. Planned saving will be equal to realized saving and realized investment, but realized investment will be greater than planned investment. On the other hand, should entrepreneurs on Tuesday offer in the market the planned amounts of goods, services, and new securities and adjust prices so as to dispose of these planned amounts in the face of unexpected increases in saving by other income-receivers, then the cash-balances of entrepreneurs will be reduced below expectations to the exact extent by which the cash-balances of others have been built up by the unanticipated saving. Realized saving and investment will still be equal to each other, but the equality will be brought about by reduction of the community's saving by the amount of the losses undergone by the entrepreneurs. Realized saving will be *less* than planned saving. As explained in the preceding section, entrepreneurs may make adjustments by a combination of both methods. In fact that is what would ordinarily be expected where production permits inventory adjustments.

In a similar fashion, in the case of the Second Supplementary Model, it is possible for planned magnitudes to differ from the realized ones because adjustments to error may be made either by changes in inventories or by changes in prices. Realized saving and investment, as before, must be equal to each other.

[30]These expressions were made familiar to English-speaking economists since 1937 by Professor Ohlin but appear to have been introduced into Swedish literature "for the first time by G. Myrdal in 1933" (A. W. Marget, *The Theory of Prices*, 2 vols., New York, 1942, II, p. 177n.). See this note (pp. 177-8) for an account of the development of the use of these terms.

The importance of this logical equality for the realized magnitudes will be apparent only at an advanced stage in the analysis. There it will show itself to be one of the conditions for the system which make it possible to claim a unique solution for the variables of the system, once the mathematical relations for the equations and the quantity of money are given.

The difficulty of weaving one's way among the complexities of the Supplementary Models is manifest. Wherever we can make approaches to reality through the Fundamental Model, we shall find it serviceable to do so.

One more preliminary task remains to be completed. In the succeeding chapter, we shall explore the concept of expectations.

NOTE TO CHAPTER II

Professor Ohlin in "Some Notes on the Stockholm Theory" (p. 237), has the following, among other things, to say of Mr. Keynes' income, savings, and investment concepts:

". . . he has defined his terms income, investment and propensity to consume as *ex-post* concepts. Perhaps he has meant them *ex ante?* But there is no such a relation between expected income, planned consumption and planned investment as he indicates. Thus, either Keynes' reasoning is *ex-post*, and then it explains nothing, or it is *ex-ante*, and then it is entirely wrong. There is no reason why the planned investment plus the planned consumption should be equal to the expected total income for society as a whole. In other words, the planned investment will differ from the planned saving, unless they should happen to be equal by mere chance. Owing to this difference, expectations will not be fulfilled. At the end of the period people will find that their incomes, investment and savings during that period have not been what they expected them to be. Consequently, the expectations, plans and actions with reference to the next period will differ from what they were in the last period. The economic situation will change in a way which can only be explained through a study of how these differences between expectations and the actual course of events during one period influence expectations and actions in the future."

Within Professor Ohlin's schema our Supplementary Models appear to fit perfectly and have the added merit of imputing errors within the short plan to two different types of time-lag. To make the set of equations set out in chapter II fit as perfectly it would be necessary to add symbols and equations for the First Supplementary Model to represent *anticipated* demands for goods, services, and securities on Monday, and to the Second to represent *anticipated* supply conditions for the factors of production. In both, since there may be net transfers within the Week as well as "over the Week-end" between the transactions and savings balances, it would be necessary to keep the L_1 and L_2 functions separate and to add symbols for net hoarding (or dishoarding).

In the Fundamental Model, entrepreneurs may become aware of errors in their longer plans during the Week and make new plans "over the Week-end," but the short plan is assumed to be sound in view of market conditions prevailing on Monday. In the Supplementary Models, the short plans too may contain errors. The Supplementary Models are obviously closer to the real world. But as stated above, so far as we may approach reality within the terms of the Fundamental Model, we shall be spared many complexities in reasoning.

CHAPTER III

THE ROLE OF EXPECTATIONS IN THE KEYNESIAN SYSTEM

(1) EXPECTATIONS AND THE PSYCHOLOGICAL-INSTITUTIONAL COMPLEX

SHORT-TERM and Long-Term Expectations in the Keynes-Lange System. Changes in the psychological-institutional complex between Weeks will affect the shapes of the functions L, ϕ, and F, and hence in relation to any given quantity of money in the system, measured in wage-units, these changes will affect the solution of the system of the equations and thus the levels of income, consumption, investment, saving, and employment. Such changes may arise for reasons which may appear to producers, income-receivers, and holders of property-rights generally to be temporary only, and the state of expectations based upon the change may be covered under the term "short-term expectations." On the other hand, these changes may be such as to impel producers and others in the aggregate to alter their longer plans, and under these circumstances we may refer to the state of expectations based upon them as the state of "long-term expectations."[1]

Within the terms of our own development of the Keynes-Lange model, the states of both short-term and long-term expectations will merge in a general state of expectations which will give us the values of the functions L, ϕ, and F for a given Week. If we knew all the facts, we could express these functions in their proper mathematical terms. If the quantity of money measured in wage-units were in addition known to us, we should be in position to set out a complete solution for the set of equations given in Chapter II as the basis of the system we are expounding. The levels of income, consumption, investment, and saving, and the rate of interest would all be determined. As Week by Week pushed by the present and into the past, changes in the values of these levels and rates could be studied in terms of changes in the mathematical relations of these functions and in the quantity of money measured in wage-units.

[1]For references to short-term expectations in the *General Theory*, see pages 46-8, 50-1, 148; for long-term expectations, see pages 47-8, 51, 147-64, 246.

Autonomous and Economic Influences on the System. We cannot, however, know all the facts. Some of the changes in the states of expectation will arise out of changes in the psychological-institutional complex which must be classed as autonomous influences as far as economic analysis is concerned; others may be made to varying degrees the subjects of economic reasoning.[2] Expectations with respect to the occurrence of war, to the progress of a given war, to probabilities of peace, to the likelihood of the ascendancy of certain political parties to power, and many other political and social factors may have effects upon the psychological-institutional complex of even a closed system; a system which was a member of an international system would have many more to consider. Effects of such changes upon the functions L, ϕ, and F of the shifting equilibrium we must recognize as "caused" by factors outside economic analysis as such. Expectations with respect to changes in the size, age-distribution, and other elements of population change and with reference to some aspects of changes in technique may be brought to some extent into our analysis. But the territory to which we can apply economic analysis most closely within the terms of our system will be given by the history, and particularly by the history of the immediate past, of the economic system with which we are dealing. The facts concerning these will be the facts which we shall know.

As the Weeks pass by our point of observation into history, the actual realizations (in relation to the expectations concerning them held in previous Weeks) of prices, profits, interest-rates, conditions respecting the supply of money, the size of the wage-unit, and the quantum of sales and the level of employment become conditions influencing the state of expectations, both long and short, for *future* Weeks. Because of the importance of these elements, we must reduce our handling of them to such order as we can, and we must develop certain tools to assist us in this process. As a preliminary, it is advisable that we begin to define the i rate of interest included in the set of equations of the preceding chapter.

(2) DEFINITION OF THE i RATE OF INTEREST

Any entrepreneur facing the market for factors of production on the one hand and the market for goods, services, and new securities on the other is not only an entrepreneur but also a saver, consumer and holder (potential or real) of existing property rights. He will

[2]See J. R. Hicks, *Value and Capital* (Oxford, 1939), pp. 204-5, for a similar analysis respecting the nature of price-expectations.

need, so far as he acts rationally and so far as rigid elements in a business enterprise do not restrict him from so doing, to compare the rates of return over cost on new investment with the returns to be earned by buying debts or equities in the market, with the satisfactions and possible gains to be made by holding property rights, at least temporarily, in the form of money, and with the joys of consumption, and to adjust his distribution of capital and income assets among these in accordance with this comparison. Rentiers and wage-earners will have similar choices to make. The bidding and trading of all such persons within an economic community will tend to equalize rates of return for equal advantages throughout the system of relationships. Thus we find within the system a multiple margin of substitution.

This margin of substitution is to be identified with the rate i which was included in the system of equations presented in the preceding chapter. Under the conditions of the Fundamental Model, we can identify this rate on each of the margins to which it applies. In the short-term money market under conditions of temporary equilibrium it will be equal to the rate of interest on risk-free loans. For the long-term money market, the rate will represent the net risk-free rate of yield which is expected by marginal holders for holding a bond from this Monday to next Monday, including expected changes in the market value of the bond. In the equities markets it will be the risk-free rate of yield which is expected by marginal holders from holding an equity for the same period, including the expected change in capitalized value. For marginal savers from income it will represent the premium which they may expect to receive for deferring consumption until next Monday. For marginal holders of existing savings balances it will represent the advantage expected in holding a savings deposit until next Monday rather than using it for purchases this Monday in one of the markets named. There is implicit in each of these statements the assumption that there are no elements of monopoly or imperfections of competition which prevent the rate in one market from coming into complete temporary equilibrium with the other margins of substitution. Though we shall give no special attention to that market, the i rate will also be the margin of substitution binding the *consumers'* durable goods markets to the other markets we have listed. It should be added that by "equity" in this study we mean the title to any investment good and by the "equities markets" the markets in which such rights are bought and sold, whether they be titles to shares of stock, to raw materials, to lands, or to other property.

In Chapter VI, we shall study more definitely the relations which exist between this rate and the prices of assets in the various markets. In the current chapter we go on to study the processes of valuation in the debts and equities markets and the relations between interest rates for various durations.[3] In the course of this discussion we shall show the place of risk and uncertainty elements in the valuation series.

(3) EXPECTATIONS IN THE ASSETS MARKETS: DEBTS

The Formula for the Valuation of a Debt: Orthodox Expression. We can perhaps best approach an analysis of valuations in the debts market as it fits into our system by beginning with the commonplace formulation of such valuations ordinarily included in elementary

[3]This section of the general analysis is built upon ideas suggested in the main by three writers. The first comes from an article by Peter Bauer, "Die Allgemeine Theorie von Keynes und ihre Kritiker," *Zeitschrift für Nationalökonomie,* Band IX (1938-9), Heft 1, pp. 99-108. In this the relation of the assets markets to the Keynesian system is pointed out carefully. The second comes from Professor Hicks' *Value and Capital,* pp. 144-52. In this, methods are described for building whole systems of interest rates with either the short or the long rate as the unit. Our method in this study will be to use the short rate for the unit but the method will differ from that of Professor Hicks in that we shall regard costs for default risks as modifications of the absolute sizes of money yields rather than as modifications of rates of yield. It will follow from the practice of using the short rate as the unit rate that where two debts have different durations the rates earned by them for the period in which they run concurrently will be the same and any differences in "pure" rates earned are to be imputed to interest-expectations for the period in which one debt is still current and the other has been paid off. This latter suggestion, of major importance for the character of the analysis which follows, came from Section II (pp. 303-8) of Mr. T. de Scitovszky's article, "A Study of Interest and Capital," *Economica,* VII n.s. (1940), pp. 293-317.

Other books and articles of importance in this literature which have been consulted are as follows: A. G. Hart, *Anticipations, Uncertainty and Dynamic Planning* (Chicago, 1940), "Anticipations, Business Planning and the Cycle," *Quarterly Journal of Economics,* LI (1936-7), pp. 273-97, "Failure and Fulfillment of Expectations in Business Fluctuations," *Review of Economic Statistics,* XIX (1937), pp. 69-78; F. H. Knight, *Risk, Uncertainty, and Profit* (New York, 1921); H. Makower and J. Marschak, "Assets, Prices, and Monetary Theory," *Economica,* V n.s. (1938), pp. 261-88; L. G. Melville, "The Place of Expectations in Economics," *Economic Record,* XV (1939), pp. 1-16; G. L. S. Shackle, "Expectations and Employment," *Economic Journal,* XLIX (1939), pp. 442-52; P. M. Sweezy, "Expectations and the Scope of Economics," *Review of Economic Studies,* V (1937-8), pp. 234-7.

text-books on principles of economics and by modifying that formula in such ways as will fit it to the variables of our system. If we take a bond with principal P, running for n years, paying an annual amount A and capitalized at r rate of interest, the school-book formula would run:

$$\text{Present Value} = \frac{A}{1+r} + \frac{A}{(1+r)^2} + \ldots + \frac{A+P}{(1+r)^n}. \qquad (1)$$

In order to adjust this valuation to our own system, we shall make the assumption usually that A is a weekly income paid each Monday. No essential change in reasoning is involved but there is convenience in this arrangement of terms.

Revision of the Formula: the Influence of Interest-Expectations. As a first approach to revision, we must realize that the rate i which will be a part of the Keynes-Lange system as we shall expound it is not the same thing as the single rate r which is the rate assumed to be earned by the bond in question over its period of life. Our rate i represents *a margin of substitution prevailing only from this Monday to next Monday* and subject to change with the passage of time. This must be true because change in the psychological-institutional complex will be causing shifts in the values of both the independent and dependent variables of our equations. On each Monday income-receivers and property holders will have the opportunity of making mutual adjustments to a new situation. If this series of adjustments leaves the rate i in the solution of the equations the same as that of the preceding Week it will be a coincidence rather than something to be expected.

We have said before that one of the strongest influences shaping the system of equations will be expectations arising out of the history of the system itself in the immediate past. The fact that rates *have* changed may be considered to be a ground for expectations of future changes. It is therefore quite to be expected that on a given Monday there may be expectations of changes in i during forward Weeks. These expectations may in some sense depend upon the size of i for the current Week, but because of the degree of perfection assumed for the market in the Fundamental Model, we may expect that the size of i will be known relatively early on Monday morning and once it is known interest-expectations may be taken as given for the current market.

Upon the basis of these expectations, we may make our first revision of the school-book formula:

$$\text{Present Value} = \frac{A}{1+i_0} + \frac{A}{(1+i_0)(1+i_1)} + \ldots\ldots + \frac{A+P}{(1+i_0)(1+i_1)\ldots\ldots(1+i_{n-1})}. \quad (2)$$

In this formula the subscript 0 stands for the current Week, and the other subscripts for weeks of a futurity indicated by the subscript.[4]

The revision of the formula is not yet complete. We must allow for anticipations of possible default and for varying degrees of satisfaction with the estimate of interest-expectations. For this purpose we attach the symbol d to the various A's of the series to cover default risks, and the symbol e as a coefficient of correction on interest-expectations.[5] Since default risks are likely to rise with futurity and degrees of satisfaction with interest-expectations to decline with futurity, these coefficients will change with the passage of time. For that reason we give them separate subscripts.

In addition to these subscripts, one other modification of the formula is required. If a holder or potential holder feels that it may become necessary or desirable at some future date to sell the asset, he will pay regard not only to his own valuation but also to the probable valuations to be set by others upon the asset at such times as he may wish to sell the asset. Some assets will be well known and will have a wide market. Others, perhaps just as essentially sound, will be little known and have a narrow market. In accordance with the degree of estimated illiquidity for each particular asset, because of market imperfections, we make subtractions from the present value under the symbol l in the amended formula.[6]

[4]The method of deriving forward rates is that shown by Professor Hicks, *Value and Capital*, p. 145.

[5]In general, the wider the dispersion of interest-expectations, the lower the degree of satisfaction felt with the estimate and the higher the correction on the "pure" rate and the lower the price of the asset.

[6]Where Mr. Keynes talks customarily of *liquidity premiums*, we shall on the other hand use *illiquidity penalties* in comparing asset prices. These penalties will represent the difference between the marginal liquidity-premium rates on money (i) and the marginal liquidity-premium rates on other assets. In this way we are able to avoid the rather awkward concept of "own-rates of interest" used by Mr. Keynes (*General Theory*, pp. 223-31) and are able to use the rate i as a margin of substitution throughout the entire system of values. The reasons why holdings of money have a liquidity-premium rate equal to the general margin of substitution for the system will be developed in Chapter VI.

The amended formula now stands:

$$\text{P.V.} = \frac{d_1A}{1+i_0} + \frac{d_2A}{e_1(1+i_0)(1+i_1)} + \ldots\ldots + \frac{d_n(A+P)}{e_1e_2\ldots.e_{n-1}(1+i_0)(1+i_1)\ldots.(1+i_{n-1})} - l. \quad (3)$$

Relation of the i and r Rates. We have still to consider how the series of i rates of formulae (2) and (3) are related to the rate r of the original formula. The present values which emerge from series (1) and (3) are the same. The rate r is the rate which *would* give the same price to the same series when all risk factors, uncertainty coeffiicients (except the e's), and expectations respecting the future course of the rate of interest are brought together as modifications of a "pure" rate. Quotations of market yields will tend to show the rate r, but the rate which fits the Keynes-Lange system will be the rate i as determined Week by Week, or e_1i_1, e_2i_2, . . . , where interest-uncertainties are involved.

The Valuation of Infinite Series. The implication throughout the above has been that such debts will always represent finite series, with repayment of principal at the end of a definite series of time-units. This is not really true, since we know that consol-type bonds exist. But market values and yields quoted for these indicate that present values and r rates of yield exist. This fits within the logic of the above series, however. Since interest-expectations tend on the whole to be inelastic,[7] and since there is a relatively narrow range within which rates tend to move, the i rates too must have a relatively narrow range and the process of valuation even for consols will result in finite values.

The Relation of the Marginal Holder of Specific Assets to the Formation of Market Rates. This analysis does not imply that all holders or potential holders of a specific asset will have like valuation series. Similarly, among *different* specific debts only the current i_0 rate representing the marginal rate of substitution for the given Week will need to coincide and then only for *marginal* holders of the specific assets for the Week. Intra-marginal holders may have higher i_0 rates on their holdings of specific assets. Potential holders may have remained potential only because they have estimated the i_0 rate of return on an asset under the general margin of substitution for the system. It is the willingness of the marginal holders to hold specific assets at the i_0 rate forming the general margin of substitution which is the ultimate determinant of what

[7]See Hicks, *Value and Capital*, p. 262.

the price and the i_0 rate will be. This is in accordance with the elementary reasoning respecting the pricing of butter and eggs as well as assets in the market.

When therefore at the close of Monday's markets, all holders of debts feel that there is no net advantage to be gained by disposing of an asset in order to move into the equities market, into new investment, into money, into an expansion of consumption, or back into the debts market to purchase another debt whose prospects are held to be more favourable, then the market is from the standpoint of the market for debts in equilibrium. With respect to the last option, it is to be observed that there will be in any market a hierarchy of r rates, which may differ with the duration of the debts and with the size of coefficients representing default risks. It is also to be observed that where two debts have different durations but the same Weekly payments and default coefficients, they will under formulae (2) and (3) above earn the same rate of return for the period in which they run concurrently.[8]

Something will be said hereafter about the effects of market imperfections resulting from time-lags. In the meantime we must consider the valuation process in the equities market.

(4) EXPECTATIONS IN THE ASSETS MARKETS: EQUITIES

The Dispersion of Expectations in the Equities Market. The valuation process for equities will differ from the process for debts only for reasons arising from the fact that the periodic payments made as a return to ownership will not be stipulated in amount, and may vary widely where corporations or other business units do not follow stable dividend policies. Because of these conditions, the expectations of yield from the ownership of a specific equity for any forward Week will not be a single, definite figure but rather a "bundle" or zone of such figures, with each member of the dispersion having a greater or lesser degree of probability (it is perhaps better to say "possibility"[9]) attached to it. The main problem for analysis here is therefore the problem of reaching a figure to represent this bundle of expectations.

Since definite prices for equities do exist, there must exist at least in the minds of holders of equities some method of comparing the outcomes of various lines of action in order to make choices between them. Each equity will have a series of anticipated returns attached to it similar to the series for debts used in the preceding

[8]See footnote 3, page 29, above, for reference to Mr. T. de Scitovszky.
[9]See *General Theory*, p. 152.

section of this chapter. A single figure in a series of returns will represent for the purchaser of equities as well as for an entrepreneur undertaking new production during a given Week "that expectation of proceeds which, if it were held with certainty, would lead to the same behaviour as does the bundle of vague and more various possibilities which actually makes up his state of expectation when he reaches his decision."[10] Each of these figures will represent the reduction of the dispersion to a single value, with any probabilities attached to given outcomes accorded their due weights in reaching the mean. The series of net returns to be expected from a given purchase of an equity on a given Monday, we shall denominate by the symbols a_0, a_1, a_2, . . . , the subscripts representing the futurity of the Week in the same manner as in the formulae of the preceding section. Since there may be a greater or a lesser degree of satisfaction with the estimate made, we shall use a correction symbol s to indicate this. The width of a dispersion may be regarded either as a favourable or an unfavourable factor by a valuator, since there is the possibility that the individual "may feel either 'risk aversion' or a liking for danger."[11] If the wider dispersion allows for "prizes" the likelihood that the dispersion may be regarded favourably is increased. For an owner or a potential owner of such assets, this situation will be related to the character of other assets owned and the quantities of each. Such circumstances change the s coefficients for individual valuators. Since dispersions about the mean will tend to widen with the degree of futurity, there will be a series of these correction coefficients, as in the case of the default coefficients previously described. Widening of dispersions because of growing futurity will be classed as an unfavourable influence and will tend to diminish the mean values set on anticipated yields.

The Equities Formula. We are now ready to set out the formula for the valuation of an equity upon a similar basis to those of the debts market. Symbols identical with those used for the debts valuations will have the same meanings as before. The new formula reads:

$$\text{P.V.} = \frac{s_1 a_1}{1+i_0} + \frac{s_2 a_2}{e_1(1+i_0)(1+i_1)} + \dots$$
$$+ \frac{s_n a_n}{e_1 e_2 \dots e_{n-1}(1+i_0)(1+i_1)\dots(1+i_{n-1})} - l. \quad (4)$$

[10] *Ibid.*, p. 24. See also Hart, *Anticipations, Uncertainty and Dynamic Planning*, pp. 52-3.

[11] Hart, *Anticipations, Uncertainty and Dynamic Planning*, p. 55.

As before, the series may have an infinite number of terms but it will still have a finite value due to the limitations on expectations of interest changes in either direction. To this is to be added the fact that for Weeks of very great futurity, correction coefficients s and the size of the time discounts will be so large as to reduce expected yields to insignificance in the valuation series.

As before, the valuation series may differ among different holders (or potential holders) for the same equity. Also, as before, it is the valuation series of marginal holders which must be brought into equilibrium with other choices on the market, and it is the marginal rate i_0 which is important for the short-term equilibrium of the system. Again at the close of Monday's market there will be no net advantage to be gained by holders of any specific equity in disposing of the equity in order to move into debts, new investment, money, or consumption markets or to purchase some other specific equity.

(5) "PURE" RATES OF INTEREST

The i rates in the foregoing formulae are "pure" rates representing the short-period margin of substitution which fits the Keynes-Lange system of equations. We call them "pure" not in the sense of orthodox economic theory but because they are free of the charges which the market makes for default risks and for all allowances for dispersions and uncertainties other than the uncertainty respecting the course of the interest rate itself.

The Effects of Transfer Costs. The r rates require only one further modification in order to fit the yields on the various types of assets which will be quoted in the markets for these assets. If in the market there are costs, objective or subjective, in transferring from one type of asset to another type of asset, the prices for the various assets may come to differ over a range in accordance with the nature of these costs. Where such conditions are present, in order to keep the i rates "pure" a term would require to be added to the foregoing formulae to cover this condition. For purposes of simplification we shall omit this symbol in valuation series but the qualification needs to be remembered.

The Derivation of "Pure" Rates for Assets of Various Durations. In addition to this, we shall find it useful when we reach discussions of the Liquidity, Multiplier, and Investment Functions to have definitions of "pure" rates of interest for longer periods than the Week. For any given series of Weeks, these "pure" rates, hereinafter to be called the r' rates, will be the average i rates (current and expected) for the series. The expected i rates must, however, be corrected by the e coefficients which apply.

The method of deriving the r' rates from the i rates will differ in accordance with the period on which the rates of interest are compounded in the institutional framework which applies.[12] If income is paid Weekly and the Week is also the compounding period, for a debt having a currency of two Weeks, the r' rate would be found by the formula $\frac{2i_0 + e_1 i_1}{3} = r'$, while for a series of three Weeks under similar assumptions, the r' rate would be $\frac{3i_0 + 2e_1 i_1 + e_2 i_2}{6}$. Analogous methods would be used for debts of longer currencies and for equities where the same assumptions prevailed. In getting the average rate each i rate would be used the same number of times it appeared in the debts or equities formula which applied under the principles worked out in the preceding sections of this chapter.

If the Week is shorter than the period for compounding, the rate for each compounding period will be the simple arithmetic average of the i rates of the compounding period. For example, if the compounding period were three Weeks long and a debt were payable with interest and principal at the end of one compounding period, the r' rate for this debt would be $\frac{i_0 + e_1 i_1 + e_2 i_2}{3}$ and the present value of the debt would be $\frac{d_3(A + P)}{1 + \frac{i_0 + e_1 i_1 + e_2 i_2}{3}}$. Where the debt has a duration of more than one compounding period and interest payments are made during the interval, combination of the method of this paragraph with the method of the preceding paragraph will be necessary to get the r' rate which applies.

The structure of the r' rates and their relation to the i_0 rate will therefore have some dependence on the institutional framework. For simplicity's sake again we shall regard the Week as the period for compounding interest payments.

(6) EXPECTATIONS IN THE THREE MODELS

The foregoing analysis appears to cover with a fair degree of completeness the variables of the assets markets under the conditions of the Fundamental Model. In the Supplementary Models there may be a further degree of imperfection, due to time-lags, to which

[12]See Hicks, *Value and Capital*, p. 145. Geometric means would give closer approximations for the r' rates. The general formula would be:

$$r' = \left[i_0^n (e_1 i_1)^{n-1} (e_2 i_2)^{n-2} \ldots (e_{n-1} i_{n-1})\right]^{2 \cdot n(n+1)}$$

the concept of expectations may also be related. In the First Supplementary Model, for example, since contracts for services of factors are made on Monday, borrowing for purposes of the Week's production will presumably be done on Monday. But the markets for goods and securities will be open on Tuesdays only. Rates agreed upon for short-term lending on Monday may be out of line with conditions for the sale of goods and securities on Tuesday. Similarly in the Second Model, prices and rates settled in the goods and securities markets on Monday may turn out on Tuesday to be out of line with the supply conditions for factors including terms for short-term borrowing. In both Models, contracts made in Monday's markets are based on *expectations* of what will happen on Tuesday and these expectations may be erroneous in varying degrees.

It is evident that under these conditions, the condition of temporary equilibrium implicit in the Fundamental Model may never be reached but will exist only as an underlying condition to which the market tends to conform. The degree to which the real world exhibits these imperfections will depend upon, first, the degree to which it exhibits the conditions of the three Models, and, second, the degree of error present in expectational forecasts included in production plans.

We shall use the Fundamental Model as the basis of reasoning in most of the analysis which follows, upon the assumption that the degree of error within the short plan, or Week, is not likely to be great enough to invalidate our general reasoning. It is admitted that many of our concepts will be non-operational, at least at the stage to which we can carry the analysis in this study, but it is submitted that the character of the analysis exposes the nature, and the frequent crudity, of many of our operational concepts.

We are not done with the analysis of expectations when we show the place of expectations in the assets market. Expectations will have a place throughout the whole system, shaping and setting the positions of each of the sheaves of functions which make up the Keynes-Lange apparatus. We must come to these one by one. In the next group of chapters we begin the attack through study of the factors determining the rate of interest and the demand for money.

CHAPTER IV

RATES OF INTEREST AND LONG-PERIOD EQUILIBRIUM

THE following group of three chapters is devoted to a study of Equation (1), namely, $i = L(M, Y)$. The method of approach will be through orthodox equilibrium analysis. The following chapter will explore the relation of the interest-rate structure to general equilibrium under static conditions. In the second chapter we shall study the nature of the demand for money under conditions of orthodox theory, and in the third chapter of the group the same demand will be studied in a world characterized by the necessities for forecasting and by the imperfections to which references have already been made. When we have completed these chapters we shall not, however, have completed our study of the determination of the structure of interest-rates. The rate structure itself emerges from the whole system of equations and further from the conditions surrounding the determination of the quantity of money, the size of the wage-unit, and the nature of interest-expectations.

In this chapter, we study the relation of the interest-rate structure to general equilibrium under three different sets of assumptions. Under the first set, we consider the conditions required for long-period equilibrium where the system can come to a point of stationariness with a positive rate of interest. Under the second set, we consider the differences brought into the situation where the degree of thriftiness in the community is so great as to make a negative rate a theoretical condition for stationariness. Under the third set, we consider the forces which determine the long-period quantum of capital where in a money economy there is an institutional minimum on the rate of interest which is higher than the rate which would otherwise be associated with stationariness. In a concluding section we suggest the application of this reasoning to the problems of the real world.

(1) LONG-PERIOD EQUILIBRIUM AND POSITIVE RATES OF INTEREST

Assumptions. We start our consideration of orthodox analysis with an analysis of the conditions necessary for the maintenance of a stationary state under marginal productivity theory. We set out at the beginning the usual assumptions connected with the concept

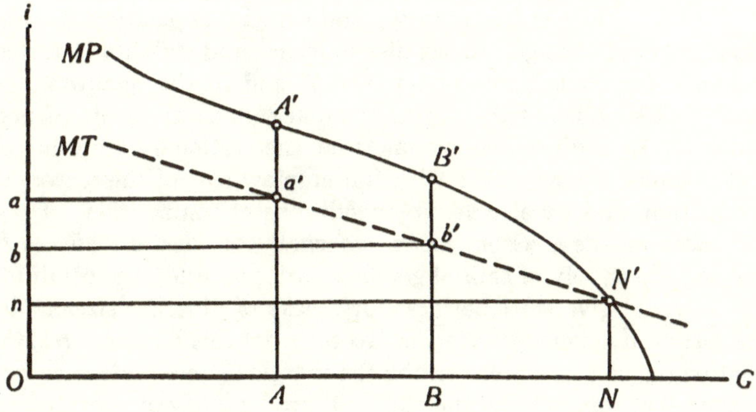

FIGURE I

Symbols:

MP = marginal productivity curve with capital forms adjusted to size of capital stock. *MT* = maintenance or marginal time-preference curve.[1] *OG* = index of size of capital stock. *i* = for *MP*, rate of return over cost; for *MT*, time-discounting rate. See text for other symbols.

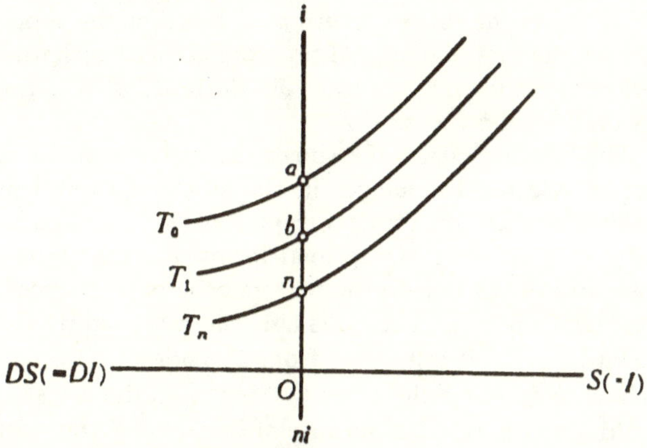

FIGURE II

Symbols:

S = saving per unit of time, measured in wage-units (= investment). *DS* = dis-saving per unit of time (= dis-investment). *ni* = negative interest rate. T_0, T_1, T_n = saving-dis-saving schedules attached to stocks of capital *OA*, *OB*, and *ON* respectively at the rates of interest shown.

---

[1]The idea of the maintenance curve was developed from Professor A. C. Pigou's *The Economics of Stationary States*, pp. 169-72 and Appendix IX. For a general development of the idea that the rate of marginal productivity and the rate of marginal time-preference coincide only at zero-saving in long-period equilibrium, see F. P. Ramsey, "A Mathematical Theory of Saving," *Economic Journal*, Vol. XXXVIII (1928), pp. 543-59.

of the stationary state, namely, stability in population factors, including size, and age and sex distributions, and stability in tastes, technical knowledge, aversion to work, and in the quantity and quality of supplies of the various primary physical agents of production. In addition, we assume that the stationary state in the first instance is compatible with full employment of the factors of production, and we also assume conditions of competition. Upon the basis of these assumptions, we shall consider the effects of varying the supply of capital goods in order to study the condition which would give stationariness for stocks of different sizes under the assumptions made. We wish to get from this picture, first, the relation of the curve representing the marginal time-preference rate to the curve representing the marginal productivity of instruments, and second, the connection of this relationship with the long-term equilibrium rate of interest.

Graphical Description of Relations. To accomplish these tasks we set up our relations in the form of graphs. Upon the horizontal axis of Figure I we indicate the size of the capital stock. The vertical axis has a double service to perform. For the demand curve *MP* it shows the rate of return over cost; for the supply curve *MT* it shows the rate of marginal time-preference which would be associated with stationary conditions.[2] Both *MP* and *MT* require fuller explanations, however.

The demand curve *MP* shows the changes in the marginal product in relation to changes in the stock of capital over long-run conditions where the forms of capital are assumed to be instantaneously adjusted to their optimal forms for the size of the capital stock and in relation to the factors otherwise assumed to be fixed. That is, if the capital stock is *OA*, the marginal return over cost is shown by *AA'*; if influences from the side of time-preference were such as to establish the stock *OA* as the stationary stock, then *AA'* would give the equilibrium rate of interest for the stationary state.

The marginal time-preference curve *MT* (hereinafter to be called the "maintenance curve"), as indicated on Figure I, shows the rates of interest which would be associated with stationariness from the side of time-preference when the population and other factors are

[2]The curve *MT* is very like Mr. de Scitovszky's curve for "stationary time-preference" used in his article, "A Study of Interest and Capital," previously referred to on p. 29. See pp. 309ff. of that article. Nevertheless the curve of this study was derived directly from the work of Professor Pigou, as indicated in note 1 of this chapter, some time before Mr. de Scitovszky's article became available through publication.

as assumed for *MP*. The method by which the curve *MT* is developed may be derived from Figure II. On this figure, three hypothetical supply curves of saving are set up, based on an index number measuring the absolute levels of savings. The first (T_0) is connected with capital stock *OA*, the second (T_1) with *OB*, and the third (T_n) with *ON*. The vertical axis measures the rate of interest, the portion below the horizontal axis representing negative rates of interest. Since a change in the rate of interest will normally be accompanied by a change in distribution and may also (because of these changes in distribution and because of differences in the elasticity of the supplies of the physical factors[3]) be accompanied by changes in the equilibrium level of income (*Y*), we subsume such differences in distribution and in income in the shapes of these curves.

Under the conditions of these curves and under conditions of full employment, if the capital stock were *OA*, the savings curve would be T_0. If *Oa* as shown on Figure II happened to equal *AA′* as shown on Figure I, the conditions of the stationary state would be fulfilled and unless and until there was some change in one of the factors we have assumed to be stable, the supply of capital would not be pushed beyond that level. For capital stock *OA*, we call *Oa* the maintenance rate and it gives us point *a′* for Figure I. Similarly, in relation to capital stock *OB* we find point *b′* from supply curve T_1 on Figure II. By like reasoning, we find rate ***On***. Since rate ***On*** coincides with rate *NN′*, and since *N′* therefore lies on both curve *MP* and curve *MT*, it will be the long-period rate of interest for the economic community for which we have made the underlying assumptions of stability in various magnitudes.

Reasons for the Fall of the Maintenance Curve. We show the maintenance curve as forward-falling on Figure I in spite of the fact that on Figure II we show the individual supply curves as forward-rising.[4] For the maintenance curve to be forward-falling, the essential point is that T_1, connected with capital stock *OB*,

[3]That is, we recognize that with a labour-supply curve having a negative elasticity, a change in distribution in favour of labour may lower the physical output because of labour's preference for increased leisure at a higher real wage-rate. Thus we cannot connect an absolute equilibrium level of income (*Y*) with capital stock *OA* before we *know* what the rate of interest is.

[4]It is perhaps desirable that we should set out here also the reasons for giving the savings-supply curves forward-rising shapes. Such shapes appear plausible. In the first place, at higher rates of interest, the saving classes tend to have higher incomes. Such a change in distribution under conditions of full employment with the forms of capital fully adjusted to the other factors, will tend to increase the inequality of distribution and this, for reasons to be developed

under the conditions given, should cross axis *i-ni*, representing zero-saving, at a point lower than that at which T_0, connected with capital stock *OA*, crosses it. We have the following reasons to present for holding that this is true. In the first place, up to the point where marginal productivity is zero or negative, total real income per time-unit under the assumptions given should be increased by the increase in capital. In the second place, it is inferred as a fundamental proposition that, *ceteris paribus*, larger absolute levels of saving, per unit of time, will be made at each given rate of interest from the larger incomes. This proposition will mean also that the *same* level of saving will be attained with a lower rate of interest when the stock of capital has been increased. It follows that as the capital stock increases, and with our assumptions of stability in certain factors listed previously still holding, the zero-saving level will coincide with lower and lower rates of interest.

---

in future chapters, will tend to increase the quantity of saving. This therefore is one reason for allying a higher rate of saving with a higher rate of interest.

As a second reason, connected with this change in distribution, if the supply curve of labour has negative elasticity, the lowering of the rate of real wages which accompanies the change in distribution will tend to enlarge the physical output of goods under conditions of full employment. This condition in turn will tend to ally a higher absolute level of saving, measured in wage-units, with a higher rate of interest when distribution becomes more unequal because of a rise in the rate of interest.

As a third reason, a supply curve, as contrasted with a maintenance curve, must be related to a definite unit of time. Within such a limited unit there will be competition between the demands for consumption and saving. Even in a society where a lower rate of interest might cause representative individuals to plan to save more over their whole saving lives, nevertheless *within the single time-unit* we cannot see the supply curve of saving attached to a definite supply of capital as falling indefinitely toward the right. With the elasticity of the labour-supply and the size of the capital stock as *given* factors, for each rate of interest for a given unit of time, there will be a definite level of output measured in wage-units connected with the level of full employment. If we consider only time-units long enough for us to hold the propensity to save a stable function of output and interest rate, it is not possible that the community should save 100 per cent of its output for the given time-unit. The individuals of the community will normally wish to continue living and some consumption is inevitable under normal conditions even where we interpret consumption in the market sense.

Therefore though it is possible that the savings curve attached to a definite stock of capital and a definite unit of time should fall in its early stages, in the course of its progress to the right it must start to rise for the same reason that any supply curve governed fundamentally by the law of diminishing returns must rise. Theoretically it should finally reach complete inelasticity, though social factors would make the extreme right section of the supply curve irrelevant to the problems of actual economic life.

Thus we get T_0, T_1, . . . crossing the zero-saving axis at successively lower rates of interest. On this assumption we are able to inscribe a forward-falling maintenance curve for capital, at least as far as the point where marginal productivity becomes zero.

To recapitulate, with the slope of the maintenance curve *MT* established on the basis given in Figure I, the equilibrium supply of capital in the long-term for a society under the conditions we have assumed will be given by the point where *MT* crosses *MP*. With supplies of labour and natural resources given, and with techniques and tastes established, the system will come to a point of rest at the interest rate *NN'*, with the demand price of capital instruments as based upon their marginal productivity equal to their supply price as based upon the marginal time-preference rate. A system of general-equilibrium equations fitted to this situation will give the value *NN'* for the equilibrium rate of interest upon this basis.

Relations within the Rate Structure for a Stationary System. In terms of the formulae developed in the preceding chapter for the valuation of assets, it is to be observed that under these stationary conditions and in this riskless universe, all assets have perfect liquidity, all other correction coefficients (besides l) are equal to unity, and the r, i, and r' rates will be equal to each other throughout the universe of rates. It is because of this equality that we may speak of "the" rate of interest here.

Bases for Expansion of the Quantum of Capital. For all stocks of capital lower than *ON*, it is the fact that the marginal demand price as based upon marginal productivity lies above the maintenance rate of interest as based upon time-preference which gives the economy an expansionary form.[5] The degree of growth per unit of time will depend upon the operation of the laws of cost in the production industries in relation to the specific forms which capital is taking at that point and the modifications necessary to adapt them under existing technical knowledge to the forms they must take under the ideal combinations for the enlarged stock of capital instruments. With instantaneous adjustment of factors, the ideal adjustment would be approached continuously and there would be no frictions. But even under such ideal conditions the period taken in moving from capital stock, say *OA* to *ON*, might be very long indeed, since for every unit of time the demand for consumption goods would be competing for the services of the factors of pro-

[5]F. P. Ramsey, "A Mathematical Theory of Saving," p. 556. See also Nicholas Kaldor, "Professor Pigou on Money Wages in Relation to Unemployment," *Economic Journal*, XLVII (1937), p. 747.

duction and only a limited proportion of the supply would be turned over for purposes of producing goods for the future. In the real world, the rate of growth of capital would be further conditioned by the existence of institutional frictions and by the changes in the level of economic activity which characterize the business cycle. Moreover, in the real world we could not expect the various types of stability in population and other factors which we have assumed in this section of the analysis.

Relations within the Rate Structure of a Moving but Riskless System. Under the ideal conditions for a system moving from stock *OA* to stock *ON*, the r and r' rates would still be equal to each other for assets of the same duration, but the i_0 (current) rate would be above all the r and r' rates for assets with a life extending more than one Week. This relation arises because of the expectation of falls in the marginal productivity of capital with expected increases in its quantity. The rate of interest used for the capitalization of permanent assets with capital stock *OA* as shown in Figure I would not be the rate *AA'*. Rate *AA'* is equal to i_0 or the rate used to find the present value of assets available for consumption on Monday Week and it would be the rate which would rule capitalization of permanent assets only if capital stock *OA* were actually the equilibrium stock. If we are considering the problem in terms of moving equilibria of the Keynes-Lange type but based upon correct expectations and full employment of factors of production, future changes in the marginal productivity of capital as the capital stock was modified in form and increased in quantity would form part of the conditions to be made the basis of valuations after the fashion of the analysis laid down in the preceding chapter.

In an economic universe where institutional frictions were present but known, the marginal productivity of any given quantity of capital would be reduced by the added costs but the general relation of the r, r', and i rates to each other would not be changed. Where correction coefficients have the character described in the preceding chapter, however, no generalization can be made at this point beyond those set out in that analysis. To complete the analysis of such conditions we must await examination of the Investment Functions.

(2) LONG-PERIOD EQUILIBRIUM AND NEGATIVE INTEREST RATES

By implicit assumption in Figure I we have shown *MT* cutting *MP* at point *N'*, a point which represents a positive rate of interest. There is nothing in the set of relations presented which requires this relationship. We have expressly ruled out by assumption the changes in population, physical factors, techniques, and tastes which might put new variables into the situation. If the degree of thriftiness is high enough in the community, the curve *MT* may cut the horizontal axis before the curve *MP* does so. In such a case, the rate of interest associated with the theoretical long-period equilibrium would be a negative rate.[6] The nature of this relationship is set out in Figures III and IV below.

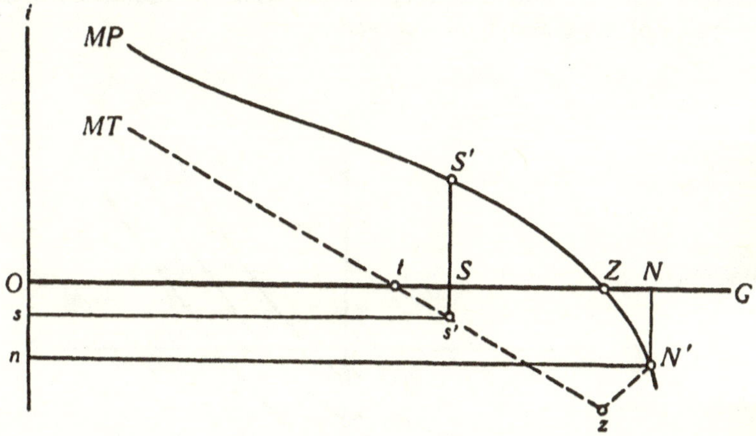

FIGURE III

Graphical Description under Changed Assumption. In Figure III we set up hypothetical conditions, based on the same assumptions with respect to stability of population and other factors as we made for Figure I. The fundamental difference in Figure III is that *MT* crosses *OG* before *MP* does, namely at *t*. Figure IV gives the supply curves of saving connected with capital stocks *OS*, *OZ*, and *ON* on practically the same bases as was true for Figure II. There is only one exception; in Figure III as set out, it is recognized that beyond the point *Z* on axis *OG* we have no general principle to guide us in the inscription of the maintenance curve. This is therefore indicated only experimentally beyond this point upon a hypothe-

[6]The idea that a negative rate of interest may be required for various types of economic equilibrium is a familiar one in current economic literature. For example, see A. C. Pigou, *The Theory of Unemployment* (London, 1933), p. 213; also *The Economics of Stationary States* (London, 1935), p. 55; also Joan Robinson, *Essays in the Theory of Employment* (New York, 1937), p. 140.

For a discussion with reference to the problem of the valuation of infinite series of income increments where there is a negative rate of interest, see S. S. Slichter, *Modern Economic Society* (New York, 1931), pp. 685-6n.

sis that the subsidization of inefficient plants by the negative rate will make the maintenance rate higher than where marginal productivity is zero.[7] The equilibrium rate for the system, however, will still be given by the point where *MT* crosses *MP*. In the graph this is given as -*n*%. The condition will arise because for any given supply of capital, at a rate higher than that shown for the maintenance curve, the desire to save is so strong that saving will be positive and thus not in correspondence with the fundamental assumption of the maintenance curve.[8]

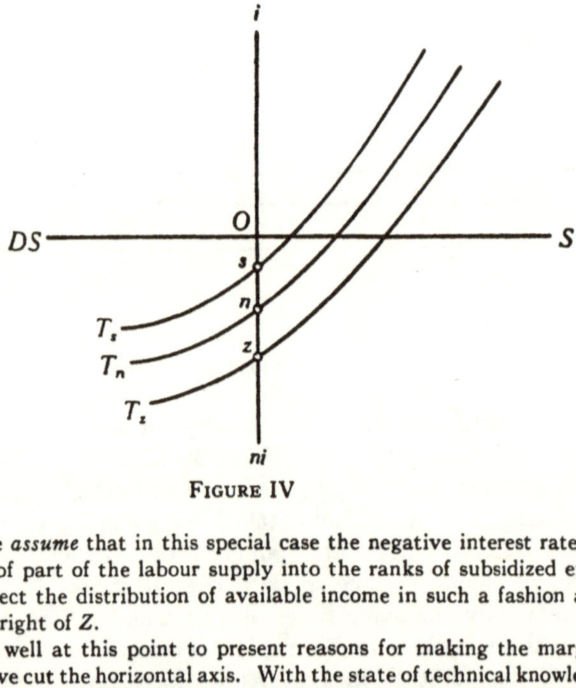

FIGURE IV

[7]That is, we *assume* that in this special case the negative interest rate and the withdrawal of part of the labour supply into the ranks of subsidized entrepreneurs will affect the distribution of available income in such a fashion as to raise *MT* to the right of *Z*.

[8]It may be well at this point to present reasons for making the marginal productivity curve cut the horizontal axis. With the state of technical knowledge, population factors, and tastes assumed to be given throughout, the fall of the interest rate which accompanies the increase in the supply of capital will provide new uses for capital in two directions. First, some lengthier processes may be adopted which were not feasible at the former rates. Second, *more* units of capital may be used with a given number of units of labour in processes made no lengthier than before, because under the cheaper rate the combinations can now cover costs. The former might, without too much stretch of the imagination, be called an expansion of use on the extensive and the latter on the intensive margin.

With reference to the limits upon the lengthening of the capitalistic process, these are given by the wastage which comes with the passage of time. As Mr. Keynes points out, "Lengthy processes are not physically efficient because they are

Description of Hypothetical Society with Negative Rate. Let us, in order to demonstrate the properties of the community with a negative rate, set up a small hypothetical society of this character on the simplest possible terms. All the assumptions we have set out for the stationary state are assumed still to be true. Capital supply is *ON* and the interest-rate ($-n\%$) is -2%, compounded annually. All business units are organized, let us say, as corporations which issue preferred stock only, called every five years and with the negative interest, duly compounded, payable at these five-year intervals. Each original purchaser of a share pays $1000 for it direct to the entrepreneur, and at the end of five years the current holder gets $903.90 for it, when it is called, since that is the value at the end of five years of $1000 compounded annually at a rate of -2%. The difference between $1000 and $903.90 is available to entrepreneurs (who are really only organizers, since the system is riskless) to add to the proceeds of sales of consumption goods in order to cover costs. Because this source of income is present in addition to the income from sales proceeds, business units are able to survive which could not survive at any positive rate. Other units are able to push production further than they could do at a positive rate, if this expansion of production gives them the basis for selling more securities each quinquennium. The saving part of the population will be subsidizing the remainder of the consuming public to the extent that they offer them an increase of goods in the *present* for a claim to goods in the future. Futurity of income has become in itself an asset having a value in the economic system.

In a perfect market, the rate could not depart from -2%. With correct expectations, it will be held at that point by the

long. Some, probably most, lengthy processes would be physically very inefficient, for there are such things as spoiling or wastage with time" (*General Theory*, p. 214; see also Alfred Marshall's note on Böhm-Bawerk, *Principles*, p. 583, to which Mr. Keynes makes reference). When all the processes have been adopted wherein the annual yield exceeds the annual wastage of capital, the remaining processes will not be worth adopting except in a society in which futurity of return is in itself an asset bearing a value.

On the intensive margin, technical knowledge being given, the operation of the principle of diminishing returns will finally exercise such force, when one factor in a combination or series of combinations is increased indefinitely, that the total physical product is actually decreased by further substitutions of the factor whose quantum is being varied.

For both these reasons we must show a limit established by economic forces to an increase in *total* income arising out of additions to capital, and at this limit the *MP* curve will cross the horizontal axis.

operation of the ordinary laws of supply and demand as demonstrated from the elementary principles.

The picture presented of this community is, however, highly unreal for a money economy. In such an economy, where money may be used as a store of value and where it has no or very low carrying costs, no one will be willing to pay $1000 *now* for an income of $903.90 five years from now, if he can get money now and *keep* it for five years! The lowest practical rate of interest will be zero or just sufficiently below it to cover the costs of safe-keeping for funds in some sort of money warehouse. Under such conditions, if the time-preference curve cuts the marginal-productivity curve below the horizontal axis or indeed at any rate not practicable under current institutional conditions, the system must be brought into equilibrium in some other way. This possibility of an inconsistency between the rate of interest institutionally possible and the rate which will bring the system into equilibrium at the level of full employment of all factors, will occupy a key position in the analysis we are to present in the ensuing chapters. For that reason we turn in the last section of this chapter to consider the problem of what will be the equilibrium level of capital stock, under conditions where the minimum institutional rate is higher than the rate which will bring full equilibrium of the type ordinarily analysed in orthodox general equilibrium theory.

(3) THE QUANTITY OF CAPITAL AND THE MINIMUM INSTITUTIONAL RATE OF INTEREST

For the purpose of analysing the forces which determine the long-period equilibrium stock of capital under conditions where the minimum institutional rate of interest is higher than the rate which brings full equilibrium under orthodox analysis, we set up Figure V. This figure is the same as Figure III and carries the same explanation with the exception of the fact that we have added the positive rate of interest *Om* as the minimum institutional rate for the society in question. Study of this figure may help us to determine what would be the long-period equilibrium stock under such circumstances.

The Equilibrium Stock of Capital and the Rate-Structure. Since the minimum rate *Om* is the *maintenance* rate for capital stock *OW* by our curves and definitions, it would at first sight appear logical to assume that the long-period capital stock connected with the rate *Om* will be stock *OW*. But this is not true. Analysis will show that the long-period equilibrium stock for rate *Om* under these conditions will be capital stock *OM*. If capital stock were *OW*, the rate of interest for the Week for which the capital stock stood at *OW* would not be *Om* but some rate above *Om*. The rate *WW'* is the i_0 rate for that Week in terms of the analysis of Chapter v. The *r* and *r'* rates will be equal to each other for assets of the same duration and will be lower than i_0 for all durable assets and securities by an amount determined by the rate of fall in the marginal productivity of capital foreseen during the life

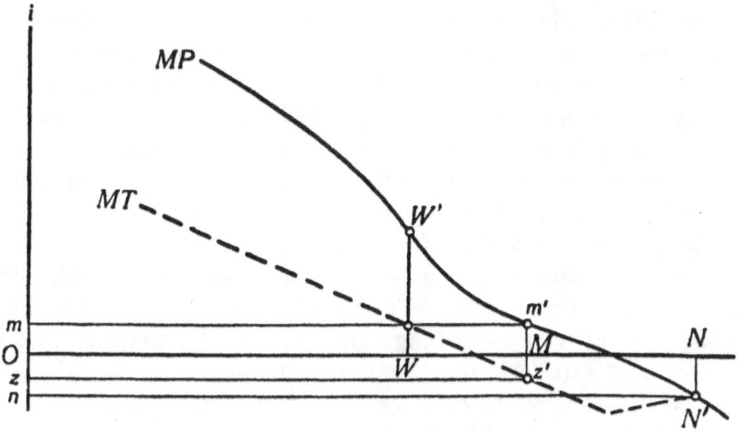

FIGURE V

of the debts and equities concerned. But since the *i* and *r* rates will all be higher than *Om*, both saving and investment will be positive and the economy will have an expansionary form.

There will be a tendency for the stock of capital to increase by Weekly increments up to the point where the inducements to invest at the objective rates of interest are zero. The stock of capital will therefore be pushed forward up to stock *OM*, at which level the marginal product of value earned by indirect applications of factors will be equal to the institutional minimum rate of interest. While all the assumptions with respect to physical supplies of factors, population elements, tastes, techniques, and aversion to work hold, and in the absence of social interventions designed deliberately to modify these conditions, there will be no inducement to push investment further. All the *i* rates, current and forward, will be equal to the marginal productivity of the capital stock *OM* and to the *r* and *r'* rates. All rates of yield on securities, whatever their duration, will be the same.

Implications. Such an equilibrium implies chronic unemployment among the factors of production, and this unemployment, we shall find later, falls upon those who offer their services to entrepreneurs at a money wage. If all who offer themselves *were* employed when capital stock is OM, their level of saving could be brought into equality with investment only through entrepreneur losses. Part of the money paid out to factors for their services (and also part of the money received by entrepreneurs as personal income rather than business proceeds) would fail to return to entrepreneurs as sales proceeds. Entrepreneurs' marginal costs would exceed the selling prices of goods. In the Fundamental Model, the amount of prevision assumed would prevent such circumstances from occurring at all. Entrepreneurs would not put into the income-circuit money which could not be recovered from it. Only business-units would hoard in this Model. (They may instead of hoarding reduce the quantity of money by reducing indebtedness to the banking system.) In the Supplementary Models personal hoarding (or dishoarding) would take place if entrepreneurs made errors in their short plans. But under the assumptions of stability made for this chapter personal hoarding (or dishoarding) could not long continue. If, for example, entrepreneurs put into the income-circuit more money on Monday than they recovered from it on Tuesday, their transactions or business balances would be drawn down by as much as the savings balances of income-receivers were built up. Entrepreneurs under the spur of such conditions would as speedily as possible adjust their production plans to the new situation. This would involve reducing production, and hence employment and income, to the level where business receipts would cover marginal costs of production. Under these conditions, the rate which would bring zero-saving as well as zero-investment would be rate Om. Income and employment would adjust themselves to this minimum institutional rate.

On the other hand, dishoarding by the public under conditions of full employment would result in price rises which would reduce the number of wage-units to which the remaining savings balances were equivalent and would tend to cause a backwash into the savings deposits again. If the original dishoarding were the result of error, we should expect these errors to be adjusted and the "correct" division of money holdings between transactions and savings balances to be established again. More will be said of these relations in the ensuing two chapters.

(4) CONCLUSION

We shall find when we get back to the world of uncertainty and variable expectations that the possibility of an inconsistency between the rates of interest required for full employment and those which are institutionally possible will hold a much more important place than it holds in the unreal static world we have analysed in this chapter. For example, if an expectation of a stable or declining population succeeds a period of fairly rapid expansion, many types of existing capital may be felt to be more than sufficient and depreciation funds may be diverted to new types of capital goods. Under such conditions very low or negative rates of interest might be required to induce entrepreneurs to undertake any new investment and the fact that such rates were institutional impossibilities would prevent the achievement of full employment as long as this inconsistency was present. We cannot get the full development of this situation until we have completed the analysis of the Liquidity, Multiplier, and Investment Functions and have assembled them into the so-called shifting equilibrium. But the analysis of the relation of the rate of interest to the capital stock which we have given in this chapter lays the basis for the later analysis.

The possibility of the presence of this inconsistency rests upon the existence of a money which can be used as a store of value. We discuss in the next two chapters the nature of the demand for money and its connection with the rate of interest. When we have completed these we shall have explored the nature of the Equation $i=L(M, Y)$. We begin again with the simplest analytical conditions.

CHAPTER V

THE DEMAND FOR MONEY AND THE CONSTITUTION OF THE LIQUIDITY FUNCTION L_1

THE first equation of the shifting equilibrium, namely $i=L(M, Y)$, will be studied in two general sections. The first of these will describe the nature of the Liquidity Function L_1, or the part of the demand for money which could exist even under the conditions which form the basis for static analysis.[1] The second will describe the nature of Liquidity Function L_2 or the part of the demand for money which arises in economic systems where money is desired as a store of value. We begin our analysis of the nature of the demand for money with a discussion of the nature of the hypothetical demand in a thorough-going stationary state with equilibrium already attained upon the basis of a positive rate of interest.[2] We shall relax the assumptions connected with this equilibrium by degrees until at the end of the next chapter we shall be dealing with the conditions of the Fundamental Model and to some extent with the conditions of the Supplementary Models and of the real world. In connection with the stationary state we shall take up, first, conditions where no frictions are assumed to exist, and second, conditions where certain minimum frictions are postulated.

[1]It might have been more correct formally to have included two equations in our system in place of Equation (1). We might have written the equation for L_1 as $M_1=L_1(i, Y)$ with M_1 meaning the quantity of money held for other reasons than as a store of value. The L_2 equation then would read $i=L_2(M_2, Y)$. This treatment would, however, prevent us from erecting one general demand function. Since the stocks of money held for one set of reasons may be affected in size by the amounts held for other reasons, it appears desirable for this reason to keep both equations in the same form. For the Supplementary Models, it would be necessary to keep them separate, since in those Models flows from the transactions to the savings balances, or *vice versa*, may occur within the Week with consequences for the variables of the system.

[2]We omit discussion of the demand for money in a stationary state with a negative rate of interest because, as pointed out in the preceding chapter, the existence of such an equilibrium under conditions of full employment is incompatible with the use of a money whose carrying costs are zero or nearly so.

(1) THE DEMAND FOR MONEY IN A STATIONARY STATE

Demand in a Frictionless System. In a frictionless economic system with equilibrium attained under the conditions of the stationary state, no stock of money will be required. With no frictions, there are no special costs involved in the purchase of equities and debts and no inhibitions against the trouble necessary for the investment of small amounts.[3] Some unit constituted by law or custom would be required as a money-of-account, but money-units would not actually pass from hand to hand, since in this frictionless universe, sellers of goods would instantaneously acquire income-producing securities which they would hold until they wished to sell them for consumers' goods. In such cases the securities themselves might pass in exchanges since in a riskless universe one security would be just as good as another.[4] Under such conditions there would be no reason for the existence of any stock of money-units.

The Quantity of Money in a System with Minimum Frictions. If we stipulate that in this universe of perfect foresight there exist minimum institutional frictions, the occasion will arise for the holding of cash-balances. Thus we may suppose that institutional arrangements call for payment of some of the factors of production at intervals set by custom, as by the week or month, while expenditures by these factors upon consumption and the transfers of existing securities (debts and equities) are spread fairly evenly over the intervals between paydays. If there are also costs connected with the investment of small amounts, either objective or subjective or both, holdings of cash will be substituted for holdings of securities until there is equality at the margin of substitution. The conveniences obtained and the inconveniences and costs avoided by the possession of these balances would be equated at the margin against the incomes which could be earned by turning them into the market for securities. Thus we shall have room in the economic system for the holding of a finite amount of money and the first appearance also of the triple margin of substitution, namely among consumption, investment, and the holding of money-balances.

Measured in money-units, any finite amount of money would serve these purposes. With expectations correct, the money-unit will be given a value in real terms (say in wage-units) which will

[3]P. N. Rosenstein-Rodan, "The Co-ordination of the General Theories of Money and Price," *Economica*, III n.s. (1936), pp. 271-2.

[4]*Ibid.*, p. 271.

make the balances carried adequate to the needs under the price system and the institutions which apply. Any amount of money which happens to be in the system when it reaches stationariness should continue to be the amount which is there.

We base this conclusion upon the following reasons. If the system is an unclosed system under stationary conditions, exports and imports will be balanced in terms of value without flows of capital. If it is a closed system (as we are assuming in this study unless the contrary situation is indicated), no money *can* be entering from outside. If the money is a reproducible commodity money of a durable kind, there will be no incentive to increase the stock under the conditions of the stationary state, since under correct expectations, the value of the money-unit would be depreciated instantaneously in proportion to the addition to the stock, and costs of production incurred at the old level of value for the unit would not be covered, while at the new the production would not be undertaken.[5]

If the money is a bank-deposit money and we hold to the assumption of correct foresight, there will be no incentive for the banks to increase the quantity of money by making additional loans because foresight will show that any otherwise apparent advantage of such an increase will be lost by depreciation of the value of the money-unit through rising prices. In terms of *money-units*, the demand for money under these conditions may be represented by a function having unit elasticity (the "rectangular hyperbola") which is contained by implication, if not otherwise, in the crudest forms of the quantity theory.

The Quantity of Money and the Rate of Interest: Static Analysis. In order to get the relation of the rate of interest to the quantity of money, let us suppose, first of all, that all money is bank money and, in order to hold our assumption of competition throughout the whole system, that we have a free banking system, with free flow of factors into and out of banking, as into and out of other enterprises, at the rates of remuneration given to factors of similar grades of efficiency throughout the system. Next, while holding the assumption of correct expectations for the remainder of the system, let us permit bankers to make mistakes. Let us suppose further that owing to the minimum institutional frictions we have predicated, the banking system has been advancing money for the payrolls of entrepreneurs before the latter have recovered the entire

[5]That is, under the conditions of the stationary state, the assumptions of the strictest form of the quantity theory would apply. See *General Theory*, pp. 208-9.

amounts from their customers. For this service they have been making a charge. The demand and supply conditions for these services will form the basis of one of the general equilibrium equations and the price of loans will be determined on the same basis as other prices. Factors of production engaged in banking will earn the same rates of return as others of the same grades of efficiency in other industries.

If the error in expectations is in the direction of thinking that the current rate of interest is too low, the only way in which entrepreneurs providing banking services can raise the rate of interest is by raising the terms on which they make these advances. Marginally placed entrepreneurs among their customers will not be able to pay the higher rates. Since their expectations are by assumption correct, these entrepreneurs will not engage in undertakings which will result in losses. They will reduce their demands upon the banks for cash. Intra-marginal entrepreneurs will also tend to reduce output in order to make marginal costs again agree with marginal revenues, and will likewise reduce their demands upon the banks for cash. Because of these reductions, the banks will fail to match their own marginal costs to their marginal revenues. Under conditions of competition, with correct expectations by all customers and a positive rate of interest, the rate cannot be maintained above the equilibrium level.

If on the other hand, the banking system[6] attempts to push the rate below the equilibrium level, and the quantity of money is increased by additional demands on the banks, revaluation of the prices of factors, goods, and services will depreciate the value of the money-unit in such fashion that the new quantity of money measured in wage-units instead of money-units will be no greater than the old. When revaluation has been completed, the banks will find that at the lower rate of interest they will earn lower rates of return than factors used in other industries. Their profits will be unmaximized under these conditions.

[6]Under the assumptions made, no one bank can make errors unless all banks make similar errors. Thus if one bank charged higher rates than its fellow banks, it would lose all its customers to the others; if it charged lower rates, it would attract to it the customers of the others. If time-lags allowed one bank to gain profits by charging either higher or lower rates than the others, these advantages would pass away in the course of time by the generalization of the error with the results above outlined.

The only way in which the rate of interest[7] could be kept below the equilibrium rate for any length of time would be where the supply of money was continuously increased but time-lags kept banking costs from rising sufficiently to cut off extra profits. Even here it must be assumed that the demand for cash must be elastic enough to make interest returns to the bank larger at the lower rate of interest than they had been at the higher rate by an amount more than sufficient to cover any additions to current costs. To the extent that we hold to the assumption of correct forecasting by the remainder of the community, such an elasticity does not appear likely. But under conditions where such a continuous inflation could take place, we should find the "money rate" of interest below the "natural rate" in a Wicksellian sense.[8]

As the adjustment takes place, there will be a continuous revaluation of the quantity of money-units by a rise in the value of the wage-unit, or other "real" standard, which nullifies the increase so far as any effects upon the economic system are concerned.[9] *Except in relation to the economic system through some such concept as the wage-unit, the quantity of money as such will not have a meaning for the system of economic relations.*

If there is an element of monopoly in the banking field and bankers succeed in holding the rate of interest above the equilibrium rate, it will only be at the cost of reducing employment of the factors of production to a point where savings are at the zero-level at the selected rate of interest. The same general conditions will apply as those analysed under the institutional minimum rate of interest in the preceding chapter.

If the assumptions of a stationary state with minimum frictions are rigidly maintained, no other but the equilibrium rate of interest can hold. The demand for money proper, measured in wage-units, will be for a definite finite amount determined at that level of the rate of interest by the nature of the institutional frictions.

This completes the first stage of our examination of the demand for money under static conditions. In the next section we begin to build the graph for the demand for money, measured in wage-units, which we shall finally apply to our concept of the Week.

[7]We recall that we may speak of "the" rate of interest here because under stationary conditions the i, r, and r' rates will all be equal to each other.

[8]Knut Wicksell, *Lectures on Political Economy*, II, pp. 205ff.

[9]*General Theory*, p. 291.

(2) THE CONSTITUTION OF THE LIQUIDITY FUNCTION, L_1

In the *General Theory*, the Liquidity Function L_1 is described as being mainly dependent upon the level of income.[10] We shall hold here that it has some connection with the rate of interest also. We start with Figure VI below which shows the nature of the demand for money, measured in wage-units, in a given stationary state with minimum frictions assumed to be present. The vertical axis measures the level of the rate of interest, and the horizontal axis shows the quantity of money measured in wage-units.

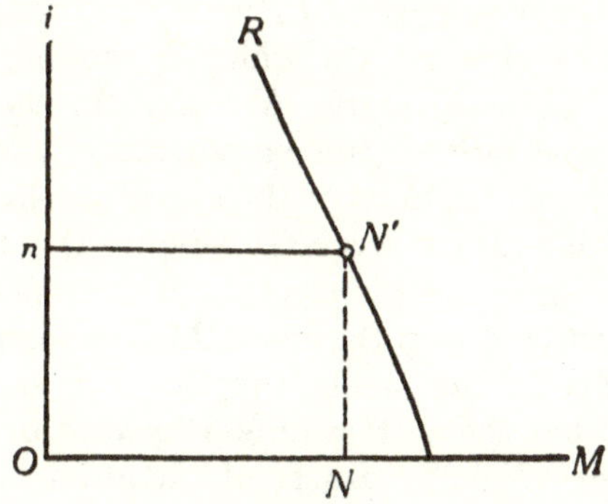

FIGURE VI

Demand for Money in the Stationary State. We assume for the purposes of this demand, in terms of Figure I above,[11] that the stock of capital has been pushed up to the equilibrium level *ON* and that the equilibrium interest-rate is *NN'* ($i = r = r'$ for all durations) as shown on that figure. In Figure VI, the curve *R* is a hypothetical curve given by the willingness of the public in this community to hold a stock of money measured in wage-units in order to have the conveniences afforded by the possession of the cash-balance for the timing of purchases and sales and in order to avoid the specific objective costs connected with the making of investments in small sums and the subjective costs which arise from inertia connected with making investments for small gains only. Holdings of cash will be pushed until there is equality at the margin with the rate of interest which holds the system in equilibrium, namely *NN'*. Thus in Figure VI, the quantity of money, measured in wage-units, is *ON* and the rate $On = NN'$.

[10] *Ibid.*, pp. 199-201

[11] See p. 39.

Once this amount of money is *in* the system, no disturbances to the rate of interest can arise from its presence under the assumptions we have made for Figure I. With no changes in the conditions upon which our assumptions are based, the system will retain its stationariness even though some persons find it worth while to hold cash-balances instead of rights to property. If any accidental force destroys part of the stock of money or adds to it, there will be a revaluation of the wage-unit which will change the quantity of money measured in wage-units in such fashion that it is again consistent with the demand curve at rate NN'.

Demand for Money under Conditions of Moving Equilibrium. At the next step of our analysis of L_1, we wish to adapt this demand curve to the needs of a system which is moving through time toward a given stationary state. We shall in the first instance assume correct expectations, full employment, competition, and minimum institutional frictions of the types previously suggested. We shall start with a capital stock OA (Figure I) and move toward stock ON and will measure the changes in the stock of money by the wage-unit connected with the stock OA, assuming the necessary degree of elasticity in the money-supply. For simplicity's sake, we shall assume that the system moves forward over time on the convention of our Week by a sort of quantum mechanics. We shall thus be able to seize upon its moments of rest in order to study its relations. We also for the short periods for which we take up the relationships identify the capital stock with a level of income and a price system as determined by the conditions of the Week.

We show the character of the relationships involved in Figure VII. For the base Week, we have the demand curve R_a, rate of interest Oa, and quantity of money OM_a, measured in wage-units. Let us say that this is the quantity of money connected with capital stock OA in Figure I. The curve R_a is similar to the curve R in Figure VI though it may differ in elasticity in a moving system.

We must not, however, identify the rate Oa for Figure VII with the rate Oa of Figure I. The rate Oa of Figure VII is the i_0 rate for the Week in which capital stock has reached OA. It is therefore equal to AA', the marginal product of capital for the current Week for capital stock OA as shown on Figure I. The r and r' rates will be equal to each other for securities of the same durations under the assumptions set out, but they will be lower than the current or i_0 rate in accordance with the average fall in the i rates over the lives of the equities and debts in question. Hereinafter when we speak of "the" rate of interest, we shall have reference to the current, or i_0, rate.

As Week by Week passes, the capital stock will grow gradually from OA to OB. If we hold to the assumptions of stability in population factors, tastes, techniques, and perhaps also in the nature of financial institutions for a moving system with frictions, we should expect the growth in the capital stock to be accompanied by a fall in the rate of interest. We shall therefore hold that the

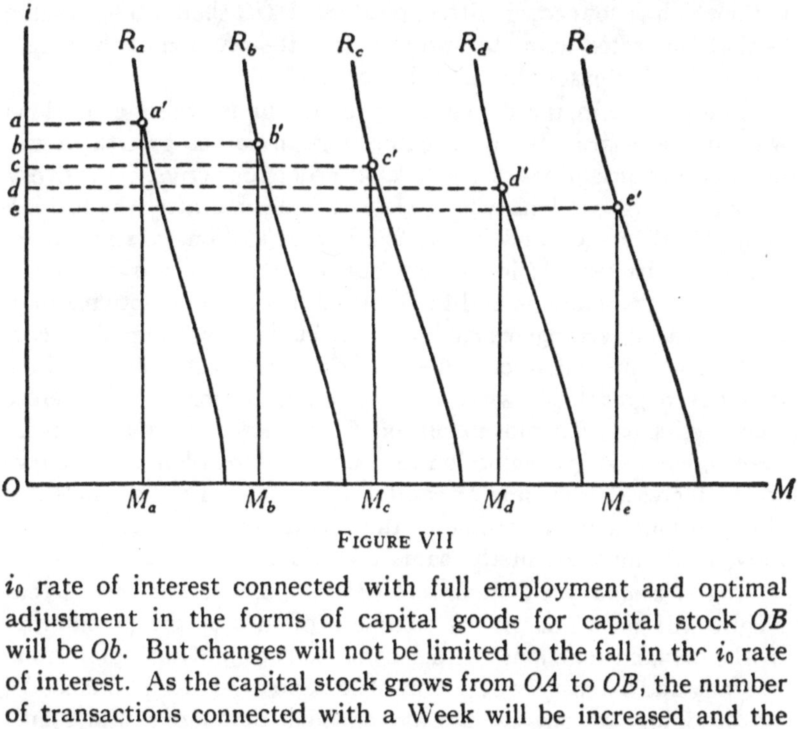

FIGURE VII

i_0 rate of interest connected with full employment and optimal adjustment in the forms of capital goods for capital stock OB will be Ob. But changes will not be limited to the fall in th^ i_0 rate of interest. As the capital stock grows from OA to OB, the number of transactions connected with a Week will be increased and the requirements for a money stock in terms of the basic wage-unit will grow, assuming that the institutional frictions keep the same general character over time. If we assume demand curve R_b, the quantity of money measured in wage-units will be OM_b. Similarly for capital stock OC, it will be OM_c, with i_0 rate O_c; for capital stock OD, it will be OM_d with rate O_d, and so on.

It is not to be inferred in these cases, however, that the quantity of money under conditions of full employment will be a factor determining the structure of the rates of interest. The interest-rate structure will be given by the underlying economic factors governing the rates of investment and saving, and the quantity of money measured in *money*-units will determine, not the interest-rate structure but the value of the wage-unit. Under conditions of correct expectations any variation in the quantity of money measured in money-units in relation to the level of economic activity will be reflected in an offsetting and instantaneous adjustment of the wage-unit.[12] It is quite possible, contrary to the assumption we have made with reference to the elasticity of the money-supply, that the quantity of money measured in money-units which is connected with capital stock *OE* should be the same as that connected with *OA* and that it is the revision of the wage-unit which increases the quantity to OM_e.

The growth in the demand for money under these conditions will not necessarily be in strict proportion to the growth in the number of transactions or the level of economic activity. At every stage some transactions will be cleared somewhat after the fashion in which all are cleared in the frictionless stationary state, even if only by barter. It is entirely possible that the growth in the number of transactions and in the level of economic activity may make clearing arrangements based on institutional organizations, if these are present, more effective, or at any rate effective in a different degree from what had been true formerly. Therefore when we show the movement of *R* connected with a series of Weeks, we make no deduction respecting the relation of the curve to the increase in income or capital stock beyond the obvious one that without a modification in the character of institutions, the movements must be in the same direction.

The Demand for "Finance." It is possible, however, that Figure VII may not give a complete picture of the possibilities of the demand for money under conditions of moving equilibrium. We may add a new type of potential demand to be called "finance."[13] By so doing, we suggest a way in which new money-units may enter the system. Suppose that entrepreneurs, preparing for an

[12]If such an adjustment is to be continuously maintained there must be immediate adjustments of contracts as well as of the prices of factors currently sold. We may solve this difficulty as Professor Hicks does a similar one in *Value and Capital* (Oxford, 1939) by assuming that contracts run for a Week only. See his description of the "pure spot economy" on page 148 of *Value and Capital.*

[13]J. M. Keynes, "Alternative Theories of the Rate of Interest," *Economic Journal*, XLVII (1937), pp. 246-8. This concept does not appear in the *General Theory* but was added by Mr. Keynes as an additional source of demand for money after certain criticisms by Professors Hicks, Robertson, and Ohlin. Mr. Keynes makes extensive quotations from these criticisms in the article cited.

increase in activity in order to maintain the rate of growth in the system, make their financial arrangements a Week in advance of their expectations of undertaking new investment. They will arrange this Monday with the banking system (directly or indirectly) for the creation of certain new deposits in order that they may be sure of being in position to close contracts with factors and customers without delay upon the Monday of next Week. If the rate of interest actually ruling is low enough to induce entrepreneurs to make such a provision, by the "stroke of a pen" the

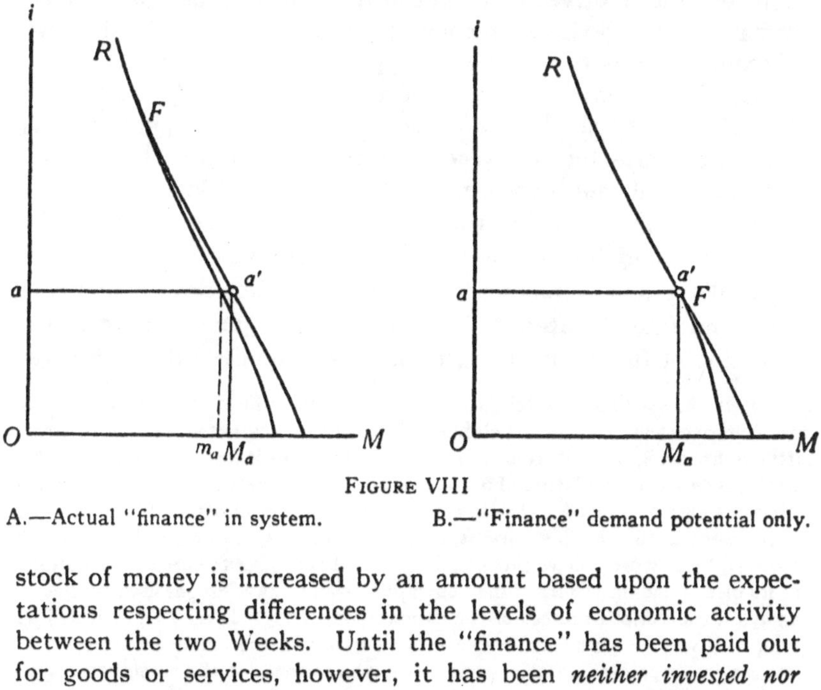

FIGURE VIII

A.—Actual "finance" in system. B.—"Finance" demand potential only.

stock of money is increased by an amount based upon the expectations respecting differences in the levels of economic activity between the two Weeks. Until the "finance" has been paid out for goods or services, however, it has been *neither invested nor saved.* The process of investment will always be connected with the making of a contract for the services of a factor of production. The process of saving will always imply failure to spend income on consumption goods during the Week it has been received.

Figure VIII sets out two different conditions under which a demand for "finance" exists. In case A, the entrepreneurs will actually make such an arrangement for the Week to which the demand R applies and the quantity of "finance" in the system will be m_aM_a. Under case B, the demand for "finance" is potential only. The rate of interest Oa is too high for the entrepreneurs to be planning an extension of the level of economic activity for the succeeding Week. Only if the rate fell below the point given by *F* would such an extension of activity be worth while.

If we were considering a demand for "finance" in a system closer to the real world, we should find that entrepreneurs would be cancelling bank-deposit credits by paying off loans as well as expanding their deposits by making new ones. It will be easiest in reference to a given unit of time such as our Week to regard the cancellation of loans and hence of money-units as a response of the supply of money to a reduction of demand for the transactions or other motives and to keep the "finance" category for net demands for supplies of money for future extension of the level of economic activity.[14] Where entrepreneurs borrow for this Week's transactions from the banks this will mean that the banks buy "securities" of one Week's duration carrying the "pure" rate i_0, with the r rate for the Week varying according to the specific risks of default and expenses connected with the loan.

In the simple world of the moving equilibrium perfectly maintained, demand for "finance" will represent an expansion of the demand for money measured in wage-units but not an influence upon the rate of interest. If the supply of money is inelastic, provision of funds for "finance" in this simple world will involve

[14]Mr. Keynes has the following to say on this subject: ". . . if [the entrepreneur] accumulates a cash balance beforehand (which is more likely to occur if he is financing himself by a new market-issue than if he is depending on his bank), then an accumulation of unexecuted or incompletely executed investment-decisions may occasion for the time being an extra special demand for cash. . . . Investment finance in this sense is, of course, only a special case of the finance required by any productive process; but since it is subject to special fluctuations of its own, I should (I now think) have done well to have emphasised it when I analysed the various sources of the demand for money. It may be regarded as lying half-way, so to speak, between the active and the inactive balances. If investment is proceeding at a steady rate, the finance (or the commitments to finance) required can be supplied from a revolving fund of a more or less constant amount, one entrepreneur having his finance replenished for the purpose of a projected investment as another exhausts his on paying for his completed investment. But if decisions to invest are (*e.g.*) increasing, the extra finance involved will constitute an additional demand for money.

"Now, a pressure to secure more finance than usual may easily affect the rate of interest through its influence on the demand for money; and unless the banking system is prepared to augment the supply of money, lack of finance may prove an important obstacle to more than a certain amount of investment decisions being on the tapis at the same time. But 'finance' has nothing to do with saving . . . . Credit in the sense of 'finance' looks after a flow of investment. It is a revolving fund which can be used over and over again. It does not absorb or exhaust any resources" (*ibid.*, pp. 246-7).

revaluation of the wage-unit in terms of the money-unit. If the supply of money is perfectly responsive to the demand for "finance" there will be a growth factor in the supply of money equal to that in the other elements of the economy and there will be no revaluation of the wage-unit. In neither case will the rate of interest be affected under these simple conditions as it might be in a world in which the assumptions of full employment, adjustment of forms of capital and of the terms of contracts, and correct expectations are not all fulfilled.

The Interest-Rate Structure and the Quantity of Money. The structure of interest-rates for each unit of time in the world with correct expectations and full employment, under the conditions of the moving equilibrium, will be determined by the possibilities of expansion and the relative rates of change in costs in the investment and consumption industries. The money-supply measured in wage-units will adjust itself to these conditions. Per unit of time, production will tend to be pushed in each type of industry until there is equality at the margin between the present estimates of the results of labour and equipment directly and indirectly applied.[15] Moreover, with expectations correct and employment of factors fully maintained, every individual act of saving will be attached, directly or indirectly, to some act of investment whose results are foreknown. There will be no losses. The charge for *user* cost which is an element of marginal cost will be truly estimated upon the technical elements determining the dis-investment in instruments which results from their use, and it will be entirely objective in its nature. The i_0 rate of interest will be determined by the elements which determine the size of the current marginal product of capital for the Week and will constitute the margin of substitution for the Week. The r and r' rates will be equal to each other for securities of the same duration and will be determined (on methods to be shown in the next chapter) by the average fall in the size of the marginal product during the currency of the securities.

So far we have held to the assumptions of stability in population and other factors which we set out at the beginning of Chapter IV. If we relax these but retain the assumptions of correct expectations and full employment, the demands for money will still be of the same nature, even though the system may be moving now toward a normal position which is constantly changing because of changes

[15]See Oscar Lange, "Interest in the Theory of Production," *Review of Economic Studies*, III (1935-6), pp. 187-9; also Oscar Lange, "Professor Knight's Note on Interest Theory," *ibid.*, IV (1936-7), pp. 231-2.

in population factors, tastes and standards of living, desire for leisure, technical knowledge, degree of thriftiness, or any other factor. It is, however, difficult to retain the assumptions of correct expectations and full employment in the face of such changes and we shall presently abate these.

The Demand for Money for the Precautionary Motive. The next and last stage for purely static analysis takes us to the condition where unemployment of factors may occur during a given Week but where the assumptions respecting the size and velocity of the use of money are such as to keep the size of the money-income constant over time. Under such conditions, expectations regarding the general situation may be assumed as data. There seems to be no point in giving any great amount of attention to the demand for money and the rate of interest in a model world built upon this assumption. It is a useful assumption for the study of the particular forces operating upon the value of the individual good or the individual business enterprise, but for the study of total reactions in an economic community, it provides us with no path from the world of static analysis into the world we know.[16]

There is, however, one further type of demand for money which would appear in such a system which we should not find in a world in which individual firms, as well as the system as a whole, were carrying on operations under conditions of correct expectations, as has been our assumption. With *MV* constant, expectations may have a given character for the system as a whole, but the operation of autonomous factors in a system in which unemployment can occur will be unpredictable for individual income-receivers and individual business-units. Under such conditions, there will be a call for a further type of cash-balance, namely one based upon the "precautionary motive."[17] In order "To provide for contingencies requiring sudden expenditure and for unforeseen opportunities of advantageous purchases, and also to hold an asset of which the value is fixed in terms of money,"[18] both business-units and individual income-receivers may seek to carry

[16]Thus see Gottfried von Haberler, *Prosperity and Depression* (1st ed., League of Nations, 1937), pp. 226-7, and note Professor Haberler's opinion that the constancy in *MV*, assumed or implied in most theory running in real terms, in the world we know "may require very drastic interventions which are hardly possible without far-reaching changes in the present institutional framework."

[17]*General Theory*, pp. 170-2, 196.

[18]*Ibid.*, p. 196.

funds somewhat beyond their calculations of *regular* needs for the evening off of payments. The margin to which the holdings for this purpose will be pushed under any given state of expectations will also be related to the structure of the interest-rates and have particular reference to the rate i_0. The total demand for money, measured in wage-units, will be increased by the new demand for each level of income.

Graphical Representation of Liquidity Function L_1. When the demand for the precautionary balance is added to the demands

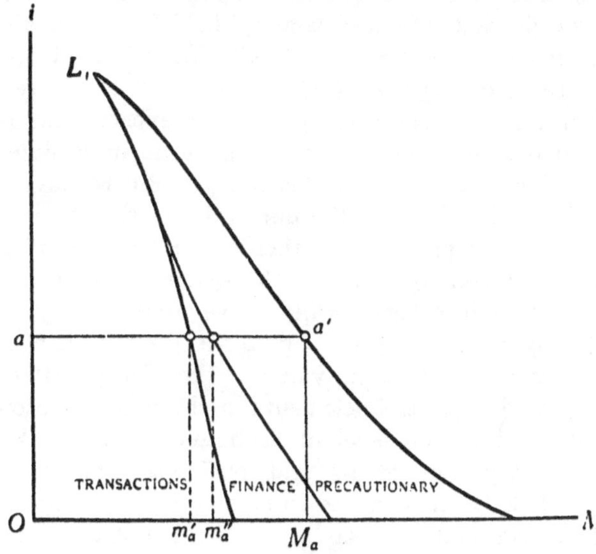

FIGURE IX

for transactions and "finance," the demand for money attached to *one of our Weeks* may appear to have the nature set out in Figure IX. In this figure, L_1 stands for the total demands for money which could occur in a society in which there was no uncertainty with respect to the future value of the money-unit, but where institutional frictions and the uncertainties of individuals respecting their own individual fortunes called for the keeping of certain cash-balances. Under the demand curve L_1 as set out, with interest-rate *Oa* established by the total factors of the economic situation, the quantity of money measured in wage-units will be M_a. Of this quantity, Om'_a will result from demands for the transactions balances, $m'_a m''_a$ from the demand of the current Week for "finance," and $m''_a M_a$ to satisfy the precautionary motive.

We are, however, getting perilously close to dynamic conditions which will make our assumption that there is no uncertainty respecting the future value of the money-unit impossible to maintain. If the various degrees of uncertainty felt by individuals regarding their own futures should undergo any degree of general change, we should expect an expansion or a contraction of the demand for money for precautionary motives. In the face of an expansion of such a demand, for example, unless the money stock, measured in wage-units, were perfectly responsive to these changes in demand, there would be tendencies upon the part of individuals to withdraw portions of their balances held for transactions purposes into inactive balances, which withdrawal would result in a change in the money-value of the wage-unit. If we were maintaining our former assumption of correct expectations for individuals and business-units, there would be an immediate adjustment throughout the system to this change. But we have assumed that the change is *caused* by the uncertainties of individuals. We are faced with the problem whether or not the uncertainties of individuals have consequences for the system as a whole.

We have therefore gone as far as we usefully may upon the basis of purely static analysis. Up to the present changes in the quantity of money and in the value of the money-unit have not been represented as possible elements in the determination of the interest-rate and in the level of economic activity. But in a pecuniary society, individuals and business-units may find it desirable to hold savings in the form of a stock of money, or to expand or to contract past savings so held, not only because of uncertainties connected with their particular situations but because of expectations respecting the course of the general situation and because of the possible reactions of this general situation upon their own positions as entrepreneurs, income-receivers, and holders of property-rights.

To the study of that demand we turn in the succeeding chapter. It will be primarily a study of under-equilibrium where the size of the wage-unit is not immediately and instantaneously responsive to change in the quantity of money measured in wage-units. The study we have set out in the last two chapters of the situation in which we have full employment and immediate response of the wage-unit to changes in the quantity of money will remain to give us the limiting positions upon the movement of the shifting equilibrium within its field. We shall come back to these limiting positions again in Chapter XIII. In the meantime we proceed to the study of Liquidity Function L_2.

CHAPTER VI

THE RATE OF INTEREST AND THE DEMAND FOR MONEY

IN this chapter it is proposed, first, to analyse the nature of the function L_2 which represents the demand for money as a store of value; second, to combine the functions L_1 and L_2 into the general function which represents the total demand for money as a stock; and third, to bring the concept of the Liquidity Function L into the form we shall require for our analysis of the shifting equilibrium. We shall do this last by drawing up a graph whereon we shall exhibit a sheaf of Liquidity Functions as the potentialities for a Week which is emerging into the present at the end of a series of Weeks having a definite history.

(1) THE DEMAND FUNCTION L_2: INTRODUCTORY

Limits on Monetary Management. Limits upon monetary management of the economic system through changes in the quantity of money have already been suggested by the general character of the preceding analysis. Upon the one hand they may result from institutional barriers to indefinite decreases in the level of interest-rates. Upon the other they arise out of offsets to changes in the effective quantity of money for L_2 balances originating in changes in the size of the wage-unit or other "real" standard. Between these limits there will be an area within which monetary management may be used with varying effectiveness to sustain or to raise the level of economic activity. This is the world of under-equilibrium, normally subsumed in orthodox equilibrium theory under the categories of frictions and transitions and summarily dismissed.

Assumptions with respect to the Supply of Money. The institutional character of monetary and banking arrangements will determine the quantity of money-units available and the elasticity of the supply of money. If the standard money were gold, for example, the output of gold mines and the flow of this output into monetary uses would be determined by ordinary cost-price principles in relation to the quantity and quality of physical sources of supply, conditions of competition applying in the mining industry and elsewhere, and the fixed legal price of gold in money-units.[1] If the standard money were a representative money whose issue was subject to arbitrary control by the central bank or other authorities, the nature of these controls would determine the quantity of money-units available and the elasticity of the money-supply.

For simplicity's sake we shall ordinarily assume throughout this analysis, unless otherwise stated, that determination of the quantity of money-units is subject to arbitrary control by the monetary authorities and that the quantity of money-units for a given Week is a datum, though it would be relatively easy to add equations to the system to provide for a variable money-supply. The shape of the L_2 function itself will be based upon price- and interest-expectations developed in part by the elasticity of the money-supply of the past.

Nature of the Demand for Money as a Store of Value. The demand for money as a store of value which we bring under function L_2 would not occur under the static conditions which we analysed in relation to the institutional demand for money in the preceding chapter. Demand L_2 springs partly from uncertainty respecting the future, and partly from a particular form of subjective certainty connected with variations in the rate of interest and in the value of the money-unit.[2] Both sources of demand are related to the ways in which men wish to hold their accumulated property-rights.

[1]For Mr. Keynes' treatment see *General Theory,* pp. 230-1, 234-6.

[2]We have departed somewhat from Mr. Keynes' treatment in dividing the L_2 functions into two categories. The division made here is similar to though not identical with the division of savings deposits into categories A and B in the *Treatise on Money* (New York, 1930), I, p. 250. We differ also from Mr. Keynes' analysis by making the "specified period," to which liquidity preference rates are primarily attached, the Week. We shall in this manner be able to make the relation of rates of interest of different durations and of different types (i, r, and r' as defined in Chapter III) to the Keynesian system of analysis much more specific. See the *General Theory,* foot-notes on pages 137 and 167, and notice the general looseness of definition of "the" rate of interest. For further references respecting the development of the determination of the interest-rate in Mr. Keynes' philosophy, see *General Theory,* chaps. XIII-XVII inclusive, and also pp. 245-9, 298-9, 306-9.

For articles and notes by Mr. Keynes on the specific subject of the interest rate, see: "Alternative Theories of the Rate of Interest," *Economic Journal,* XLVII (1937), pp. 241-52; "The 'Ex-Ante' Theory of the Rate of Interest," *Economic Journal,* XLVII (1937), pp. 663-9; "The Theory of the Rate of Interest," from *The Lessons of Monetary Experience* (ed. A. D. Gayer, New York, 1937), pp. 145-52; A Comment "On Mr. Keynes and 'Finance,'" *Economic Journal,* XLVIII (1938), pp. 318-22.

In Chapter III, property titles were divided into three categories, equities, debts, and money, the latter including bank-balances. From the standpoint of the debts market, we described the requirement for short-period equilibrium as a condition where all holders of debts feel that there is no net advantage to be gained by disposing this Monday of specific assets held in order to move into the equities market, into new investment, into money, into an expansion of consumption, or back into the debts market in order to purchase another debt whose prospects are held to be more favourable. The condition for equilibrium in the equities market was described similarly, *mutatis mutandis*. The margin of substitution which emerged from these series of valuations is identified with the rate of interest, i, which emerges from the solution of the Keynes-Lange system, and the symbol for any current time-unit, or Week, is i_0. The study of the Liquidity Function L_2 brings us to the consideration of the relation of the demand for money as a store of value to this margin of substitution.

(2) THE CHARACTER OF THE RATE i_0

Before we proceed to a consideration of the relation of the demand for money as a store of value to the demands for various debts and equities available in this market, we may make our reasoning clearer by defining more precisely the relations existing among Weekly yields (the A and a series of Chapter III), current and expected prices for debts and equities, and the current substitution rate i_0. We use the same symbols as before but we must add symbols for the current and expected prices of debts and equities. The current price for any specific debt or equity we shall symbolize by P_0; expected prices will be symbolized by P_1, $P_2, \ldots$ subscripts as before indicating the position of the Week in a sequence of future Weeks.

Expected prices for debts and equities may be derived from the formulae of Chapter III by simple modifications. For example, P_1, the expected price for a debt next Monday, would be given by the formula:

$$P_1 = \frac{d_2 A}{e_1\,(1+i_1)} + \frac{d_3 A}{e_1\,e_2\,(1+i_1)\,(1+i_2)} + \ldots + \frac{d_n(A+P)}{e_1 e_2 \ldots . e_{n-1}\,(1+i_1)\,(1+i_2) \ldots . (1+i_{n-1})} - l. \quad (5)$$

The i_0 Rate of Interest; No Expectations of Interest-Changes. We divide our consideration of cases in this section as follows. We shall consider, first, cases where expectations have such a character that the i and r' rates are always equal to each other. Whatever the current margin of substitution, that margin is expected to persist. For the formulae of the debts-equities markets, therefore, under these conditions $i_0 = i_1 = i_2 = i_n$. Under this convention, the relation of the i_0 rate to the current and expected prices of securities will be studied, first, where payments are made Weekly, and second, where they may be made irregularly. We shall follow up this analysis by relaxing the assumption that the i rates are all equal to each other and consider the qualifications which must be brought into the analysis where differences between the i_0 and r' rates exist. Lastly, we shall consider conditions where the a series of an equity forms a rising or falling sequence.

A debt whose income is payable Weekly will pay next Monday the sum d_1A in money-units, d_1 representing the adjustment of the periodic interest payment named in the debt by any existing risk of default. The ratio of advantage in holding this debt from this Monday to next Monday would be given by the ratio of the expected yield to the current price, or d_1A/P_0. As long as the calculation of d_1A remains the same, changes in the ratio can occur only through changes in P_0, the current price, and such changes can occur only with actual changes in $i_0 = i_1 = i_2 = i_n$. It will be a condition for short-period equilibrium that, for marginal holders of specific debts at the end of this Monday's trading, the ratio d_1A/P_0 will be equal to i_0, or the margin of substitution for the system for the Week. This is just another method of expressing the condition of temporary equilibrium implicit in the Fundamental Model and explained in Chapter III.

If a debt promises no payment next Monday but is expected to accumulate value because it will be a Week closer to payments specified for some future Monday or Mondays, there must be an expected increase in the price of the debt on next Monday which will be sufficient to equal the advantage of holding any other property-right for the Week. Therefore the condition for short-period equilibrium here is that for marginal holders of the debt $\frac{P_1 - P_0}{P_0} = i_0$.

We may by similar reasoning derive formulae for the equities market. The formula $s_1a_1/P_0 = i_0$ will describe conditions for short-period equilibrium for specific equities promising a payment next

Monday, a_1 representing as in Chapter III the mean value given the dispersion of yields for next Monday and s_1 the correction coefficient as explained in that chapter. For equities which may promise no payment next Monday, we may use the formula $\frac{P_1-P_0}{P_0}=i_0$ as in the debts market.

Since the rate i_0 forms part of the formula for the derivation of both P_0 and P_1, it is possible that an imputation of circular reasoning may be made respecting the above relationships. It is easily met. On any Monday morning before the markets open there may be as many i_0 rates in valuation series as there are potential traders in the markets for new and old equities and debts. Each may have his *own* expectation of what will happen next Monday. But as the market situation discloses itself, expectations may become modified and by the time the market has reached temporary equilibrium, the prices established by the market will be those which are in line with the expectations of *marginal* holders. At the close of trading, the available stock of any equity or debt will be in the hands of those whose price- and interest-expectations are such that they expect returns at the rate of i_0 *or better*. Each property holder will have made what appears to him the best possible distribution of property-rights for the current Week.

The formulae of this chapter express not a method of *determination* but a *relationship* which will exist when the jockeying for position has been completed. The total situation is one of interdependence.

The i_0 Rate; Expectations of Changes in Interest-Rates. Cases where the expected forward i rates form a falling or a rising series[3] will require combination of the two general types of formula described above. Where the i rates, duly corrected by the e coefficients which apply, form such series, the r' rates will differ from the i_0 rate and expected forward prices will differ from current prices in the debts and equities markets even where there are no reasons connected with the timing and sizes of income payments to cause such differences. Where the i rates, for example, constitute a falling series, there is an expectation of falling interest-rates and current and expected r' rates will lie below i_0, and expected r'

[3]The possibility of a "hump" or "slump" in the shape of the expected i series must be admitted. We shall, however, not complicate analysis by considering such series. Moreover, since the main relation for the Week will be the relation between this Week and next Week, analysis of a "humped" or "slumped" series is not very important. For next Week, i_1 must be *either* above *or* below i_0.

rates below current r' rates for the same durations. Moreover, under these assumptions, the longer the currency of a debt or equity, the lower the r' rate will be, with the consol rate lowest of all, *ceteris paribus*. Such a state of expectations carries with it an expectation of rising prices for debts, and also for equities unless offset by some other expected changes. Where the i rates form a rising series, the current and expected r' rates will lie above i_0 and there will be an expectation of falling prices for debts, and for equities unless offset as before. Such states of expectation for marginal holders of property-rights will have consequences for the current rate of substitution i_0.

By combination of the two general types of formula we make adjustments for such expectations. For example, in the case of the formula d_1A/P_0, we must make an adjustment to provide for the possibility of an expected fall in the price of a specific debt between this Monday and next Monday which will reduce the expected yield for holding it for the Week. Alternatively we must provide for the possibility of an expected rise in the price which may increase the expected net yield. The expectations in question are those of marginal holders of the assets since it is such persons or business-units who will be sensitive to these changes and who will wish to shift holdings in accordance with any net expectation of gains to be made or losses to be avoided by so doing. For debts, the amended formula will read:

$$\frac{d_1A + (P_1 - P_0)}{P_0} = i_0.$$

We may show what this means by an example. If the Weekly payment on a consol bond is $3.00 each Monday and if the current r' rate on consol bonds is 3%, the current price P_0 will be $100. If the i series has such a character that the expected consol rate one Week forward is 3.05%, the expected price next Monday for the bond will be $3 ÷ .0305 or $98.36. Application of the above formula gives $\frac{\$3.00 + (\$98.36 - \$100)}{\$100} = 1.36\%$ as the current margin of substitution or i_0 rate of the i series. This is the current margin of substitution if trading has brought the prices and rates of return, current and expected, of this consol bond into short-period equilibrium with the other possibilities for holding property-rights or spending money for the Week.

There is no intention in the above example of implying that the long-term rate in any sense "determines" the short-term rate any more than the short-term rate "determines" the long-term rate. Basically it is truer to state that if the psychological-institutional complex is among the "given" factors of the situation, interest-expectations will have such a character that once the i_0 rate is given, the r' rates attached to that i_0 rate will be subsumed under the functional forms as determined by that psychological-institutional complex. The total situation, it is to be emphasized again, is one of interdependence. But the i_0 rate which emerges this Week may be a powerful factor in determining the nature of the psychological-institutional complex for next Week.

We have still to consider conditions in the equity market where the a series form rising or falling sequences. While the A payments for debts are assumed to be equal to each other, the a series representing expected yields for the equities market will be subject to varying expectations in accordance with the expected trends of net profits in the industries whose equities form the market stock. Expectations may be based either upon specific elements in the firms or corporations represented by the equities or upon factors of the general economic situation which lead to expectations of a rising or falling level of economic activity accompanied by general changes in cost-price relationships. Expectations of either type may result in rising or falling a series. P_0 and P_1 and other expected prices may bear somewhat different relations to each other because of such expectations. For short-period equilibrium between this Monday and next Monday, the formula which will fit the equities market for a current Week will be:

$$\frac{s_1 a_1 + (P_1 - P_0)}{P_0} = i_0.$$

With reference to equities, therefore, it is to be noticed that the term $(P_1 - P_0)$ may have a positive or a negative value for reasons connected *either* with interest-expectations *or* with expectations regarding the character of the a series.

Relation of Forward to Current i Rates. So far we have given attention only to short-period equilibrium for a current Week. It is probably desirable to indicate the relation of the forward i rates to the current or i_0 rate. We do this by showing the method of deriving the rate $e_1 i_1$ from a valuation series of the debts market. The formula for the place taken by this rate in the expectation series is as follows: $\frac{d_2 A + (P_2 - P_1)}{P_1} = i_1$. Since $(P_1 - P_0) + (P_2 - P_1) = P_2 - P_0$, the place of the i_1 rate in the series is consistent with the place of the i_0 rate. We have already under the conventions of the Fundamental Model assumed that once the i_0 rate is known, the forward i rates attached and hence the r' rates will be determined by the nature of the psychological-institutional complex. Under these assumptions we may restrict our analysis to the examination of the conditions that determine which i_0 rate will emerge from a set of given conditions.

Differences in the states of expectation which may be assumed under the psychological-institutional complex will have consequences for the L_2 function. We defer consideration of these differences until we have analysed the general reasons why holders of money as a store of value may impute to such holdings advantages which give a yield equal to the i_0 margin for a Week.

(3) DESCRIPTION OF THE L_2 FUNCTION

The Basis of the Demand for Money as a Store of Value. We have already described the demand for money under function L_2 as being determined partly by uncertainty and partly by a type of subjective certainty. We may think of demand L_2 under these two categories as consisting of a central core of savings deposits held as a sort of hedge against a possible rise of value in the money-unit and based upon fairly long-term expectations, and of a more variable marginal portion related more specifically to short-term expectations. As we shall see, there may be circumstances under which even the hard core may be dissipated by transfers to the institutional or L_1 balances.

The holder of a cash-balance at any time is retaining his freedom of choice respecting disposition of his property or its decumulation without loss of principal in terms of money. That freedom to move carries with it certain satisfactions in a world in which the future is highly unpredictable.[4] Because of these satis-

[4]In a riskless universe subject only to institutional frictions and characterized always by full employment, these options would have no value. They would on the contrary mean unnecessary losses of income without subjective or objective offsets.

The balances carried under the hard core are hard to differentiate from the balances categorized under "precautionary" for demand L_1. But this is a difficulty in which any system of categories finds itself involved at the margin between classifications. Perhaps we should put into L_1 the precautionary balances held for reasons which are related to the specific prospects of individuals or business-units. Demand under L_2 we would then relate to the *general* state of uncertainty which characterizes a society subject to *general* changes in the levels of economic

factions, possession of the balances will carry an economic value to be measured by income foregone in order to hold them. For a given economic society at a given time, therefore, there may be a disposition to carry a certain proportion of the annual income or of the remaining property-rights quite consistently in the form of claims to money-balances.

The demand for the hard core of savings holdings in the form of money will be based upon a history of instability in the system of economic relations normally of very long standing. Even if conditions of full employment were to persist for some time, it would probably take some fairly long time to develop confidence in the stability of the system at the level of full employment. Only as this confidence grew would the balances forming the hard core be dissipated under these conditions by transfers to the transactions balances and hence into the income-circuit. Under conditions of instability in the system, there are, however, certain states of expectation which would also cause such transfers. These will be described in their place. It is to be observed that transfers from the savings to the transactions balances under conditions of full employment (or previously, if "bottle-necks" exist)[5] must result in rises in prices, including the price of the labour-unit, which will reduce the quantity of any given number of money-units measured in terms of the wage-unit.[6]

The Marginal Demand for Money as a Store of Value. The marginal demand for L_2 is the demand which is related in part to a type of subjective certainty through the balance of "bull" and "bear" sentiment in the community for a given Week. A growing party of "bears" means a growing party of individuals with degrees of subjective certainty that there is increasing danger in holding property-rights in forms other than as cash-balances and an advantage of a nature to be analysed hereafter in holding cash-balances. A growing party of "bulls" means growing sentiment of

---

activity, prices, and interest-rates. In such a world an individual may find it clearly advisable to carry a portion of his bundle of rights in a form not subject to price changes. The difficulty in laying down the boundary between L_1 and L_2 holdings is intellectual only, for we shall presently merge the two functions into one general demand function in which money-units held by one individual or business-unit for one purpose may serve to lessen demand for money-units held for another purpose.

[5]*General Theory*, pp. 300-1.

[6]*Ibid.*, pp. 209, 301-2, 304-5.

the opposite nature.[7] In part also the marginal demand may reflect a growing desire for hedges.

Terminology. The human attitude which causes human beings to build up these balances, whether it springs from subjective uncertainty or certainty, we shall call *liquidity preference.*[8] The values which we attach to such balances we shall call *liquidity premiums,*[9] and the schedule of the quantities of money attached to the various liquidity premium rates which form potential margins of substitution for the system as a whole we shall call the *liquidity preference schedule.*[10] It is obvious that other assets may have their own liquidity preference schedules and liquidity premiums. We have already adjusted the system of valuations to this circumstance in Chapter III by the "illiquidity penalties" we used to reduce the prices of assets under the symbol l in accordance with the differences between the liquidity of money and the liquidity of other assets.

At this point in the analysis we must make more precise than is done in the *General Theory*[11] the relation of the Liquidity Function to a precisely defined unit of time. We choose the Week and therefore the i_0 rate of the foregoing analysis. This is reasonable because balances which it is planned to hold for longer periods than the Week will be included in the demand for the Week, while balances which it is planned to hold for the Week only will also be included. Upon the basis of the Week and of the i_0 rate, therefore, we proceed to a closer description of the L_2 function. With respect to this description, it is to be recalled that we are assuming that when the i_0 rate is given, the r' rates are given by the nature of the psychological-institutional complex.

General Description of the Function and its Elasticity. If we set up the L_2 function upon a graph of the same type as that used to describe L_1, we should find the elasticity of the function determined by the state of the psychological-institutional complex. This complex will determine what rates of interest are considered "normal" under the state of expectations which applies. Within the range of

[7]*Ibid.*, pp. 169-74. For a discussion of the relation of short-term expectations to the state of long-term expectations in market valuations of investment, see *ibid.*, pp. 152-64.

[8]*Ibid.*, pp. 166, 168. For the general discussion, see pp. 166-74 and all of chap. XV, pp. 194-209.

[9]*Ibid.*, pp. 226-9.

[10]*Ibid.*, pp. 168, 171-2, 197-200, 205. These deal generally with the idea of the schedule under the concept of the Liquidity Function.

[11]See foot-note 2, p. 68 above.

normal rates, the i_0 and r' rates previously described will tend to be equal to each other, since as long as the rates are within this range there will be as much likelihood of their moving up as moving down, and *vice versa*. The $(P_1 - P_0)$ section of the preceding formulae, so far as it depends upon expectations of changes in the r' rates of interest, will have a value of zero. Substitution at the margin under such conditions will tend to be based upon the economic factors of the situation and not upon speculative expectations. So far as the desire to hold money is concerned, within this range of normal rates, the L_2 function will have a strong tendency to be inelastic.

Within this range of rates, if changes in the quantity of money measured in money-units tend to coincide with conditions of under-employment in the system, such changes will tend to change the rates of interest and to inspire transfers of money to or from the transactions balances with consequences presently to be analysed for the levels of employment and economic activity. An increase in the amount of money is likely to be followed by an enlargement of the transactions rather than the savings balances or at least the major effect will be on the transactions balances. The effect upon employment and economic activity will depend upon the expansibility of the system at the level of employment which exists. If the system is perfectly expansible, the whole effect will be upon employment and economic activity. If, on the other hand, a condition of full employment already exists, the whole effect will waste itself in effects upon prices and the size of the wage-unit. If the situation is intermediate, and some parts of the system are perhaps perfectly expansible and others show varying degrees of rigidity, the effects will be in part to increase the level of employment and economic activity and in part to raise absolute and change relative prices. If the initial change is a *decrease* in the quantity of money, the effects may be worked out, *mutatis mutandis*. The full understanding of the reasons for this relationship must await again the assemblage of the whole apparatus.

Outside the normal range of rates, identity between the i_0 and r' rates will not obtain. High i_0 and high r' rates will go together, but if the complex of rates is thought to be near or outside the limit of rates considered to be normal, falling rates of interest are more likely to be expected than equal or rising rates in the future and the i_0 rates will tend to be higher than the r' rates. Since falling rates mean rising prices for securities, *ceteris paribus*, so far as such an expectation exists, it will give the term $(P_1 - P_0)$ of the formulae a positive value which will tend to increase the advantages of holding debts and equities rather than money, at least as far as anticipations of falling *a* series do not offset for equities anticipations of rising rates. Under such states of expectation, if the anticipation of rises in the values of debts and equities is very active, even the hard core of money held for hedging purposes in the L_2 balances may soften up and disappear into the transactions balances to be used in the Financial Circulation for trading in the debts-equities markets[12] or alternatively into new investment if the inducements to invest justify. If the psychological-institutional complex is given, as the range of i_0 rates rises above the level coincident with the complex of normal r' rates, the L_2 function will be growingly elastic.

At the other extreme of the function, it will be the marginal demands based on short-term expectations which give the demand function extraordinary elasticity. This is a consequence of the fact that where money has no carrying charges, or practically none, the effective limit upon the fall of interest-rates must be *zero* rate—if not above that level—since at that point there could be no purpose in holding debts or equities rather than money. All increases in the quantity of money measured in wage-units, once that limit was reached, would go into inactive bank-balances *without effect upon the rates of interest* or upon the levels of employment and economic activity.

Under these conditions the relations between the i_0 and r' rates would be the reverse of those described above. At rates considered abnormally low, there would be a net expectation of a rise in the complex of interest-rates. So long as such an expectation exists, the term $(P_1 - P_0)$ will have a negative value, as far as the effects of interest-expectations determine it. Any d_1A or s_1a_1 amount due next Monday must be reduced by the amount of the $(P_1 - P_0)$ term which applies. The i_0 rates will tend to be the lowest of current rates under these conditions. The rewards foregone by holding property in the form of money from this Monday to next Monday will be so small (if they exist at all) and the risks so one-sided that at some minimum rate for i_0 the desire to hold property-rights in the form of money will be absolute. As the complex of the rates of interest falls into the range which gives the i_0 rate this minimum, monetary authorities will find themselves increasingly unable to influence the levels of employment and output.

[12] I know of cases in the "great bull market" of the twenties where even church choirs and football teams transferred idle deposits to New York in order to loan them in the call-market!

We have already referred to the fact that the marginal demand for savings balances may be in part a demand arising from subjective certainty and in part an increasing desire for hedges arising from uncertainty. Some holders of money impelled by subjective certainty will be so "bearish" that they feel that decreases in the market prices of debts and equities will be sufficient, or more than sufficient, to wipe out the running yield from this Monday to next Monday. For example, if $i_0 = 3\%$ for the system as a whole, there may be some holders of inactive balances who feel that $(P_1 - P_0)$ for available securities and equities will show a negative value equal to or exceeding 3%. It is obvious that if the psychological-institutional complex is given, as the rate falls from 3% to 2% and down, there will be a larger and larger number of "bears." Thus growing subjective certainty increases the elasticity of the function at lower rates.

With reference to those influenced to hedge by the falling complex of rates, it is also obvious that as the interest-rate complex falls lower and lower below the normal range, the probability of further falls grows weaker and of rising rates grows stronger. Under these conditions there will be an increasing disposition on the part of holders of property-rights to increase the proportion of savings deposits held for hedging purposes in the "bundle" as the complex falls.

Illustration. An arithmetical example will help to make these relations clearer. Let us suppose that a consol bond brings a payment of \$1.00 on each Monday and let us suppose further, in order to relate the rates of interest given to the ordinary quotations of the market for r rates, that the Week is twelve months long and that the r rates equal the r' rates. In the first instance let us assume that the current r' rate for consols is 10% and that there is an expectation on the part of marginal holders that on next Monday (one year from today) it will have declined by one-fourth of one per cent to 9.75%. The problem is what i_0 rate must have found its place in such a state of expectations. By application of the formula, the rate i_0 will be found to be 12.6%. Since the current price, capitalizing at 10%, will be \$10 and the expected price P_1, at 9.75%, will be \$10.26, the solution of the formula gives $\frac{\$1.00 + (\$10.26 - \$10.00)}{\$10.00} = \frac{1.26}{10.00} = 12.6\%$. Current (P_0) and expected (P_1) prices for debts and equities of shorter durations than consols but longer than one Week will be such, when short-period equilibrium has been reached, that the i_0 rates on these will be the same as for consols. But their current r' rates will be higher than 10% (the consol rate) and lower than 12.6% (the short-term or i_0 rate) in accordance with their respective durations. Again there is no imputation of causality with respect to the relations of the rate structure, but rather of total interdependence.

The strength of the impulses carrying money from the savings balances into that part of the transactions balances used in the debts-equities markets (or alternatively under specified conditions into the investment market) is obvious. If in the next Week expectations are confirmed by an actual fall in interest-rates, the condition may continue as long as the anticipated forward or r' rates are lower than the current margin of substitution for the system. Sooner or later, however, rates must fall into the normal range, or the idea of normal must change, and the i_0 and r' rates must move closer to each other and finally coincide.

At the other extreme of the interest range, conditions are markedly different. Thus let us suppose that the consol rate, rather than being 10% is only 1%. The current price of a $1.00 income will then be $100.00. Let us suppose this time that there is an expectation of a *rise* of *one hundredth of one per cent* in the consol rate between this Monday and next Monday. The expected consol rate one Week from this Monday will therefore be 1.01%. The expected price of the consol one Week forward will therefore be $1.00 ÷ .0101 or $99.009. The running yield on the bond is practically wiped out by an expectation of a very small rise in the consol rate. The i_0 rate which forms part of the formula must be only 9/1000 of one per cent! Under such conditions the demand for money would become practically absolute and we should expect any increases in the quantity of money to be absorbed into the savings balances without effect upon the rates of interest and levels of employment and economic activity.

It is obvious that before we could inscribe a function for L_2, we should require to know, first, what rates of interest are considered by the community to be "normal," and second, the way in which interest-expectations change as the constellation of rates moves above or below the "normal" range.

Effects of Interest-Payments on Bank Deposits. Beyond this we must recognize that if the banks pay income to holders of L_2 balances, the tendency will be for the demand function for money as a store of value to become absolute at an i_0 rate which represents this income plus the actual costs for commissions and so on of transferring a claim from a savings deposit to some other asset-holding. There is no point in holding an asset from this Monday to next Monday whose return is lower than this. The margin of substitution for the system cannot fall below this rate. Those who own money will keep it rather than offer it in the assets or production market this Week at any i_0 rate below this rate. Any type of monetary management which aims at control of economic relations through manipulation of the rate of interest will find its ability to control the situation grow weaker if it requires pushing the complex of rates to the point where the short-term "pure" rate gives the demand for money an infinite elasticity. In the remainder of this study we shall ignore the complication brought into the analysis by the fact that the banks may pay income on savings deposits. This institutional habit raises the institutional minimum on the margin of substitution for the system, but it does not change the essential reasoning.

Rate-Relationships. The foregoing analysis indicates that we should expect short-term rates of interest to have a wider range of variation than longer-term rates. This appears in fact to be true. It appears as a corollary that the shorter-term and longer-term rates may have different rates of change in accordance with changes in interest-expectations regarding forward rates. Limitations on space and advantages of continuity in analysis have ruled out a comparison of movements of i_0 and r' rates with the r rates, or market yields, as these were defined in Chapter III. The possibility of expected falls or rises in the correction coefficients d, s, and l, as described in Chapter III, may cause the r rates to move divergently from the movements in the i_0 and r' rates.

Price-Expectations. Finally, we have in the foregoing related the L_2 demand for money to *interest*-expectations almost completely and have given practically no consideration (except to enter a *caveat* with respect to prices of equities occasionally) to *price*-expectations as a factor of the situation. Obviously again an emergence of an expectation of rising or falling prices may cause revision of the a series included in equity valuations and may lead to expectations of rising or falling equity prices on forward markets. Such expectations may cause a revision of the demand schedules for both debts and money as well as for equities and it may be a *cause* of changes in the i_0 margin of substitution for the system, since at all times the entire complex of schedules forms an interdependent set of relations with substitution at the margin of one kind of asset-holding for another tending to produce equality between rates of return after the correction coefficients have been accounted for.

The "Liquidity Preference Theory." Mr. Keynes speaks of the rate of interest as being "determined" by liquidity preference in conjunction with the quantity of money,[13] but this is true only because under given conditions and within the limits set out previously in this chapter it is possible for the banking system by a change in the quantity of money to modify this rate of substitution. In conditions of under-employment, an increase in the quantity of money measured in money-units may not be followed by an equal and opposite change in the monetary equivalent of the wage-unit. To the degree that this is true, the effect of the change in the quantity of money may be a change in the complex of rates of interest representing the preferences of the community with respect to the holdings of property-rights for the current Week.

Graphical Representation of L_2. Before we can see how these demand curves interact, we must inscribe the graph L_2, show graphically how it is affected by changes in the idea of the normal range of rates and then proceed to build up the general demand curve which combines L_1 and L_2.

In Figure X below, a graph of the demand L_2 for one of our Weeks is set out, with the quantity of money measured as usual in wage-units. Rate of interest Oa measures the rate (i_0) at which the hard core begins to melt and to be transferred to the L_1 balances under the common processes of inflation. At this rate, it is assumed that the r' rates are far enough below $Oa = i_0$ to encourage speculative activity in the assets and goods markets, while the r rates or market yields may actually have previously fallen because of decreases in estimated risks and increases in estimated liquidity. Below rate Oa the demand curve for some distance is represented as relatively inelastic. This is the range where the rates will be considered to be just as likely to go up as down, and where the predominant holdings in savings deposits would be limited, first, to the holdings of savers unfamiliar with investment whose subjective costs for investing are fairly high and, second, to holdings which are normally held as more or less of a hedge against changes in prices and the rates of interest by investors or business-units who may feel that the carrying of certain liquid reserves is a matter of advantage as well as strictly a "precaution." Even where there is a fairly wide range between the rate of income paid by the banks on savings deposits and the rate of income to be earned by purchases

[13]*General Theory*, pp. 167-8.

in the assets markets, there may be a fairly stable core of savings deposits not disturbed by these conditions.

Rate *Om* in the graph shows the i_0 rate at which the demand for money is assumed to become perfectly elastic because of the conditions set out previously. At this rate if the central bank through the purchase of part of the existing stock of assets, such as bonds, or through other means, attempts to increase the quantity of money measured in wage-units in an endeavour to make credit conditions easier for entrepreneurs, the additional supplies of money will disappear into the savings deposits without any effect upon the rates at which the holders will turn to the industrial bond or other markets as purchasers of assets. As this rate is approached, the loss of control of the central bank over the situation is shown by the increasing elasticity of L_2.

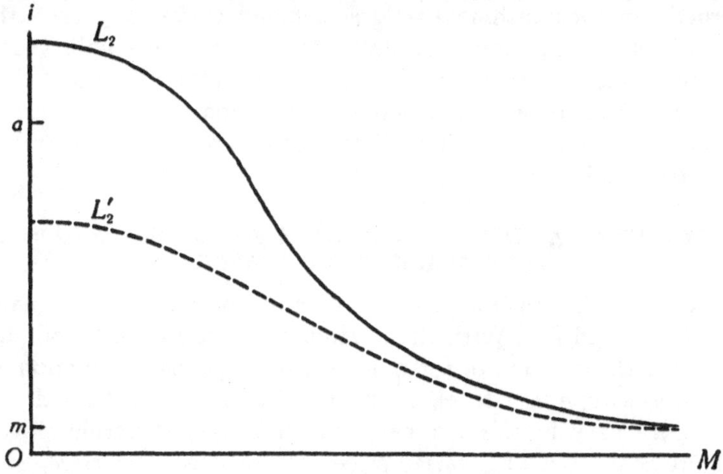

FIGURE X

As already indicated, the position of the demand function L_2 may vary with both place and time. For example, everything else being equal, the rate which was "safe" for a country with an expanding population would not be considered "safe" for a country with a stable or contracting population because of the differences of expectational forecasts between the two countries. For inter-connected countries with currencies related to some fixed common standard, the variations among demand curves would be less than where exchange rates between currencies were highly variable. In the first case, changes from autonomous factors occurring in one country would be translated through prices and the exchange rate to the other in a much higher degree than in the second.

From the standpoint of time, the history—and particularly the recent history—of the system, is the strongest determining element. Range, direction and frequency of interest-changes in the immediate history of the system will all condition psychological reactions which determine the demand for money L_2 at each potential i_0 rate for the Week. Thus a long period of stable interest-rates may narrow the dispersion of rates which is considered to be "normal" in such fashion that the demand curve may take the form L'_2 shown in Figure X also. In such a case stability and substantial identity between the i_0 and r' rates for a period of time have caused an expectation that any deviation from this narrow normal range will almost immediately be followed by a reversal of movement back to normal rates.

(4) THE GENERAL DEMAND FUNCTION FOR MONEY AND THE POTENTIALITIES OF A WEEK

We build the general demand function by combining demand L_2 with demand L_1. With the psychological-institutional complex given, the demand curve for money which applies to function L_1 will vary with every level of income Y. Demand L_2 will not necessarily vary in this manner, though it may if various levels of Y are connected with varied price-expectations, since changes in these may carry with them changes in the relative demand schedules for debts, equities, and money as a store of value. If the levels of income Y which are potential for a given Week do not show a very great deal of variation from each other, we may take the L_2 function as given by the history of the system and get the L function by adding to the L_1 function attached to each potential income the L_2 function which applies. What we get from the combination will be a sheaf of functions (L) representing the short-period possibilities of the system for the Week, to be reached either spontaneously or perhaps through monetary or other types of management of the system.

Graphical Representation of the Demand Function L. In Figure XI below, we set up the total demand function for one level of income and one state of expectations. In Figure XII we combine the same L_2 function, as given by the state of expectations, with several levels of income represented as hypothetically possible for the given Week. Y_a, Y_b, Y_c, . . . indicate rising potential levels of income in this and following figures.

In the terms of Figure XII, if the quantity of money, measured in wage-units, is M_a and conditions at the margins of substitution for property holdings throughout the system give the rate of interest $Oa = i_0$ for this quantity of money, then only the level of income Y_a will be consistent with the state of expectations and the quantity of money as given. If the quantity of money measured in wage-units is increased to M_b, this would be consistent with the maintenance of income Y_a at a rate of interest *Oa′* so far as the reactions of the Liquidity Functions are concerned. We have, however, to

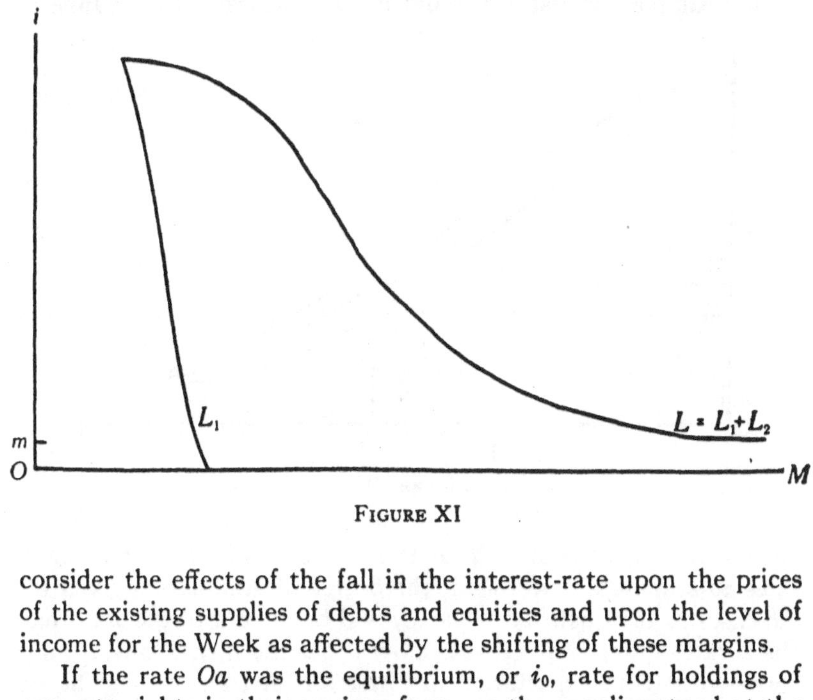

FIGURE XI

consider the effects of the fall in the interest-rate upon the prices of the existing supplies of debts and equities and upon the level of income for the Week as affected by the shifting of these margins.

If the rate *Oa* was the equilibrium, or i_0, rate for holdings of property-rights in their various forms as the supplies stood at the beginning of the Week, and if the rate *Oa* is *above* the minimum institutional rate for i_0, then the effects of the increase in the quantity of money will be felt throughout the system of demand schedules for property-rights. Multiple adjustment at the margin of substitution will prevent the i_0 rate from falling as low as *Oa′*. The rate will fall perhaps to *Ob*.[14]

[14]The rate connected with M_b cannot *rise* to *Oc* and income Y_c, because although this situation is consistent with the Liquidity Functions, there is nothing in the rise of the rate of interest to *increase* either consumption or investment and hence to increase *Y*. In fact, as presently to be explained in succeeding

Income Effects and the Rates of Interest. But the rate *Ob* and the money-supply M_b are consistent with a level of income Y_b because of the stimulus to investment by entrepreneurs given by the lower rates of interest on borrowed money connected with money-supply M_b. If there is still unemployment in the system at income Y_b and the quantity of money M_c gives a further possibility of a lower complex of interest-rates that supply of money rather than M_b will be closer to the ideal amount for the system.

Full explanation of the reasons why lower rates on borrowed money stimulate investment must await explanation of the Invest-

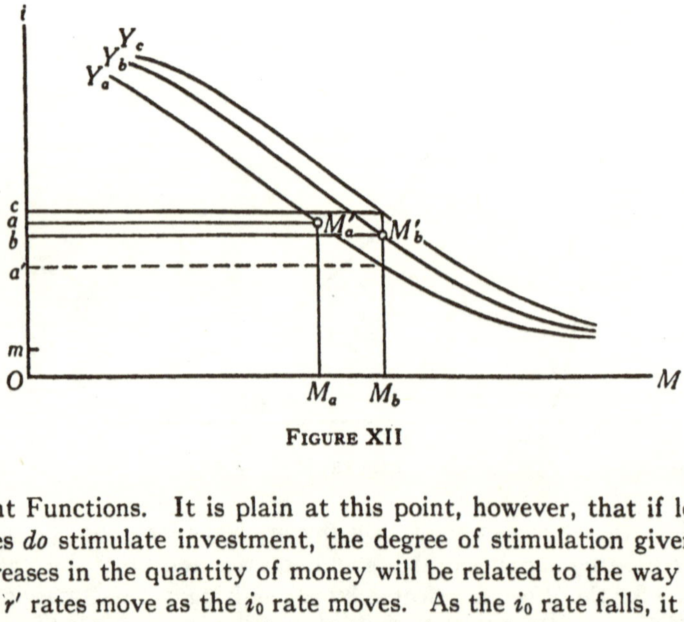

FIGURE XII

ment Functions. It is plain at this point, however, that if lower rates *do* stimulate investment, the degree of stimulation given by increases in the quantity of money will be related to the way that the r' rates move as the i_0 rate moves. As the i_0 rate falls, it may carry with it an expectation of lower forward i rates and hence lower r' rates for the system. On the other hand, there may be an expectation that the fall in the i rates is temporary and the effect upon the r' rates will be limited to the very early terms of the valuation series. In the first case the effects upon investment will be

chapters, it is a fall in the rate of interest which tends to increase both consumption and investment through reactions upon the second and third equations of the system. The Liquidity Functions deal with only one of four simultaneous equations and the solution which can be presented in this chapter is therefore only partial. Complete demonstration must remain in abeyance until we have explored the remaining equations and have assembled them into a system for purposes of demonstration.

greater than in the second case, given the assumption that lower rates of interest stimulate investment.

As the i_0 rate falls below the "normal" range and toward its institutional minimum, growing divergence between the i_0 rates and the r' rates will tend to divert increases in the quantity of money into the L_2 balances. The limits upon management of the system through manipulation of the quantity of money will be given by the fall of the i_0 rate to its institutional minimum.

Causes and Effects of Shifting of Functions. As the given Week passes into history, it has its own effects upon the character of expectations by whatever modifications it brings to the psychological-institutional complex. If, for example, the modification is interpreted optimistically, the demand function L attached to the various levels of income for the next Week may shift downward because of changes in L_2.[15] The same amount of money connected with the same rates of interest (i_0 and connected r' rates being assumed to form the same complexes as before) may be consistent with a higher level of activity than before. Other and higher levels of activity (Y_d, Y_e, . . .) may become potential for the succeeding Week. If, on the contrary, the Week's outcome is interpreted unfavourably, the modification of the state of expectations may shift the functions to the right and new and lower levels of income (as Y_{a-1}, Y_{a-2}, . . .) may become potentialities for the succeeding Week.

Figure XIII attempts to analyse the nature of this shifting. In this figure, the state of expectations is interpreted to have grown more optimistic. There is less desire at any i_0 rate therefore to hold cash-balances under L_2 than before. When the new L_2 curve is added to the series of L_1 curves for the levels of income potential for the Week in the same manner as was done in Figure X, the demand curve for money, measured in wage-units, is for each level of income further to the left than before.

In Figure XIII, quantity of money M_b and rate Ob are now consistent with income Y_c rather than Y_b, since at that i_0 rate more investment will be undertaken than under the conditions affecting L_2 for the previous Week. Consumption also will be greater for reasons to be explained in our next chapters. Therefore $C+I$ or Y will be greater than under the previous conditions. The quantity

[15]If institutional factors make necessary advance preparation for purposes of "finance," part of the shifting to the left may be offset by an enlarged demand for "finance" if the expansion of planning goes beyond the requirements for the present Week.

of money measured in wage-units will be adequate to sustain Y_c instead of Y_b because since less of M_b is required to satisfy demand under L_2 more is available for the active or transactions balances from the same quantum.

If the shifting of functions had been in the opposite direction, it might have served to nullify the effects of the increase from M_a to M_b as explained for Figure XII, and quantity M_b in the new Week might then be consistent with income level Y_a only.

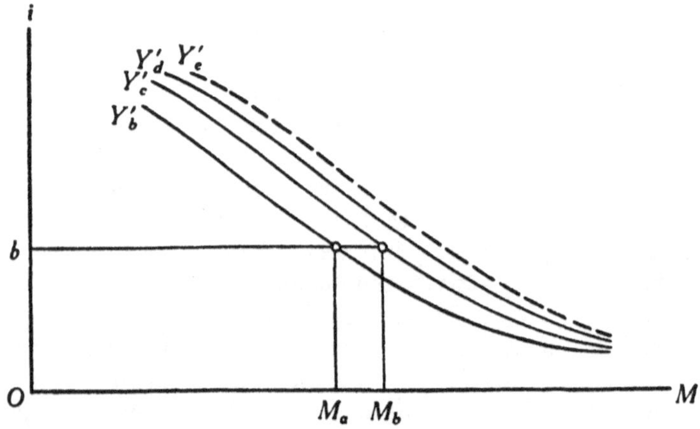

FIGURE XIII

($Y'_b = Y_b$ in its new position, etc. Income level Y_b can now be sustained by rates of interest and quantities of money formerly only adequate to sustain Y_a. Y_d and Y_e have become potential.)

The shifting of functions explained above has been a simple vertical shifting. Elasticity has been assumed to remain substantially the same except for the modifications connected with the fact that the institutional minimum rate is the same as before. It is possible also, as previously indicated, that changes in the psychological-institutional complex may change the r' rates of interest connected with given i_0 rates. If this is true there will be changes in the elasticity of functions which may or may not be connected with vertical or horizontal shifting.

What we have been trying to do in this chapter is to get a view of the process of substitution at the margin which, within the limits described, may make an increase in the quantity of money effective in decreasing the complex of interest-rates. The division between the i and r' rates which we have made in this study brings into view an aspect of management through the interest-rate which, while it is recognized in the *General Theory*,[16] is not always kept in sight in the theory of open-market operations. It would appear from this analysis that where the interest-rates required for full employment are under those considered normal for the society, permanent good effects of manipulation through the interest-rate must rest upon the establishment of these lower rates as normal ones for the society. So long as an expectation persists that the interest-rates will rise again into the estimated normal range, the r' rates will lie above i_0 and low i_0 rates will fail to give the society the buoyancy required to reach and hold the level of full employment. Perhaps simultaneous operations of the banking and monetary authorities in both short-term and long-term markets may do something to bring the r' rates down toward the i_0 rates but it would appear from analysis that this condition would require to be long enough continued to establish the low rates within the normal range if the programme is to have any relatively permanent effects. Moreover, if the lending community is acute enough to recognize the connection of low rates in the "gilt-edged" market with arbitrary monetary manipulation, the effects upon the industrial bond market may be limited to the results of certain diversions of demand from the "gilt-edged" to the industrial market without serious effects upon forward interest-expectations.

Before we complete this chapter, a certain amount of attention must be given to the relation of the Liquidity Functions to the balance of saving and investment. Through that attention we may gain some understanding of the problems involved in maintaining the equilibrium of the system at high levels of employment over longer periods of time.

(5) THE LIQUIDITY FUNCTIONS AND THE BALANCE OF SAVING AND INVESTMENT

One requisite, if the outcome of the economic operations of a given Week is not to affect the state of expectations in such a way as to cause revision of plans for succeeding Weeks, is that the equality between saving and investment which is a logical necessity for the system must be reached on bases which indicate a consistency between the disposition of the entrepreneurs to invest and the disposition of the community to save. In Professor Ohlin's language, *ex ante* and *ex post* saving and *ex ante* and *ex post* investment must all be equal to each other. This condition is fulfilled by the Fundamental Model. But it may not be in itself a sufficient con-

[16]Pages 202-4.

dition to maintain full employment: there may be revisions of entrepreneur plans "over Week-ends" which push employment below this level.

There is a second requisite for equilibrium over time if the emerging Weeks are characterized by positive investment. Someone must be willing to *hold* titles, directly or indirectly, to the increases in the quantum of capital rights on terms which keep the rates of money interest related to the inducements to invest at the equilibrium level of income. But the addition of new units of capital goods changes the conditions of supply and demand to some extent for the whole system of prices, including pricing for the system of property-rights, as this system is determined by the terms of marginal holders of equities, debts, and cash-balances. This necessity for continuous rearrangement of the conditions of substitution at the margin adds another element of instability to a system which already has a degree of instability because of the precarious character of human expectations. The quantity of new capital goods emerging from the processes of production for any one Week may be small in relation to the total quantum of rights to existing capital goods, but it may be appreciable in relation to the attitudes of marginally situated bidders for the new rights. Variations in the attitudes of marginally situated bidders may have consequences for the system, including the Liquidity Functions, particularly if there are definite time-lags between the planning of new investment and the marketing of new securities based on the investment.

Within the limits set out in this chapter, the monetary authorities will be in some degree in position to manage the rates of substitution in the desired directions by varying the supply of money. It is this ability which justifies us in speaking of a "Liquidity Preference Theory of Interest." The liquidity premium measures only one margin among the multiple margins where substitution enters into the determination of the rates of interest for the system. We give it a place of dignity only because of the possibility of applying pressures upon the system through endeavours to change the liquidity premium. Yet under given states of long-term expectation it may be impossible, because of the presence of the limits indicated, for the monetary authorities to bring the system into equilibrium at the level of full employment. Other measures would require to be used. Development of these requires examination of the other equations.

We turn in the next group of chapters to the development of the reasoning behind the Multiplier Functions.

CHAPTER VII

DEFINITIONS AND ASSUMPTIONS CONNECTED WITH THE MULTIPLIER FUNCTIONS

WE have already given our second equation as $C=\phi(Y, i)$. In words, this means that the level of consumption per unit of time is a function of the level of income and of the rate of interest.[1] Before we can set out the nature of the relationship based on this equation very extensively, however, it is desirable that we should examine more closely than has hitherto been necessary certain definitions and assumptions connected with our convention of temporary equilibrium and that we should go on from there to consider the nature of the concept of *effective demand.*

(1) THE CONCEPTS OF CONSUMPTION AND INVESTMENT

In considering the concepts of consumption and investment, we must define our categories of consumption and investment goods, and we must distinguish the categories of consumption and investment goods from the symbols *C* and *I* of our equations.

Our dividing line in the first division is entirely arbitrary. We put into the category of consumers' goods not only all perishable consumers' commodities and services but also all consumers' durable commodities with the single exception of houses. Because of the importance of the variation in residential construction in changes in the level of employment, it is probably best to hold the purchase of a house as an act of entrepreneurship.[2]

[1]Mr. Keynes sets the function out as $C_w=(Y_w)$, the subscript w standing for the wage-unit. See *General Theory*, p. 90. We follow Dr. Lange's usage in relating the function explicitly to the rate of interest. Our reasons for doing this will be analysed in the chapter following this one.

[2]See J. M. Keynes, "Net Investment in the United States," *Economic Journal*, XLVI (1936), p. 541, n.1. Mr. Keynes states here that on pages 61-2 of the *General Theory*, he should have "made it clearer that the purchase of a house is most conveniently regarded as an act of entrepreneurship." It is possible that in a country like the United States automobiles should also be called investment goods, because purchases of these appear to have a cyclical connection with employment in the consumption- as well as the investment-goods industries of the general pattern which is analysed in this study.

With reference to the relation of the category of consumption goods to the symbol *C* of our equations, the term *C* relates to consumption entirely in the *market* sense. A good is consumed *when it is purchased by the consumer on the market.* Consumption goods which are held either in consumers' hoards since some previous Week or as part of the stocks of entrepreneurs do not come within the definition of the *C* of our equations. Entrepreneurs' stocks of consumers' goods we shall call "liquid capital." If a stock of consumers' goods is purchased by an individual, not for use but *as a store of value*, and later resold, it will be held also to be part of the stock of capital, and will have the quality of "liquidity" to some degree. Goods purchased for consumption at some postponed date come under *C* for the Week in which they are purchased.

With respect to the symbol *I*, as intimated in Chapter IV, that symbol stands for *net* investment for the Week. Any activity in the investment-goods industries which is the basis of an issue of new securities or of an increase in the value of old ones, comes under the symbol *I*. Goods produced for replacement and maintenance do not, although we include them in the wider category of *gross* investment.[3] Goods produced by the consumption-goods industries for the purpose of adding to stocks of liquid capital also come under the symbol *I*. Analysis of the concept of effective demand in the third section of this chapter will make these relations clearer.

(2) ASSUMPTIONS CONNECTED WITH THE CONCEPT OF INCOME

Before we can carry the concept of *income* further than we have already carried it, we have three assumptions to set out specifically and two warnings to issue. The first two assumptions are a part of our convention of temporary equilibrium as it appears in the Fundamental Model, while the third has the nature of a general "law" in the economic sense of the word.

The first assumption of our convention of temporary equilibrium, to be analysed in relation to our exposition of the concept

[3]It is to be recalled that *gross investment* means the same as Mr. Keynes' *current investment*, as defined on page 62 of the *General Theory*. Mr. Keynes relates the decisions of the entrepreneurs as producers to gross income and gross investment, but their decisions as income-receivers to net income and net saving. See *General Theory*, p. 57. I could not find a way to give a definite meaning to the equations of the construction without making a choice between the two uses. It is a merit of the choice made that when the construction is erected on the bases of symbols defined in relation to these concepts, the whole system can be more easily related to the historic development of marginal productivity theory.

of effective demand, is that the level of income, measured in wage-units, is uniquely determined by the level of employment.[4] This means for us that, under the conditions of the single Week, if the units of factors employed are given, the level of income measured in wage-units is also given.

The second assumption is a corollary of the first. In Mr. Keynes' terminology, not yet developed for our own use, we are assuming for purposes of analysis that the "investment multiplier" and the "employment multiplier" are the same.[5] For our present purposes this means that we assume that a change in relative demand between the consumption- and the investment-goods industries, under conditions where we have a single set of values for our equations, will have the same proportionate effects upon employment that it has upon relative expenditure for the two categories of goods. Thus, if nine-tenths of an increase in money-income is devoted to expenditure on consumption goods and one-tenth to new investment, of ten new factors employed, nine will be employed to increase consumption for the Week and one to increase net investment. The character of this assumption will also be explored later in this chapter.

The third assumption is regarded as an "observed tendency" to which the real world conforms. It states that when there is an increase in aggregate real income in a community, *ceteris paribus*, aggregate consumption will be increased, *but not by as much as income is increased.*[6] Some part of the increase in aggregate real income will be devoted to saving. This will mean, when we have our terms more fully developed, that either dis-investment is lower or investment higher than under conditions where real income is smaller.

The first caution is to the effect that the law which is basic to the third assumption is to be interpreted entirely in a functional

[4]*General Theory*, p. 90. This assumption would not be tenable for the Supplementary Models for reasons to be given later.

[5]*Ibid.*, pp. 115-16. Mr. Keynes states here that while the assumption "is not entirely in accord with the facts of the real world . . . there is no difficulty in rewriting the . . . argument in the more generalized form." In the Supplementary Models again the convention would tend to be untenable.

[6]See *General Theory*, pp. 27-31, for a preliminary statement of this relationship. The idea is further developed in chaps. VIII, IX, and X, pp. 89-131 inclusive, and the law is related to the general statement of the system as a whole in chap. XVIII, pp. 245-54. The generalization appears now to be accepted by general equilibrium economists. See for example, A. C. Pigou, Note on "Money Wages in Relation to Unemployment," *Economic Journal*, XLVIII (1938), p. 138.

sense. For us, this will mean that it must be related to a *given* Week with given supplies of factors in specific forms, and with a given psychological-institutional complex. What we are doing, in fact, is to interpret the law as we interpret the reactions of demand which we impound in a single demand curve. All changes over time which result from changes in variables will be treated as a shifting of the curves under which we shall presently impound the law, just as increases and decreases "in the schedule sense" are related to the shifting of demand curves. On the other hand, all *potentialities* respecting one set of conditions for the division of income between consumption and saving we may set out upon a curve, just as we set the potentialities of demand for defined conditions upon a single curve, even though in both cases only one potentiality can "come true." In this way, though the law is interpreted as a general law, it will be through the convention of the Week that we shall be able to segregate for study the set of relations embodying it from the many variables which may play upon it over time.[7]

The second warning asks us to recall that the period of our Week must be long enough for consumption and saving to be considered stable functions of income. Otherwise, as Mr. Lerner says, "some very strange results appear."[8] For an individual, we could define the Week as the shortest period for which an income-receiver has a coherent plan for the division of income between consumption

[7]See *General Theory*, chap. VIII, pp. 91-6, for Mr. Keynes' list of the objective factors which influence the propensity to consume, and see the whole of chap. IX, pp. 107-12, for an account of the subjective factors.

[8]A. P. Lerner, Note on "Saving and Investment: Definitions, Assumptions, Objectives," *Quarterly Journal of Economics*, LIII (1938-9), pp. 617-18. Mr. Lerner points out that if we take very short or atypical periods, we may get almost any combination of variables for the marginal propensity to consume and the multiplier. He says that this is merely a matter of presentation, and that "Consumption and saving can be considered to be stable functions of income only if periods are considered that are long enough for the elimination of the discontinuities that give such strange results. In other words, unless some special period is indicated, *the* marginal propensity to consume which gives *the* multiplier, and which is based upon 'psychological law,' must be understood to refer to *short period equilibrium* where the abnormalities due to discontinuities and to the failure of adjustment of the output of consumption goods to the new level of investment will have been overcome . . . . If we consider periods long enough for short-period equilibrium to be reached, the propensity to save will correspond closely enough to the habits of the people to enable us to say how much the level of employment will have moved up as a result of a given increase in the level of investment and saving."

and saving, with seasonal, cyclical, and secular swings assumed in the position of the individual function to bring it into accordance with the consumer's longer plan and with revisions in that plan. In the *real* world, however, this unit might be too short for effective combination with the planning periods of producers. We are saved from the necessity for speculating upon this problem by the nature of our own convention. With all contracts made on Mondays in a market which "proceeds quickly and smoothly to a position of temporary equilibrium" and "where everyone knows the current prices in all those markets which concern him,"[9] the problem of differences in the timing of consumers' and producers' planning is avoided.

Terminology. Before we leave this section of this chapter, we should probably set out brief definitions of the special terms to be developed in connection with our exposition of the Multiplier Functions. A function which shows potential divisions of income between consumption and investment for one Week, we shall call "the propensity to consume."[10] The *rate of change* in that function connected with any given level of income measured in wage-units, we shall call "the marginal propensity to consume."[11] From the concept of the marginal propensity to consume will be derived the concept of the Multiplier.[12] Since, however, we are in our equation representing the function C as determined not only by the level of income Y but also by the rate of interest i (which for the current Week will mean i_0), the possibility is to be kept in mind that we may have more than one function representing the propensity to consume.

We leave the latter possibility in abeyance in order to consider the concept of effective demand.

(3) THE CONCEPT OF EFFECTIVE DEMAND

Definition. By Mr. Keynes' definition, effective demand means "simply the aggregate income (or proceeds) which the entrepreneurs *expect* to receive, inclusive of the incomes which they will hand on to the other factors of production, from the amount of current employment which they decide to give."[13] Translated into the terms of the world of the Fundamental Model, this means that on

[9]See quotation from Professor Hicks, chap. III, p. 14.
[10]*General Theory*, p. 90.
[11]*Ibid.*, p. 115.
[12]*Ibid.*
[13]*Ibid.*, p. 55. Italics mine.

each of our Mondays, income-receivers will stand ready to make contracts for furnishing services in production, and for the purchase of consumption goods and new securities, or alternatively, to make additions to their cash-balances. Entrepreneurs, on their side, will be ready to make contracts for the sale of consumption goods and new securities.[14] In accordance with their plans for the latter, they will be ready to make contracts with the factors of production for services to be used either in furnishing goods to be consumed (in the market sense) during the Week or to be added to the quantum of capital—fixed, working, and liquid—to be carried from the current Week to the next. We shall define effective demand for the Fundamental Model, therefore, as the quantity of cash which receivers of income (including entrepreneurs as income-receivers) are willing to hand over for possession of the quantum of consumption and investment goods which entrepreneurs are willing to supply during the Week.

To some extent, of course, entrepreneurs may be purchasers of securities indirectly, as when they hire factors for the extension of supplies of fixed, working, and liquid capital, without offering new securities against these in the market.[15] Because of the importance of this method of financing capital extensions in some modern economies, notably the economy of the United States, we should probably include such demands for new capital claims under effective demand. If we left them out it would not be logically serious since the entrepreneur appears as both the "buyer" and "seller" of the new capital claims. However, variations in such types of investment may be important in determining the level of employment and therefore we count them in.

Mr. Keynes' Aggregate Functions. In the *General Theory* the level of effective demand is determined by the equilibrium point

[14]An entrepreneur, of course, is also an income-receiver for the Week and enters as a demander of consumption goods and similarly as a demander of new securities into the markets for the Week.

[15]This may obviously be a very large source of net investment. Thus Professor Paul Douglas points out on page 448 of *The Theory of Wages* (New York, 1934), that when the Ford Motor Company "was organized in 1903, only $28,000 of capital was paid in. By reinvesting almost all of the profits of the company, plant and machinery have been built and raw materials purchased which now have a total value of approximately $300,000,000." He calls attention also to the United States Steel Corporation, "which has probably ploughed back into its plant and equipment at least a billion and a quarter dollars." New securities will be issued against such increases in net investment only periodically, as "melons."

between the so-called Aggregate Demand Function and Aggregate Supply Function, the latter being defined as the function showing the relationship between the aggregate supply price of output and employment as employment varies.[16] In the current study it does not appear necessary to include these complicated functions. The substitution of the short-period margin of substitution for the interest-rate of undefined duration used in the *General Theory* makes it possible to connect the operations of the *firm* straightway to the margins of substitution in the system without building up the intervening apparatus of these aggregate functions.

Effective Demand and the Models. We may consider what effective demand is for our series of relationships in terms of our Models. In the Fundamental Model we have on a given Monday morning given quantities of capital and labour and given potential consumers, savers, and investors for the Week. We have also a given psychological-institutional complex, including a given system of property-rights. Because of the degree of perfection assumed for the market, entrepreneurs will reach a knowledge of the price situation as it affects each one of them fairly quickly and will be able to plan short-period operations with full knowledge of the current market situation. Under such conditions, they will each match marginal costs to marginal revenues perfectly. Sales proceeds in the market will therefore determine the quantity of employment offered to the factors of production and the scale of output of consumption- and investment-goods industries. There will be no *individual* hoarding for the Week. If any amounts are abstracted from the transactions balances and used either to increase the savings balances or to liquidate bank loans, such actions will be taken by the entrepreneurs themselves as heads of business-units, who will not wish to pay over to the factors of production sums which would be hoarded rather than paid out for the consumption goods and new securities offered from output of the Week. Such action will be taken "over the Week-end."

When every entrepreneur has matched his marginal costs to his marginal revenue, we shall have a definite level of income under conditions where the marginal supply prices of output equal their demand prices. This is exactly the same situation which applies

[16]*General Theory*, p. 25. For general discussion of these aggregate functions, see *General Theory*, chaps. III and XX. As first completed in the summer of 1940, the study presented in this volume contained an elaborate structure covering the relationship of these aggregate demand and supply functions. For reasons given in this chapter, this section has been omitted in the revised analysis.

in the *General Theory* when the Aggregate Demand Function is in equilibrium with the Aggregate Supply Function. Under the Fundamental Model, the equality between saving and investment will be established without error, so that planned (*ex ante*) saving will equal realized (*ex post*) saving, while planned (*ex ante*) investment will be equal to realized (*ex post*) investment and to planned as well as to realized saving. Under the Fundamental Model, effective demand will be the demand for goods, services, and securities associated with this equilibrium.

The margin of substitution operates within this production market as well as in the assets market. Consumers' divisions between consumption and saving in this relatively perfect world will be determined by the relative strengths of the desires for present goods and for future goods in relation to the premiums which may be earned by deferring marginal units of consumption. If the i_0 and r' rates show different yields, short-period substitution over time may enter to affect the situation. Consideration will be given to this possibility in the following chapter.

For this world it does not appear inconsistent to accept the first assumption of the convention of temporary equilibrium set out in Section II of this chapter, namely that the level of income, measured in wage-units, is uniquely determined by the level of employment, so that a definite quantity of employment may be attached to each potential level of income.

Weaknesses of the Assumptions for the Supplementary Models. For the Supplementary Models the case is different. If, for example, the level of income measured in wage-units is exactly the same as under the conditions of the previous Model but some entrepreneurs have over-expanded and have marginal costs greater than realized prices while others have produced less than the short-period optimal outputs, it is entirely possible that the plants in question may be labour-using in different degrees and yet aggregate output may have the same value in wage-units as under the conditions of the Fundamental Model. On balance effective demand appears to be the same as before, though it has been brought to the same figure by the fact that one set of incomes has been diminished below Monday's expectations by the same amount by which the other set has been increased beyond them. There will be no *net* individual hoarding under these conditions. Any hoarding by the customers of one set of enterprises will be offset by dishoarding by the customers of the other, to the extent that these customers are not the same persons who have transferred demand from one set of enterprises to the other set.

If the degrees of error do not offset each other, the definition of effective demand is more complex. In the First Model, entrepreneurs may over-estimate on Monday the demand schedules for goods, services, and new securities which appear on Tuesday. The particular enterprises which have made errors must choose on Tuesday between unplanned investment or the reduction (probably) of their transactions balances by the amounts which their customers have transferred to inactive accounts, or they may decide upon some combination of the two methods of readjusting marginal costs and revenues. Thus net individual hoarding may eventuate. Under the opposite conditions, demand for goods, services, and securities may be supported by net individual dishoarding. Under the Second Supplementary Model the same general types of error may be made where entrepreneurs make contracts on Monday to deliver goods, services or new securities during the Week under conditions where their calculations of Tuesday's prices for the services of the factors of production are in error. Where such situations occur, there is one level of effective demand which entrepreneurs *expect* on Monday and another level of effective demand which is *realized* on Tuesday. Neither need agree with the level of effective demand which *would* have eventuated had the situation contained no errors in short-period forecasting. The whole concept takes on a rather ragged appearance in a world where such errors are common. We shall make little definite use of it for this reason but present it because of the degree of attention given to it in the *General Theory*.

The assumption that definite levels of income are associated with definite levels of employment is obviously even less tenable when the degrees of error are large. Neither is the assumption tenable that the investment and employment Multipliers are equal to each other. Under the conditions of the Fundamental Model, we *may* be able to assume that all industries are equally labour-using and that as all expand their outputs, this expansion is so synchronized that the changing labour-capital combinations keep pace with each other. If entrepreneurs are allowed to make mistakes in the scales of their outputs, however, the only situation under which we could see their labour-capital combinations remaining the same, despite the degrees and directions of error, would be where all industries were producing under conditions of constant cost, an assumption even more unreal than the others we have been using. Yet if the law of diminishing returns operates differently in different industries or is at a different stage of its operation because of errors in forecasting which make the marginal products unequal to marginal revenues, then the assumption that the "investment multiplier" and the "employment multiplier" are the same is patently an artificial one.

We do not challenge the nature of the assumptions we have made in order to bring down the structure of our reasoning but rather to help us to keep clearly in mind the differences between the world of the Fundamental Model and the real world. We cling to the Fundamental Model because its structure can be *seen* and because analysis of its structure may bring us to a clearer understanding of the workings of that intricate and vast structure of the real world which *cannot* be seen in its entirety. The two chapters which follow are directed almost wholly to a consideration of the nature of the average and marginal propensities to consume and the Multiplier as these are related to the operation of the Fundamental Model.

CHAPTER VIII

THE AVERAGE AND MARGINAL PROPENSITIES TO CONSUME

(1) THE NATURE OF THE CONSTRUCTION

OUR first task in this chapter will be to set up a construction for the propensity to consume based upon a single rate of interest or margin of substitution for the system. Our second task will be, within our convention of temporary equilibrium, to relate the function as rationally as we can to the levels of the interest-rate. When we have set up this construction upon a basis which illustrates the meaning of our second equation of the shifting equilibrium, we have then to develop the concepts of the *average* and *marginal* propensities to consume. In the succeeding chapter we shall go on to expound the concept of the Multiplier.

Graphical Representation of the Propensity to Consume. We begin with Figure XIV. On this the horizontal axis measures the net income for the Week as given in terms of wage-units when production is carried on, as assumed, under the conditions of the Fundamental Model, with the connected assumptions set out in the last chapter holding good. The vertical axis measures the level of consumption for the same Week in the same manner. We select an i_0 rate for the Week and call it i_c. On a given Monday morning, with a given psychological-institutional complex, we suppose that an income represented by the arbitrary point Y_r is connected with the marginal rate of substitution i_c. At that margin there will be a demand for goods and services for consumption during the Week which we indicate by C_r. Thus C_r/Y_r gives the proportion of consumption to net income for the Week. If income Y_r is the level of output which actually emerges from the solution of the system of equations as the income of the Week, then both saving and investment for the Week will be equal to OY_r-OC_r, which, as will be presently pointed out, is equal to rr'. The level of employment associated with income Y_r, measured in labour-units, is N_r by assumption. The point O(or Y_0) on the figure gives the level of zero net income. Employment N_0 associated with income Y_0 is just sufficient to maintain the quantum of capital if consumption is zero.

Under these conditions (and under the assumptions of the previous chapter) we can have positive levels of consumption for the Week with zero income only under two different conditions:[1]

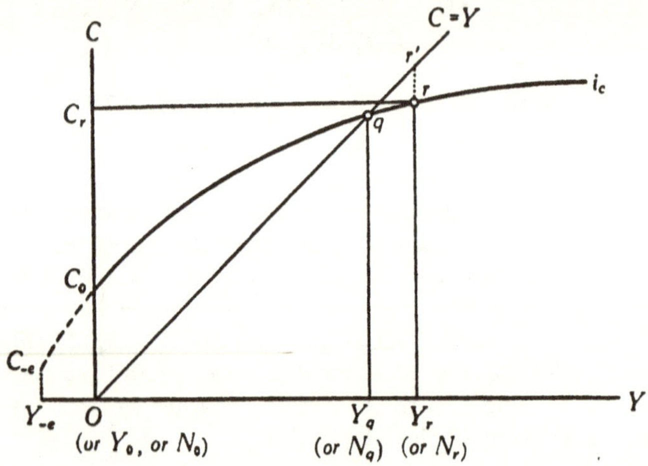

FIGURE XIV

(*a*) Labour devoted to *maintaining* stocks of fixed, working, and liquid capital may be diverted to increasing the output of goods passing into consumption during the Week. Thus consumption is offset by a decline in the quantum of capital stocks due to the passage of time. $C+(-I)=0$.

[1]Under this convention we get two possible measures of dis-investment for the system caused by the excess of consumption. Since labour will not be withdrawn from maintenance unless the cash-returns from dis-investment make it advantageous for entrepreneurs to prescribe the transfer, the minimum value which can be set in wage-units upon any dis-invested stocks of liquid capital or extension of output of consumption goods at the expense of maintenance will be given by the wages bill for the units of labour so transferred. No goods would be offered for consumption at the zero level of income whose proceeds did not cover this opportunity cost. But this minimum value will not necessarily be the proceeds to be expected. Another term will be given by the expectation of proceeds in future Weeks which has the highest net value in the present (*General Theory*, pp. 70-1). The degree of dis-investment for the system will be measured by the higher of these two terms. Each of them is an opportunity or user cost which rests upon the expectations of entrepreneurs with reference to the future prospects of economic activity and to the proceeds to be gained from conservation of stocks of fixed, working, and liquid capital from this Week to some succeeding Week.

(*b*) Stocks of liquid capital as such may be drawn upon. Excess of consumption over income is offset by a *dis-investment* in liquid capital. In this case it must be assumed that the quantum of labour required for selling, delivering, and other services connected with the transfer of stocks of liquid capital to consumption must be withdrawn from labour otherwise devoted to maintaining the same stocks. Else we could not maintain the assumption that employment N_0 is the employment connected with Y_0. $C+(-I)$ is again zero.

The locus of point r as Y_r shifts along the horizontal axis indicates the levels of consumption which would be associated with the given levels of income at the given margin of substitution with the other conditions of the Model as assumed. Such a curve we call the propensity to consume or consumption function, or alternatively, the Multiplier Function.

Zero-saving. The linear function of 45° indicated on Figure XIV shows for each potential level of income the relation of consumption to income at which net income and the level of consumption would be equal to each other. These are the theoretical levels of zero-saving for the Week. Under the conditions of the Week assumed in Figure XIV for margin i_c, income Y_q and employment N_q would be associated with zero-saving. The condition of zero-saving will actually emerge only if the values of the full set of equations bring the level of effective demand (as defined for the Fundamental Model) to rest at the point where the function showing aggregate demand for consumption crosses the linear function $C=Y$. It is because this function *does* represent zero-saving that rr' represents saving for income Y_r.

In the graph as given, for incomes smaller than Y_q the Multiplier Function lies above the function representing zero-saving. This means that if such incomes emerge from the system of relationships, consumption will exceed income and there will be net dis-investment in the system for the Week. The relative size of the deficit is indicated by the distance which the Multiplier Function lies above the zero-saving function.

(2) THE RELATION OF THE PROPENSITY TO CONSUME TO RATES OF INTEREST

We come thus to our second task for this chapter, namely the relation of the function representing the propensity to consume to the interest-rates of the system. It has already been pointed out that we have elected to follow Dr. Lange in presenting the propensity to consume as a function of *both* the level of income and the rate of interest.[2] It should be noticed, however, that Mr. Keynes does not deny that there is a connection between the interest-rate and the propensity to consume.[3] It appears to be his desire to throw the hitherto neglected factor of the level of income into its proper focus which causes him to omit the interest-rate variable from the formal statement of the relationship in his equation. The problem arises therefore as to what is the relation between the interest-rate complex and the propensity to consume. Dr. Lange brings the variable of interest directly into his equation and in his Figure 2 he gives the propensity to consume an *inverse* relation to the rate of interest.[4] In his text, however, he points out that it is possible that the relation *may* be the other way.[5] Neither Mr. Keynes nor Dr. Lange relates the propensity to consume to definite conditions based upon a definite unit of time as is done in this study. The isolation of variables under the concept of the Week and the substitution of the short-period margin of substitution for a loosely defined "rate of interest" permit us to make some additional generalizations in terms of our own construction.

Under our own construction, when we consider the effects of the rates of interest upon the position of the propensity to consume under the terms of the Week, we are able to consider these in relation to the presumed history of the system over the immediately preceding Weeks. In other words, the factor of expectations as based upon the immediate history of the system is prominent in the determination of the construction for the Week. This condition has consequences which will help us to make assumptions respecting the probable relation between the rates of interest and the propensity to consume within the construction for the Week.

We recall the general assumption made for the Liquidity Functions that if the i_0 rate is given, the r' rates will also be given by the state of the psychological-institutional complex. It is to be recalled also that high i_0 rates and high r' rates go together in spite of the fact that the short-term rates (and hence the Weekly margins)

[2]Oscar Lange, "The Rate of Interest and the Optimum Propensity to Consume," *Economica*, V n.s. (1938), p. 13.

[3]*General Theory*, pp. 93, 178.

[4]Lange, "The Rate of Interest and the Optimum Propensity," p. 15. It is to be noted that while Dr. Lange in his text makes dC/dY diminish as income increases, his Figure 2 shows the function as linear in form.

[5]*Ibid.*, p. 13.

vary more than do the longer-term rates.[6] As the i_0 rate moves up or down, the whole complex of interest-rates is therefore presumed to move up or down to some degree. It is under these assumptions that we must consider how the position of the Multiplier Function varies with the complex of the interest-rates.

There are at least four reasons for urging that the Multiplier Functions will have an arrangement which makes consumption vary inversely with the i_0 rate of interest. The first is connected with windfall changes in the value of capital assets, the second with substitution of saving over time, the third with distribution effects of changes in interest-rates, and the fourth with the relation between saving and time-preference. We take these up in order. In this discussion, and hereafter in this study, we shall use the subscripts a, b, c, d, etc., in that order to denote rising rates of interest.

Effects of Windfall Gains and Losses. Let us suppose that i_c was the i_0 margin of substitution last Week and that the i_0 rate this Week turns out to be the higher rate i_d or i_e. The complex of interest-rates will move up to some degree with this change in i_0. To the extent that this is true, owners of debts will suffer losses in the capital values of their claims. Likewise, yields of the a series being assumed to remain the same, the change in the rate of interest will lower the capitalized value of holdings of land and of other equity rights. Even though these circumstances should have no immediate effects upon the potential levels of income for the Week measured in wage-units, they will, so far as they were unexpected during the Week before, influence the psychology of the holders of these property-rights.[7] They will *feel* poorer, and this will tend to lower their individual propensities to consume with consequent effects upon the general function for the community. Conversely, if the i_0 rate falls to i_b or i_a, and the change is unexpected, the effects upon the capitalized values of future rights to income will have opposite effects upon the psychology of holders.

Substitution of Saving over Time. The effects of substitution of saving over time are connected with the relative movements of the short and long rates of interest. If the character of interest-expectations is

[6]Variations in bond prices over business cycles indicate that "changes in rates of bond interest conform, in general, to the concurrent changes in call loan and commercial paper rates" (A. B. Adams, *Economics of Business Cycles*, New York, 1925, p. 88). It is probable that the shorter-term and longer-term "pure" rates would show closer correlation in movement than do the market yields (or r rates).

[7]*General Theory*, pp. 57-8, 92-4.

such that a rise in the i_0 rate is expected to be followed by a return to or toward its former position, the r' rates will move upward less than the i_0 rates and the rates for securities for long-term investment will be affected only slightly. If short-term rates have risen above the long-term, current saving promises more reward than future saving. Some saving planned for the future may be done now to take advantage of the current situation. If rates are lower than those expected in the future, incentives are in the other direction. Again as with the first influence, the effects appear to be to give the propensity to consume an inverse relation to the interest-rate, for a higher inclination to save means a lower propensity to consume, and a lower inclination to save a higher propensity to consume.

Distribution Effects. In the third place, changes in the rates of interest tend to change the distribution of income. Since it is a fundamental law that, *ceteris paribus*, a larger amount of saving will be made from a larger income, and since those who hold property-rights, on balance at least, have higher incomes than do that portion of the income-receivers who depend only on the sale of personal services, a *rise* in the complex of interest-rates will tend to divert income from lower to higher personal incomes. To the extent that this is true, it will for the community result in a lower propensity to consume for any given level of income.

In the first Week that a higher system of rates holds, this circumstance may not have much influence because the newly made contracts will be only a small proportion of the total quantity of such contracts. But if the higher system of rates persists, as the effects of the windfall losses pass away, the effects upon distribution of the higher rates of interest will tend to take their place as factors depressing the propensity to consume. With falls in the rates of interest the reverse conditions prevail.

Differences in thriftiness are possible influences here also. If the *rentier* classes of the community are on balance thriftier than the other classes, as appears reasonable, this circumstance will increase the effects of distribution changes on the propensity to consume.

The Influence of Time-Preference upon the Arrangement of the Multiplier Functions. The influence of time-preference appears to be the most important of all those urged in determining the relation of the Multiplier Functions to the complex of the rates of interest. Its operation in the short-period appears linked with the operation of "increasing costs" in the subjective sense. If the income for any Week and the psychological-institutional complex are given, it appears inescapable that higher rates of saving must be connected with higher rates of interest and hence with higher i_0 rates. As more and more of the limited income for a current Week is saved rather than spent, more and more important wants are left unsatisfied. Because of their increasing importance, operation of the principle of substitution requires that they be matched by higher and higher offsetting advantages. By definition what is not saved is consumed. This means that lower and lower propensities to consume must be matched by higher and higher i_0 rates. What we get from the distribution of the consumption functions in relation to one level of income is in effect the reciprocal of the familiar savings curve of "classical" theory. And here we are able to find a place within the Keynesian apparatus for the apparatus of "orthodox" theory. The degree of dispersion for the functions attached to any definite Week will be related to the way the r' rates move with the i_0 rates, but the character of the dispersion, if higher i_0 rates mean higher complexes of rates, appears to require an inverse relation between the i_0 rate and the level of consumption from the standpoint of increasing costs of saving as well as for the reasons hitherto set out.

The Influence of Time-Preference Factors upon the Position of the Multiplier Functions. There are other aspects of "orthodox" theory which may be used to analyse the *position* of the Multiplier Functions in relation to the i_0 rate of interest, as distinguished from the character of their *variation* with interest-rates. Let us suppose, first, two communities with the same relative provisioning for the future as based upon the size of present capital stock, but with different degrees of thriftiness from the psychological standpoint. Under such conditions the savings curves of individuals, related to given levels of income and a given time-unit, would lie lower for representative individuals in the thriftier community. The curves themselves would, however, under operation of the principle of increasing cost, have the familiar forward-rising shape. This means that in the thriftier community the Multiplier Functions would still have an inverse relationship to the i_0 rate of interest but the functions themselves would lie lower down the vertical axis.

Suppose secondly that the two communities have equal degrees of thriftiness psychologically but that one is able already to provide better for future wants because of the size of its stock of previously accumulated capital. In this case, we should expect the richer community, *ceteris paribus*, to be under less pressure to save. *For the same levels of income*, therefore, we should expect the savings curves of representative individuals to lie on balance higher. The fact that we should expect the objective rates of interest to be lower in the richer community rests upon the fact that we expect larger incomes in this community and that we expect further that income-effects will more than counterbalance the effects of the relative provisioning of the present and the future. For such a community, *for the same levels of income*, we should therefore expect the Multiplier Functions to lie higher.

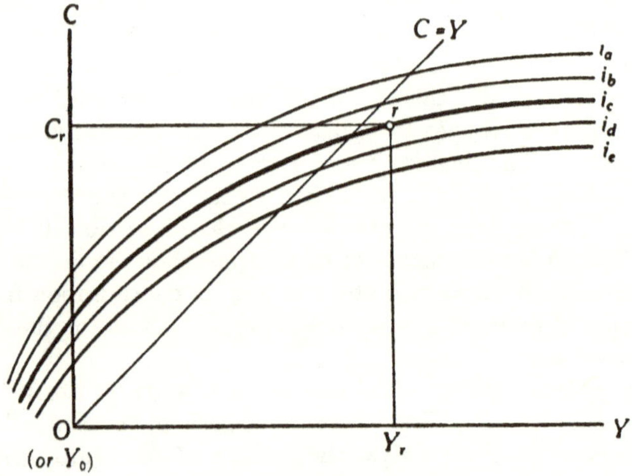

FIGURE XV

Conclusion and Graphical Representation. All the general conditions enumerated have effects which operate in the same direction despite differences in their relative importance. It is because of the cumulative effects of these sets of influences that we elect to set up our construction for the Multiplier Functions for a given Week on an assumption that for the Week, the position of the function representing the propensity to consume will vary inversely with the complex of interest-rates as represented by the i_0 rate which is attached to the complex.[8]

[8]It is further to be pointed out with reference to the factors which Mr. Keynes lists as possible influences upon the rate of interest, that his objective factors, listed on pages 91-5 of the *General Theory*, represent fundamentally changes which will operate upon the positions of our sheaves of functions between Weeks by the alteration of some element of the psychological-institutional complex. Thus the imposition of an income tax which alters the relative distribution of income in favour of lower incomes would raise the function which we attach to a given i_0 rate for a given Week. This would constitute an additional autonomous

In Figure XV we therefore show five potential functions representing the propensity to consume attached to five potential i_0 rates of interest for the Week arranged in accordance with the foregoing analysis and with the necessary assumptions made to account for the dispersion of these functions. The rate i_c is assumed to be the i_0 rate which ruled during the preceding Week. The shape and position of the i_c function indicate the divisions of income between consumption and saving which are potential for this Week, should that margin of substitution emerge from the solution of the system. The i_c margin can emerge only if there is some division of income on it which is consistent with the shapes and positions of the Liquidity Functions already developed and the Investment Functions still to be explained. If there is none, some other margin of substitution must emerge. As will be obvious after we have completed analysis of the Investment Functions and assembled the apparatus, there will be only one solution for a Week which will be consistent with the three sets of functions and with the definition that income Y is equal to the sum of investment and saving. This solution will determine the levels of the i_0 rate of interest and consumption, saving, and investment, if the quantity of money, the size of the wage-unit, and the psychological-institutional complex are given.

The conclusion embodied in Figure XV is that the level of effective demand, so far as it is affected by the Multiplier Functions, will be determined, subject to the influence of the complex of interest-rates, by the relation which consumption takes to the level of economic activity. In mathematical language, $C=\phi(Y, i)$.

(3) THE CONCEPTS OF THE AVERAGE AND MARGINAL PROPENSITIES TO CONSUME

We have for our last task in this chapter to define the terms *average* and *marginal* propensities to consume. These are purely

factor affecting rates of change between two specific Weeks. Once the new factor exercises its full effects upon the psychological-institutional complex, it becomes part of it, and we may set up the same generalizations as we have already done in this chapter for our construction of the Multiplier Functions even though the change in the psychological-institutional complex has somewhat altered the shaping and positions of functions attached to specific rates of interest. Most of the objective factors which Mr. Keynes lists would be factors which could be subsumed under shifts in the functions which we present for the Week.

The subjective factors which Mr. Keynes lists in Chapter IX are longer-term than those which govern relations for one of our Weeks. Like Mr. Keynes, "we shall not concern ourselves, except in occasional digressions, with the results of far-reaching social changes or with the slow effects of secular progress" (*General Theory*, p. 109.)

mathematical concepts and their meanings are very easily set out. We use Figure XVI for this purpose, but it is necessary to keep in mind that for any given level of income (e.g., Y_r) under our construction for the Week both the average and marginal propensities to consume are assumed to vary with the i_0 rate of interest.

Definition of the Average Propensity to Consume. The *average* propensity to consume for any level of income as based on function i_c, and for the Week to which the function i_c applies, is given by the value C/Y. Thus for income Y_r, the value as based upon the re-

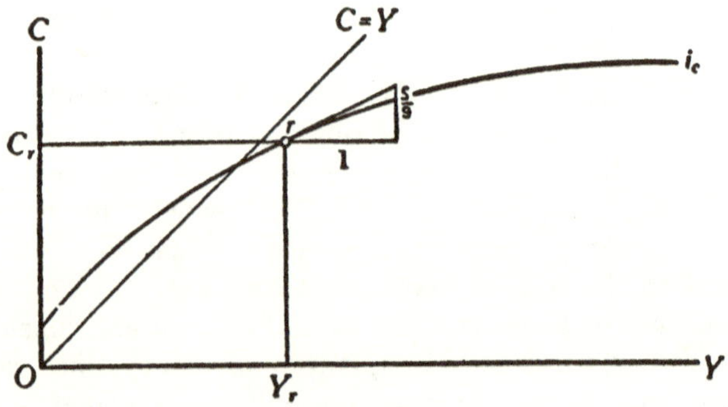

FIGURE XVI

$$\frac{C_r}{Y_r} = \frac{9}{10.5} = \frac{6}{7} = \text{average propensity to consume.}$$

$$\text{At } Y_r, \frac{dC}{dY} = \frac{5}{9} = \text{marginal propensity to consume.}$$

lations of our diagram is C_r/Y_r or $9/10.5 = 6/7$. This means that if the level of economic activity is that connected with income Y_r and the i_0 rate is i_c, net saving represents 1/7 of income and must be balanced by an equivalent amount of investment for the Week.

Under the conditions of our Fundamental Model, the income Y_r could not emerge unless the actions of entrepreneurs in their determination of the rate of investment were consistent in offering just that quantity of investment which is equal to saving at this level of income. If they show consistency at that level, only that level of income can emerge. Under the conditions of the Supplementary Models, however, with one set of contracts made on Mondays and the other on Tuesdays, it *is* possible for entrepreneurs to make mistakes even within the concept of the Week. If, for example, entrepreneurs offer the quantum of *employment* connected with Y_r on Monday, but intend to sell more than C_r goods for consumption during the Week, they will find themselves on Tuesday with an unwanted addition to their stocks of liquid capital unless they drop their prices for these goods in such a manner as to affect the propensity to consume. In this second case, this will mean losses or failure to maximize profits by those entrepreneurs who have been forced to drop prices below the amounts which represent their marginal costs. Similarly, if entrepreneurs produce more investment goods than called for by the functional division between consumption and saving for the Week in question, they will find themselves with new securities which cannot be sold at prices covering the marginal costs of the investment goods they represent. These entrepreneurs will incur losses under these conditions also which will bring investment into equality with saving at an income in terms of value lower than that attached under conditions of the Fundamental Model to the level of employment which we assume for the Week.[9] Figure XVI is, by assumption, related to the less complicated situation associated with the Fundamental Model.

Definition of the Marginal Propensity to Consume. For problems of social control, the concept of the *marginal* propensity to consume is more important than the concept of the *average* propensity. By the marginal propensity to consume, we mean *the rate of change in the average propensity to consume* as the level of income changes. As before, however, for each function the i_0 rate of interest must be given. For each level of income, there will be a *different* marginal propensity to consume associated with each level of the i_0 rate of interest.

We may illustrate the meaning of the concept of the *marginal* propensity to consume by reference to our Figure XVI. Let us attempt to find the rate of change in the function i_c at the point where income is Y_r. If we inscribe a tangent to function i_c at r and ascertain its slope or gradient by drawing a horizontal line of unit length through r and then measuring vertically to the tangent, we shall then have ascertained the rate of change of C, which is $\frac{dC}{dY}$. By measurement on Figure XVI, this gradient is about $\frac{5}{9}$.

[9]Conditions of disequilibrium bring in price changes which affect the positions of our functions because they affect the distribution of income between individuals and also the distributions which individuals make of their incomes between various types of goods and services and between consumption and saving. But whatever the conditions, there will be a functional division for the society between consumption and saving, and for any level of income under given conditions the relation C/Y expresses the *average* propensity to consume. The assistance which the Fundamental Model gives in simplifying analysis is apparent here once more.

A gradient 1 would represent a condition where an increment of income would be fully consumed. A gradient $\frac{5}{9}$ represents a condition where $\frac{5}{9}$ of an increment of income will be consumed and $\frac{4}{9}$ saved. In other words, the marginal propensity to *consume* at Y_r is $\frac{5}{9}$, while the marginal propensity to *save* is $\frac{4}{9}$ at this point.[10]

Characteristics of the Construction. Before we proceed in the succeeding chapter to extend the concept of the *marginal* propensity to consume into the concept of the Multiplier, we should probably examine the relations of the marginal to the average propensity, as these emerge from our calculations, to see what assumptions, if any, underlie our construction of the relationship which we have not as yet explicitly set out. We set these out below.

In the first place, it is to be noted that for a given level of income and a given rate of interest, the average propensity to consume will be higher than the marginal propensity to consume. Thus our average propensity to consume as given by the preceding calculation for i_c is $\frac{6}{7}$ but the marginal propensity to consume at the same value for Y is $\frac{5}{9}$. This is a necessary consequence of the assumption that at very low levels of economic activity, there will be net dis-saving and at high levels of income positive saving if the conditions of the situation are otherwise given. The fact that both conditions are probable appears self-evident.

[10]The mathematical notation for the marginal propensity to consume is $\frac{dC}{dY}$ and for the marginal propensity to save is $1-\frac{dC}{dY}$. The ratio of change in income to change in investment at the margin will be $\frac{1}{1-\frac{dC}{dY}}$ or the "investment multiplier." From the standpoint of theoretical analysis, if we know the equation for one of our functions for the propensity to consume for a Week, the marginal propensity to consume may be directly derived from the equation. Thus if the interest-rate is given, the function for that rate is $C=\phi(Y)$. If we have the equation for ϕ, we may get the derivative, $\phi'(Y)$. If we solve this for the desired value of Y, we shall get the marginal propensity to consume by direct calculation without reference to tangents.

For the original development of the formula for the Multiplier in terms of the "employment multiplier," see R. F. Kahn, "The Relation of Home Investment and Unemployment," *Economic Journal,* XLI (1931), pp. 183-6.

One of two things must follow as a corollary: either the marginal propensity to consume decreases as the function for one i_0 rate moves toward the right along the horizontal axis, or else, if the function is linear, it must cut the vertical axis above zero.[11]

In the second place, it is to be recalled that for one level of Y, we assume that the marginal propensity to consume falls as the level of the i_0 rate rises, for the reasons given in Section II of this chapter. Attached to this assumption is the correlative assumption that higher i_0 rates both theoretically and practically tend to be attached to higher r' rates.

In the third place, we must recollect also that over a series of Weeks we may have changes in our functions due to changes in the value of ϕ which arise from causes either internal or external to the system of equations. Internal causes may relate to changes in the physical supplies of factors which change the level of employment attached to a given level of income; or they may arise out of changes in expectations based on the immediate past history of the system. Thus it is possible, for example, to find evidences of cyclical shifts in the propensities to consume, and hence in the marginal propensity, based upon the effects of optimism and pessimism upon the expectations of stability in employment and real income. With respect to external influences, an infinite number of autonomous factors may influence the psychological-institutional complex and hence may influence the value of ϕ over a series of Weeks.

In the fourth place, we must never lose sight of the fact that in our Fundamental Model we are dealing with a simplified system and that in the real world conditions of disequilibrium, such as we adumbrate in our Supplementary Models, may operate to change the value of ϕ.

If, therefore, we should study movements in the marginal propensity to consume upon a statistical basis over a period of time we should find a combination of factors operating upon the value

[11]See foot-note, *General Theory*, p. 126. Mr. Keynes points out in a letter to Mrs. Gilboy quoted by her in the *Quarterly Journal of Economics*, LIII (1938-9), pp. 633 ff., that it is not necessary for the validity of his reasoning that dC/dY should decrease. It is only necessary that the *absolute* volume of saving should increase as the level of income increases, whether or not this means an increase in the *proportion* of new income saved. For a discussion of the relation of the individual propensity to consume to the social propensity which must apply to the Week, see the Appendix to this chapter.

of the marginal propensity to consume. Statistics gathered over time for an economic community may obscure the logical functional relationships because of the constant change in the determining variables of the relationship. Under the assumptions for the Week, these variables are ruled out of the picture. The variables which are left appear to justify the general shape we give the functions.

We have in this chapter set out the general nature of the Multiplier Functions. In the next chapter, we require to examine the concept of the Multiplier.

APPENDIX TO CHAPTER VIII

THE RELATION BETWEEN THE INDIVIDUAL AND SOCIAL PROPENSITIES TO CONSUME

In this study our reasoning is based not upon the conformation of the individual propensity to consume but upon the "social propensities to consume" or Multiplier Functions. The latter are modified by certain institutional habits and conditions in ways which keep them from conforming perfectly to a summation of the individual propensities to consume of a given society. The Multiplier Functions as we consider them are functional relationships applying to a situation fixed in time through the concept of the Week. At the same time, there is a third type of relationship which may be (and has been) studied which represents the statistical movements of the "social" relationships over series of short-periods.

Budget studies[1] made of the individual propensity tend to show that, in general, individuals with larger incomes save increasingly larger proportions of these, environmental factors being relatively the same. At the same time certain of the historical studies for communities show a stronger tendency toward stability in the division of national income between consumption and saving than we might expect from the individual figures.[2] For example, the study made by Richard and W. M. Stone, while it shows a strong curvilinearity in the individual budget studies, shows a stable or linear division

[1]For example, see Horst Mendershausen, "The Relationship between Income and Savings of American Metropolitan Families," *American Economic Review*, XXIX (1939), pp. 521-37.

[2]See Richard and W. M. Stone, "The Propensity to Consume and the Multiplier," *Review of Economic Studies*, VI (1938-9), p. 20, point 4; Colin Clark, "Determination of the Multiplier from National Income Statistics," *Economic Journal*, XLVIII (1938), table, p. 442. The linearity of Mr. Clark's multiplier relationships very likely depends, however, upon the drastic nature of the assumptions made. See R. W. Jastram and E. S. Shaw, "Mr. Clark's Statistical Determination of the Multiplier," *Economic Journal*, XLIX (1939), pp. 358-65.

between consumption and saving for the community over the historical cycles to which the study refers. The same linearity shows in Colin Clark's study based on the national income of Australia.

Powerful balancing factors must account for differences between budget studies and some of the statistically derived multiplier relationships. Several possible causes may be listed:

(1) *Distribution Effects.* (*a*) Adjustments of production to changing levels of activity are not made by slicing infinitesimal decrements from the employment of all factors when the level of activity falls. They are made, rather, by dismissing units of factors from employment altogether. The persons who furnish these services must, then, be furnished with purchasing power over consumption goods either by transfers from their own cash-balances or by other decrements of property-rights (as by loans or "deficits") or they must alternatively, be supported by public or private charity. The very rapid fall in the incomes of these persons will bring their marginal propensities to consume up sharply. Under such circumstances, the marginal propensity to consume of the *general*, as opposed to the *individual*, function must fall off more regularly than would be the case if unemployment were shared by all. When economic activity increases, the effects will be reversed.

(*b*) In our convention of temporary equilibrium, we have assumed for the most part that "the investment and employment multipliers are the same"; that is, that the consumption and investment industries are on balance expansible enough so that shifts of demand between investment and consumption goods may operate smoothly without changing the quantum of employment of factors associated with given levels of output measured in wage-units. In the *real* world, the consumption industries are likely to be less expansible in their output, since the operation of the "Acceleration Factor" makes instability of demand more normal for the investment industries, and hence the proportion of plant unused at the nadir of the cycle is likely to be larger in the investment industries. Under such circumstances, the operation of the price system in the later stages of an expansion will tend to support the propensity to consume by altering the rates of change between the consumption and investment price levels. Under the operation of the law of diminishing returns, the "real" wage may decline.

(2) *Psychological Effects.* Pessimism or optimism upon the part of the employed may reinforce the institutional factor described under (1) (*a*). Thus fear for the stability of employment and real income may cause a lowering of the functions representing the individual propensities to consume when the level of economic activity is falling, while optimism may have the opposite effect when it is rising. Under these circumstances the increase in Y may tend to diminish the marginal propensity to consume on the general function while the shifting of the function may tend to increase it in relation to given incomes. When the rate of activity is diminishing, the effects would be the opposite.

(3) *Windfall Effects.* The effects of windfalls upon the propensities to consume will tend to run counter to the effects of income as shown in the budget studies. Thus increases in the values of securities tend to accompany rising phases of economic activity, resulting for equities from rises in the a series, and for both debts and equities from falls in interest-rates and in corrections for risk, uncertainty, and illiquidity. These increases may cause

upward shifting of the component individual propensities to consume although the changes in the values of securities may be reflected only in part in the size of the current national dividend. A general decrease in values may have the opposite effect.

(4) *Effects of Institutional Saving.* The patterns of corporate saving and investment of profits may differ from those of individuals[3] and have definite effects upon the Multiplier as derived from the national dividend without being reflected in the budget studies. With respect to the general function, so far as corporations follow stable dividend policies, and so far as their incomes increase with Y, the effect will be to increase the distance $\frac{dC}{dY}$ lies below $\frac{C}{Y}$.

(5) *Effects of Changes in Rates of Interest.* In this study we have argued for some response of the propensity to consume to the rate of interest. Though the nature of these responses is in part covered by point (3) above, the possibility remains that there may be other effects which will alter the divisions between consumption and saving as interest-rates change over a period of time.

(6) *Effects of Time-Lags.* The world in which statistics are accumulated is not the world of temporary equilibrium in which our analysis mainly moves. In the real world, because of the time-element in production, entrepreneurs may make mistakes and push production beyond the point where the marginal product is equal to marginal revenue. To the extent that they do this, the value of investment may be reduced and the quantum of investment in terms of money may take a lower proportion to the national income than would be the case in a world where these errors did not occur. At the periods of the cycle where these errors occur, as at the peak of a boom, the statistically determined Multiplier may fail to fall as in theory it should in a period of expanding activity. Similarly, near the nadir of a cycle, failure to keep production adjusted to the upward impulses beginning to accumulate may keep the relation between investment and consumption which appears in statistical series from reaching the theoretical relationship. The rigidity of investment plans and the lags between initiation and completion may be even more important elements.

The points made do not invalidate the assumptions we make for our concept of the Week. Only (1) (*a*) and (4) affect the concepts under which we set up our functions for a Week. Nos. (2) and (3) reduce themselves to the shifting of functions between Weeks. No. (5) is accounted for by the nature of our construction. Concerning (6) we may make some generalizations within the terms of our Supplementary Models but we could not handle it within the terms of the Fundamental Model.

---

[3]Paul Douglas, *The Theory of Wages* (New York, 1934), pp. 446-52.

CHAPTER IX

THE GENERAL CONCEPT OF THE MULTIPLIER

(1) INTRODUCTION

THE concept of the Multiplier is derived from the concept of the marginal propensity to consume and has reference to the effects of variations in investment upon income. These effects operate through the connection of increase (or decrease) in the rate of investment with a correlated increase (or decrease) in the demand for consumption goods. The effects upon *demand* will tend to be there under all conditions to some degree so long as income-receivers would spend any part of an increase in money-income per unit of time upon an increase in consumption, *ceteris paribus*. But the crux of the theory is that *in conditions of under-equilibrium* with unemployed factors offering themselves for employment at the "going" wage, an increase in employment in the investment industries resulting from an increased net demand for investment will carry with it not only an increase in demand for consumption goods but an increase in employment in the consumption-goods industries.

As was true in the case of our analysis of the Liquidity Functions, here again the significant contributions made by our analysis will be in the field of under-equilibrium theory. We recognize that under conditions of full employment, investment cannot be increased without drawing factors from the consumption-goods industries nor consumption increased without drawing factors from the investment-goods industries. An actual increase in investment under such conditions will tend to raise *prices* in the consumption-goods industries, since production of these will actually be reduced. We deal fundamentally in this analysis not with such conditions, but with those where there are unemployed labour-units offering themselves in the market and unemployment in both the investment- and the consumption-goods industries.

Our general assumption that the employment and investment Multipliers are equal to each other in the sense in which we have explained these terms is, of course, much over-simplified. Actually expansion does not proceed smoothly and continuously in both investment and consumption industries up to the point of full employment and then cease, as is implied under our Fundamental

Model for the Week. In the process of expansion, there will normally be a series of "bottle-necks"[1] which will interrupt the continuity of the expansion process and disrupt the equality between the employment and investment Multipliers. We set our analysis chiefly in terms of our Fundamental Model (with some references in this chapter to our First Supplementary Model) because again it is only in terms of such simplifications that it is possible at all to build an apparatus which is at once workable and comprehensible. If we regard our reasoning with caution, it seems plausible that we shall be able to secure at least some working hypotheses from it.

It is proposed, under these conditions, that we attempt in this chapter to do four things:

(*a*) We shall first set out the logical theory[2] of the Multiplier

[1] *General Theory*, pp. 300-1.

[2] For articles and notes containing theoretical approaches to the concept of the Multiplier, see: J. M. Clark, "Aggregate Spending by Public Works," *American Economic Review*, XXV (1935), pp. 14-20, "An Appraisal of the Workability of Compensatory Devices," *American Economic Review*, XXIX (1939), Supplement, pp. 194-208; H. C. Coombes, "The Propensity to Consume: A Comment on the Note by Dr. Smithies," *Economic Record*, XIII (1937), pp. 250-6; G. von Haberler, *Prosperity and Depression* (2nd ed.; Geneva, League of Nations, 1939), pp. 222-32; G. R. Holden, "Mr. Keynes' Consumption Function and the Time-Preference Postulate," *Quarterly Journal of Economics*, LII (1937-8), pp. 281-96, and "Rejoinder," pp. 709-12; R. F. Kahn, "Public Works and Inflation," *American Statistical Association Journal*, XXVIII (1933), pp. 168-73, "The Relation of Home Investment and Unemployment," *Economic Journal*, XLI (1931), pp. 173-98; J. M. Keynes, "Mr. Keynes' Consumption Function: A Reply," *Quarterly Journal of Economics*, LII (1937-8), pp. 708-9, and LIII (1938-9), p. 160, Letter quoted by Mrs. Gilboy, *Quarterly Journal of Economics*, LIII (1938-9), pp. 633-5; F. Machlup, "Period Analysis and the Multiplier Theory," *Quarterly Journal of Economics*, LIV (1939-40), pp. 1-27; P. J. Saulnier, *Contemporary Monetary Theory* (New York, 1938), pp. 326-36; E. S. Shaw, "A Note on the Multiplier," *Review of Economic Studies*, VI (1938-9), pp. 60-4; A. Smithies, "The Propensity to Consume," *Economic Record*, XIII (1937), pp. 97-100, and "A Further Comment," p. 256.

For a few of the studies based more directly on statistical relationships, see: Colin Clark, "Determination of the Multiplier from National Income Statistics," *Economic Journal*, XLVIII (1938), pp. 435-48; Ray W. Jastram and E. S. Shaw, "Mr. Clark's Statistical Determination of the Multiplier," *Economic Journal*, XLIX (1939), pp. 358-65; Horst Mendershausen, "The Relationship between Income and Savings of Metropolitan Families," *American Economic Review*, XXIX (1939), pp. 521-37; J. J. Polak, "Fluctuations in United States Consumption, 1919-32," *Review of Economic Statistics*, XXI (1939), pp. 1-12, and "A Correction," p. 88; Hans Staehle, "Short Period Variations in the Distribution of Incomes," *Review of Economic Statistics*, XIX (1937), pp. 133-43; Richard and W. M. Stone, "The Propensity to Consume and the Multiplier," *Review of Economic Studies*, VI (1938-9), pp. 1-21.

as it applies within the concept of temporary equilibrium for one of our Weeks and shall develop the theory arithmetically under conditions where the full effects upon income are achieved within the Week.

(*b*) Next we shall take this "logical" theory of a Multiplier which changes continuously along a function representing the propensity to consume for one i_0 rate of interest and develop a method for theoretical calculation of a Multiplier which would apply to a finite *block* of new investment for a Week.

(*c*) Thirdly, we shall set out the operation of the theory under the conditions of limited disequilibrium which characterize our First Supplementary Model and show how these effects develop over a series of Weeks because of a lack of the degree of "perfection" in the market assumed in the Fundamental Model.

(*d*) Lastly, we shall indicate some of the differences between the *real* world and the worlds of the Fundamental and Supplementary Models.

(2) THE LOGICAL THEORY OF THE MULTIPLIER WITHIN THE CONCEPT OF TEMPORARY EQUILIBRIUM

Definitions of the Investment and Employment Multipliers. For us, the fundamental Multiplier is the *investment* Multiplier which "tells us that, when there is an increment of aggregate investment, income will increase by an amount which is *k* times the increment of investment."[3] The *employment* Multiplier, *k'*, on the other hand, "measures the ratio of the increment of total employment which is associated with a given increment of primary employment in the investment industries."[4] The distinction between the two is not, however, a matter of very much concern for us for the operation of the Fundamental Model. It must, however, be set out explicitly in order that we may not forget some of the differences between the conditions of temporary equilibrium which are fundamental to our concept of the Week and the conditions of disequilibrium which are more characteristic of the world in which we live.

Derivation of the Multiplier. We shall develop our concept of the Multiplier in terms of Figure XVII. On this we draw a single function for the propensity to consume which we assume to be allied with the rate i_c, taken to be the i_0 rate of the Week. Suppose

[3]*General Theory*, p. 115.

[4]*Ibid.* The employment Multiplier is the concept derived from Mr. Kahn's work to which reference has already been made. See Note 2 of this chapter for Mr. Kahn's main analyses in this field and also *General Theory*, pp. 115-16.

that we inscribe tangents on this function at points a, b, and c to derive the marginal propensities to consume at these points.[5] The gradient of the first tangent is $\frac{8}{9}$, of the second $\frac{5}{9}\left(\text{or } \frac{1.25}{2.25}\right)$, and of the third $\frac{1}{3}$.

The marginal propensity to consume is simply $\frac{dC}{dY}$ and the formula for the Multiplier is $\frac{1}{1-\frac{dC}{dY}}$.[6] Let us calculate for these three angles the marginal propensities to consume and the values

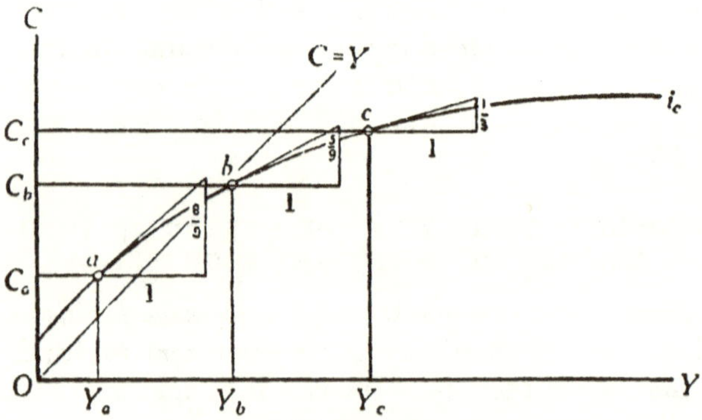

FIGURE XVII

$$\text{At } Y_a, \frac{dC}{dY} = \frac{8}{9}, \ k = 9.$$

$$\text{At } Y_b, \frac{dC}{dY} = \frac{5}{9}, \ k = \frac{9}{4} = 2.25.$$

$$\text{At } Y_c, \frac{dC}{dY} = \frac{1}{3}, \ k = \frac{3}{2} = 1.5.$$

of the Multiplier. Then let us proceed to see what the Multiplier means in terms of our Fundamental Model for the Week. At a, the rate of change in i_c being $\frac{8}{9}$, the Multiplier, k, will be $\frac{1}{1-\frac{8}{9}} = 9$.

[5] It is to be recollected that if we have the equation for the function and the values of Y for the three points, we may calculate the marginal propensities to consume at these points by finding the derivative, $\phi'(Y)$, and solving it for Y_a, Y_b, and Y_c.

[6] See note 10, p. 112. We may also write the marginal propensity as $\frac{\Delta C}{\Delta Y}$.

By a similar calculation at *b*, the marginal propensity to consume is $\frac{1.25}{2.25}$ or $\frac{5}{9}$ and the Multiplier is 2.25. At *c*, the corresponding numbers are $\frac{1}{3}$ and $\frac{1}{1-\frac{1}{3}}=\frac{3}{2}$. What then do these statements mean in terms of our Week?

We must recall at this point that under the assumptions for our Fundamental Model for the Week, all contracts for the Week are made on Monday, everybody knows the prices which concern himself, and the consumption industries are sufficiently expansible within the Week to permit them to supply goods to new consumers without changing the equality between the employment and the investment Multipliers. Because of these assumptions, the changes in investment which we shall assume in our examples will have their complete effects within the single Week. Let us take the three cases, one by one, and see what these effects will be.

At income level Y_a, with the Multiplier equal to 9, if an additional wage-unit[7] is expended for maintenance or replacement,[8] those who receive it will on balance and subject to individual differences, expend eight-ninths of the increment in income for consumption goods and devote the remainder to reducing their deficits. But those in the consumption industries who receive this additional income on Monday will themselves *also* spend eight-ninths of their additional income for the Week on consumption goods and use the remainder for reducing *their* deficits. Again the same thing will happen at the next step. When the contract markets close on "Monday evening," if we set out the sums of the additional contracts resulting from the increase in the level of investment for the Week, we have a progression like the following:

$$1+\frac{8}{9}+\left(\frac{8}{9}\right)^2+\left(\frac{8}{9}\right)^3+\ldots+\left(\frac{8}{9}\right)^n.$$

The limit on the value of this progression is 9, and *it is this limit which is the Multiplier.* For the one extra wage-unit which went

[7]We assume that one wage-unit is so small a portion of the total level of income, Y_a, that the addition of *one* wage-unit does not impair the application of the reasoning of the calculus. Necessary modifications for finite blocks of investment will be considered in the succeeding section. It is also necessary to assume that the new income falls to what we may call "representative income-receivers."

[8]Since the level of income, Y_a, lies at the left of the linear function $C=Y$, there is net dis-investment for the Week at that level.

into maintenance or replacement for the Week (in comparison, say, with the number which applied under the same function last Week), eight more will go into the consumption industries and thus a total of nine into income. Under the assumption that the investment and the employment Multipliers are equal to each other, the increase in employment in the consumption industries will be eight times the increase in the industries which maintain or replace capital goods and which we call in a broad sense the investment industries. The whole effect comes true within the Week because of the degree of "perfection" which we have assumed to apply in the market.

If we accumulate the quantities used by income-receivers to reduce deficits in the same manner, we have the progression:

$$\frac{1}{9}+\frac{1}{9}\cdot\frac{8}{9}+\frac{1}{9}\left(\frac{8}{9}\right)^2+\frac{1}{9}\left(\frac{8}{9}\right)^3+\ldots+\frac{1}{9}\left(\frac{8}{9}\right)^n.$$

The limit on this progression is 1, and thus the amount by which the deficits are reduced exactly equals the amount which was used for maintenance or replacement. Dis-saving and dis-investment are reduced by equivalent amounts.[9] Since all the effects come true within the Week, we need in this model to give no attention to any possible "tertiary" effects upon expectations because of the alteration in the level of investment.

By similar reasoning, at income level Y_b, for an additional wage-unit going into new investment, $\frac{5}{9}$ goes into consumption, and the Multiplier progression is

$$1+\frac{5}{9}+\left(\frac{5}{9}\right)^2+\ldots+\left(\frac{5}{9}\right)^n=\frac{9}{4}=2.25,$$

while the investment progression becomes

$$\frac{4}{9}+\frac{4}{9}\cdot\frac{5}{9}+\frac{4}{9}\left(\frac{5}{9}\right)^2+\ldots+\frac{4}{9}\left(\frac{5}{9}\right)^n=1.$$

Investment and saving are equal to 1 wage-unit; the consumption increase is 1.25, while the Multiplier is 2.25.

At income level Y_c, computation shows the limit on the value of the Multiplier progression to be 1.5 and on the investment progression to be 1.

[9]Alternatively we may say that gross saving and gross investment have been increased by 1 unit, or if we were to use Mr. Keynes' terminology, *current* investment and saving. Once more, we keep to our own terminology to keep our construction consistent throughout and to keep problems of maintenance explicit for the system.

Thus where these different conditions apply, any increase in investment is connected with a complementary increase in the level of consumption which increases the total income for the Week by a multiple (called the Multiplier) determined by the marginal propensity to consume.

The above reasoning outlines the so-called "logical theory of the multiplier, which holds good continuously, without time-lags, at all moments of time."[10] After we have digressed to expound the application of the Multiplier concept to finite blocks of investment,

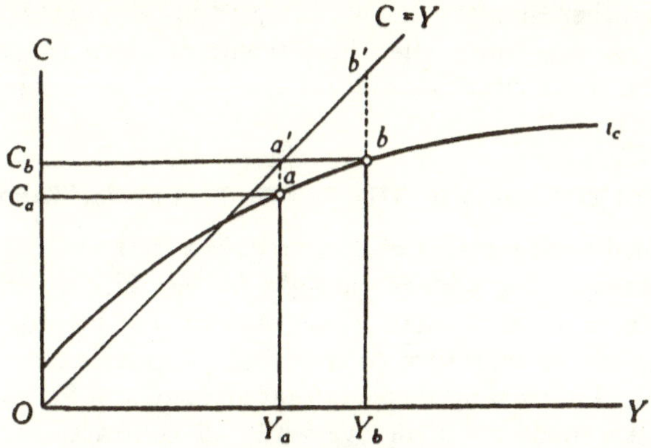

FIGURE XVIII

we shall extend the concept of the Multiplier to a world characterized by possibilities of limited disequilibrium by means of our First Supplementary Model.

(3) THE "AVERAGE" MARGINAL PROPENSITY TO CONSUME AND THE MULTIPLIER

We have already pointed out in the preceding chapter that the marginal propensity to consume may be subject to a continuous change as the propensity to consume travels to the right, becoming lower and lower as income becomes larger. If, therefore, the change in the level of investment per Week comes in substantial amounts, we must allow for this shifting in the marginal propensity to consume when we calculate the value of the Multiplier. Thus in terms of Figure XVIII, if we increase the quantum of net investment in a block from *aa'* to *bb'*, the Multiplier which will apply to the increase in income (and employment) under the assumptions can be taken from the marginal propensity to consume at neither *a* nor *b*. We

[10]*General Theory*, p. 122.

must find in some sense the *average* marginal propensity to consume for this finite change in investment and calculate the Multiplier from this average. In the foot-note below the theoretical method of making this calculation is set out.[11]

Whenever we speak of *the* Multiplier with reference to finite changes in the level of investment for a Week, we shall mean this average Multiplier. Actually, since any laws which we derive with respect to human behaviour are only *statistically* true, it is this Multiplier we *must* mean when we make definite applications of our reasoning, rather than the one we analysed in Section II. We could not be at all sure that when investment changed in very small amounts the new increments of income would fall to "representative income-receivers."

(4) THE MULTIPLIER AND THE FIRST SUPPLEMENTARY MODEL

Our third task for this chapter requires that we relax our assumptions respecting perfect foresight for the Week. In order to get the effects of incomplete foresight upon the logical theory of the Multiplier, let us return to the First Supplementary Model of our system. Let us suppose again that all contracts for the services of factors are made on Mondays while all contracts for the sale of consumption goods and new securities are made on Tuesdays. We assume in the first instance that entrepreneurs' plans for a current Week are made in the light of their experience the previous Week, and that entrepreneurs on Monday may therefore either under-estimate or over-estimate the quantum of sales measured in wage-units which they will be able to make on Tuesday.

[11]Let the consumption or Multiplier Function be $i_c = \phi(Y)$. The problem is to find the average Multiplier when the level of investment for a given Week is increased from aa' to bb'. If we find the first derivative, $\phi'(Y)$, and solve for Y_a and Y_b, we shall have the marginal propensities to consume at a and b, but the Multiplier for a will be too high and for b too low to give the average between a and b. Mathematically and theoretically we could get this average Multiplier by calculating the definite integral for the derived curve, $\phi'(Y)$, and dividing it by the distance $Y_b - Y_a$,

$$\frac{\int_{Y_a}^{Y_b} \phi' \, dY}{Y_b - Y_a} = \frac{C_b - C_a}{Y_b - Y_a}.$$

This would give the mean value of the ordinate for the derived curve between a and b and this would *be* the marginal propensity to consume when the level of investment for the function i_c was increased by $bb' - aa'$. *The* Multiplier for this block of investment could be derived from the marginal propensity to consume by substituting in the formula as before.

Effects of Single Doses of New Investment on the Multiplier Relationship. On Monday, let us say, owing to the presence of some autonomous factor, in terms of Figure XVIII, the rate of *planned* investment is increased from aa' to $aa'+1$. The marginal propensity to consume, let us say, is $\frac{3}{4}$ and the Multiplier is therefore 4 for the additional unit. On Tuesday, entrepreneurs in the consumption industries, who have made their plans in accordance with the experience of the previous Week, find that their proceeds are increased by the $\frac{3}{4}$ of the addition which the new income-receivers of Monday will spend upon consumption. *There will be disinvestment in the consumption industries amounting to* $\frac{3}{4}$ *of the new investment made on Monday. Net additional investment of the system* for the Week will be $1-\frac{3}{4}=\frac{1}{4}$. Investment is equal to saving for the Week, but the *actual* increase in investment as opposed to the *planned* increase is from aa' to $aa'+\frac{1}{4}$ instead of $aa'+1$.

In the second Week, if nothing has happened to change the position of functions, entrepreneurs in the consumption industries will seek to provide new consumption goods to the extent at least of their increased sales of the previous Week, under our assumption that they base their expectations on the outcomes of operations during the previous Week.[12] But if the dose of increased input into the system is not repeated on the second Monday, upon the second Tuesday, entrepreneurs will be confronted by the fact that final income-receivers desire to save one-fourth of the new income coming to them through the consumption industries and entrepreneurs will receive in return for the additional consumption goods produced only $\frac{3}{4}\times\frac{3}{4}$ or $\frac{9}{16}$. The difference between $\frac{3}{4}$ and $\frac{9}{16}$ must be made up by additions to their liquid capital which will restore to a

[12]If entrepreneurs in the consumption-goods industries enter into operations designed to replace stocks dis-invested the previous Week, then that increase in money-income for the Week will in itself be subject to the operation of the Multiplier. We are sliding over in all these Weeks the complication brought in by the fact that the Multiplier for the different Weeks will be somewhat modified by the changes in the curve which we analysed in the preceding section. The progressions given in this section represent only approximations.

degree the goods dis-invested the Week before, or it must be covered by reductions of prices below cost which reduce the incomes which entrepreneurs had expected to receive from the operations of the Week. But saving and investment will still be equal in either case.

If we could assume that the functions of the system kept the same position Week by Week, and that only the single dose of investment took place, the same types of progression apply as those given for the cases where foresight for the Week was perfect. The essential difference in the case of our Supplementary Model would be that it would take an infinite series of Weeks for the full effects to be felt on both consumption and investment and hence on income. If we assume that entrepreneurs do not alter their plans to restore the liquid capital dis-invested during the first Week but allow their stocks to be restored gradually, these progressions would be summarized as below:

$$
\begin{array}{lccccccccc}
 & \textit{Week 1} & & \textit{Week 2} & & \textit{Week 3} & & \textit{Week 4} & & \textit{Limit} \\
\text{Consumption:} & \frac{3}{4} & + & \left(\frac{3}{4}\right)^2 & + & \left(\frac{3}{4}\right)^3 & + & \left(\frac{3}{4}\right)^4 & + \ldots & =3 \\
\text{Investment:} & \frac{1}{4} & + & \frac{1}{4}\left(\frac{3}{4}\right) & + & \frac{1}{4}\left(\frac{3}{4}\right)^2 & + & \frac{1}{4}\left(\frac{3}{4}\right)^3 & + \ldots & =1 \\
\hline
\text{Income:} & 1 & + & \frac{3}{4} & + & \frac{9}{16} & + & \frac{27}{64} & + \ldots & =4 \\
\hline\hline
\end{array}
$$

That is to say, under the assumptions made and with no further impulses working upon the system, with imperfect foresight within the Week and with the decisions of entrepreneurs made upon the experience of the preceding Week, the strongest effect upon the system of *the single dose of new investment* will occur in the first Week, when income rises to Y_a+1. Thereafter, unless something new occurred to support or depress it, the level of income would die back toward Y_a again.[13]

[13]It is possible, if the system is volatile, that entrepreneurs may plan new investment for the second Week upon the basis of the unexpected additions to consumption in the first Week and that such an addition may set off a cumulative expansion in the system. It is also possible if these plans do not get started fast enough to raise the rate of input on Monday of the second Week over 3/4, or the extra consumption of Week 1, that the fact that an increment of liquid capital is left on their hands may cause entrepreneurs to revise expectations downward and the dying away of the effects of the added input in Week 1 may become the basis of a downward revision of entrepreneur plans. Any "overdoing" of this revision may carry the system below income Y_a. Analysis of such "dynamic" relationships is not, however, undertaken in this study.

Effects of Changes in the Rate of Investment. Let us, before we close this section and in order to recapitulate, suppose that the change was a true change in the *rate* of new investment, that the extra dose is therefore repeated, Week by Week, and that the same functions hold. What would be the effects upon income under our Fundamental and First Supplementary Models?

Under the Fundamental Model, where the full force of the Multiplier is felt immediately, income per Week would be increased by 4 units immediately, consumption would become C_a+3 and investment $aa'+1$. This would continue Week by Week. Under the First Supplementary Model, we might summarize the change in income as follows:

Investment Doses	*Income Effects* Week 1	*Week 2*	*Week 3*	*Week 4*	*Limit.*
1st	1	$+\frac{3}{4}$	$+\frac{9}{16}$	$+\frac{27}{64}$	$+\ldots.$
2nd		1	$+\frac{3}{4}$	$+\frac{9}{16}$	$+\ldots.$
3rd			1	$+\frac{3}{4}$	$+\ldots.$
4th				1	$+\ldots.$
Total Income Effects:	1,	$1\frac{3}{4}$,	$2\frac{5}{16}$,	$2\frac{53}{64}$, ..	4 per Week

That is, under the assumptions, after an infinite number of Weeks,[14] the effects upon the rate of income per Week would be measured by the full value of the Multiplier, the condition that was true from the beginning where foresight for the Week was assumed to be perfect.

[14]Over an infinite number of Weeks even without the operation of autonomous factors the increase in the quantum of capital in a system with positive investment or the decrease in a system with negative invéstment must alter the functions for our construction. This makes only a very small amount of difference to the values of our progressions, however, since the main effects of the operation of the Multiplier would pass away in a very short series of Weeks. Thus if the Multiplier is 4, more than three-fourths of the effects pass away in a series of five Weeks and 93% of them in a series of ten Weeks. In a society even moderately provided with capital goods, the increments of capital of a small series of Weeks can have only a very small effect upon the system as a whole. Autonomous factors, naturally, can cause important changes in short series both in the physical quantum of capital (as for example, a war) and in the estimates placed upon the future uses of that capital.

Once more we issue the caution that the condition of expanding income may itself become the basis of new expectations which push the rate of investment forward faster and thus multiply the effects shown.

Reverse Application of the Multiplier. There is a further warning to issue with respect to the operation of the Multiplier. We usually find its effects considered in relation to increases in the rate of investment per Week. *But the Multiplier also works in reverse.* A *reduction* in investment brings with it a train of *decrements* of income because of the reduction of incomes of the entrepreneurs in the consumption-goods industries and the consequent revisions of their plans for output.

(5) THE OPERATION OF THE MULTIPLIER IN THE REAL WORLD

Even a very faint acquaintance with the world of actuality would be sufficient to inform us that the level of income cannot be manipulated as simply as we have implied in either the Fundamental or the First Supplementary Model. The degree of foresight assumed in the Fundamental Model simply does not exist; the character of expectations assumed in connection with the First Supplementary Model is over-simplified and the functions of the system for these and other reasons will only rarely remain unmodified over any definite series of Weeks; the rates of expansion in the consumption and the investment industries may be quite different from each other, absolutely and relatively, and the system will be subject to disturbances because uneven changes in prices will result from the presence of "bottle-necks" in the expansionary phases of change and from unequal ability to adjust production in periods of recession. From outside the system an infinite variety of autonomous factors may play upon the psychological-institutional complex to change the values of the system.

Out of this welter of complicating factors we cannot bring a concept of the Multiplier as a simple unitary relationship operating directly over time. Nevertheless statistical studies based upon the concept have shown a surprising degree of stability[15] in the relationship and indicate the probable presence of powerful balancing factors.

This chapter has had in many respects the character of a digression from the main line of our analysis. It has been made

[15]See *General Theory*, p. 128, and Richard and W. M. Stone, "The Propensity to Consume and the Multiplier," p. 20, point 4, and *supra*, pp. 114-16.

necessary by the importance of the concept of the Multiplier in the literature respecting the Keynesian system of analysis. The relationship is *implied* in the structure which we are erecting upon the bases of our set of simultaneous equations. The time element which is usually made prominent in discussions of the Multiplier[16] appears frequently to obscure the real nature of the system of analysis as a set of shifting functions. For this reason we shall develop our own system mainly without direct reference to the concept.

One more task remains to be carried out before we are able to assemble our complete apparatus, demonstrate its inter-dependence, and then make it a tool for the analysis of the effects of certain types of social policy. We turn briefly in the next two chapters to the analysis of the Investment Functions.

[16]For example, see J. M. Clark, "An Appraisal of the Workability of Compensatory Devices," and note on the diagram on page 200 the method of analysing the concept through primary, secondary, and "tertiary" effects.

CHAPTER X

THE PROCESS OF VALUATION IN THE INVESTMENT-GOODS INDUSTRIES

THE third and last equation of the shifting equilibrium, namely $I = F(i, C)$, asserts that the level of new investment per Week is a function of the rate of interest and of the level of consumption. The structure which we shall build for this equation, and which will be set out in detail in the chapter to follow, will therefore show the relation of the rate of investment for one of our Weeks to the i_0 rate of interest upon the one hand and to the level of consumption upon the other. In the development of this structure throughout the next two chapters, we shall perform five general tasks: (*a*) We shall set out the general problem involved in the relation of the rate of new investment to the concept of the Week; (*b*) we shall consider the nature of demand and supply and of the process of valuation in the investment-goods industries; (*c*) we shall discuss the calculation of the schedule of the marginal efficiencies of capital; (*d*) we shall analyse the structure of the Investment Functions; and lastly, (*e*) we shall consider the causes of instability in the positions of the Investment Functions.

The current chapter will be devoted to a consideration of (*a*) and (*b*) as listed above.

(1) THE GENERAL PROBLEM OF INVESTMENT IN RELATION TO THE CONCEPT OF THE WEEK

Hoarding, Dishoarding, and the Scale of Economic Activity in the Fundamental Model. Under the degree of market perfection which we have assumed for our Fundamental Model, entrepreneurs have enough knowledge on Monday to allow them to decide upon the scale of operations which will maximize their profits for the Week. If entrepreneurs, under this convention, see on "Monday morning" that the scales of operations which have characterized their enterprises the preceding Week would result this Week in failure to recover marginal costs from market sales, they will reduce the scale of activity and make the transfers to the L_2 balances themselves from their own transactions balances.[1] If they see that the scale of activity of the previous Week, if adopted for the current Week, will give marginal revenues higher than marginal costs, they will increase the scale of activities for the current Week, finding new funds for the purpose by transferring portions of their own L_2 balances or by borrowing from the banking system or from other sources. Thus the degree of employment which they will offer for the Week will be related to their estimation of the demands for consumption goods and new securities during the Week.

Hoarding and Dishoarding in the Supplementary Models. By comparison, under the conditions of the Supplementary Models, the same general conditions apply with the exception that the expectations of entrepreneurs on Monday are subject to error with respect to the events of Tuesday. Under these conditions there may be transfers between the transactions (L_1) and savings (L_2) balances which were not planned by entrepreneurs when deciding upon the scale of activities for the Week. Thus in the First Supplementary Model, entrepreneurs may contract to pay out from their transactions balances more than will be returned to them on Tuesday for the purchase of consumers' goods and securities offered for sale in the market, the difference going to the L_2 balances. Under the opposite state of expectations, money may on Tuesday be diverted unexpectedly from the L_2 balances for the purchase of consumption goods or to make offers for the purchase of debts and equities resulting from the Week's operations. In both cases entrepreneurs as a group will have failed to match marginal costs to marginal revenues and therefore as individual operators will feel that profits have not been maximized and that plans require revision. The fact that, under this Model, expectations can be incorrect within the Week as well as over a series of Weeks gives greater instability to the system of relations but it does not change its general character. Conditions in the Second Supplementary Model are similar enough not to require separate analysis.

As we have set out before, particularly in Chapter III above, in making their choices between the disposition of savings in L_2 balances or in the purchase of debts or equities, individual savers

[1]Alternatively, if they have been using funds borrowed from the banks for working capital funds, they may reduce their indebtedness to the banks and hence reduce the quantity of money measured in money-units. Since in general we are treating the quantity of money as a datum, we omit this complication ordinarily. But we must recognize that we are omitting it and that the quantity of money is less arbitrarily determined by the banking authorities than we have assumed.

are guided by their estimates of advantage in these actions, and there will be a tendency to make substitutions at the margin until the marginal rate of liquidity-preference enjoyed from the possession of the cash-balance comes into equilibrium with the rate of interest i_0 which the marginal holders of the supply of debts require to remain holders for the Week, and with the rates which marginal holders of the various classes of equities available expect to earn from possession for the Week. In addition to this system of margins is the other general margin of substitution between consumption and saving.

In our study of the Liquidity Functions we studied the nature of the relationship between the liquidity-preference premium afforded by the possession of a cash-balance and the complex of interest-rates. In the chapters upon the Multiplier Functions, we studied the conditions of substitution between consumption and saving, first, with reference to the relation between income, consumption, and saving, and second, with reference to the time-preference margin through the arrangement and dispersion of the Multiplier Functions as attached to specific interest-rate complexes. In the chapters on the Investment Functions, our main task is to study the nature of the expectations of entrepreneurs which have issue in different levels of investment for a Week.

(2) THE PROCESS OF VALUATION ON THE SUPPLY SIDE OF THE INVESTMENT-GOODS MARKET

In this and the following section we propose to examine the motives which condition the supply of and the demand for investment goods, including the goods devoted to the maintenance and replacement of existing capital goods and the consumption goods which are produced for stocks of liquid capital.

Expectations and the Valuation Process for Investment Goods. The current level of consumption gives the basis of the current yield from existing capital. The higher this demand for consumption goods in the present, the more fully utilized the current capital equipment will be. But as the yield from current supplies of capital rises, expectations of future yields from *extensions* of the capital supply rise also. For this reason, therefore, in any structure we set out for the Investment Functions we must show the demand for investment goods as varying directly with the level of consumption.

The effects of impulses toward the expansion of either consumption or investment will differ for the system as a whole in accordance with conditions of employment. Under conditions of full employment of the factors of production, demands for factors for consumption and for investment will obviously be in competition with each other. Employment in each type will be pushed each unit of time toward the point of equality for the marginal product of value under conditions which maximize the profits of the individual entrepreneurs engaged in production. Under conditions of *under*-employment, however, the operation of the Multiplier functions as we have set these out in the preceding chapters, will push employment *upward* in *both* types of industry in accordance with the actual functional relations which apply.

If the impulse toward expansion is not checked before the level of full employment is reached, when this level *is* reached, further impulses toward expansion may change the division of employment between the two types of industry but cannot affect the level of activity itself *unless* they add some factor to the situation which changes the general equilibrium level.[2] The general force of the impulses will waste itself in price effects.[3] But the limit on expansion in the system may occur before this point if the i_0 and attached r' rates of interest are high enough to check the expectations of the rate of return over cost sufficiently. Under such conditions, demand for new investment will fail to reach the level required for equality with the volume of saving per Week at the level of full employment. Since, *ceteris paribus*, the higher the rate of interest the entrepreneur must pay,[4] the lower the amount of net proceeds he will have left over for himself, the Investment Functions when we come to set them up must show the level of investment under a given state of expectations and consumption level, as varying inversely with the i_0 rate of interest. As before, under the Liquidity and Multiplier Functions, for any given Week we must make assumptions as to the connection of the i_0 rate with the r' rates, but there will always be a general inference that a high i_0 rate means high r' rates.

The expectations upon which an entrepreneur bases his demand for investment factors rest (*a*) upon his own expectations of yield

[2]E.g., an impulse which tends to change the rates of interest (i_0 and r') will tend to change the equilibrium level of activity also.

[3]*General Theory*, pp. 118-19, 289-91.

[4]This rate of interest may be explicit or implicit, since the entrepreneur too has opportunities to purchase debts, and if he uses his own capital the rate he might receive from the purchase of a debt of the same duration as his equity enters as an opportunity cost.

from the investment over its life and in relation to present and probable future costs of producing the instrument; and (*b*) upon his expectation of the salability of this equity in the market, or really upon the "liquidity" of the equity. Different lines of action will show different combinations of these elements of yield and liquidity. Certain of these will fit in best with the entrepreneur's plans. But his decision to hire factors in the market for the purpose of making additions to the quantum of fixed, working and liquid capital will rest not only upon his judgment respecting the best combinations of yield and liquidity open to him. He has further to decide whether or not any other choice upon his whole system of multiple margins offers him a larger prospect of advantage. Even more, his decisions to hire factors to maintain the existing quantum of capital in his enterprise or to replace units passing out of use, will rest upon the same combination.[5] When we have reduced these elements to order, and have combined them with the conclusions set out respecting the nature of the variation of the demand for investment with the level of consumption and the i_0 rate of interest, we shall have our Investment Functions.

We shall find it easier to analyse the entrepreneurs' subjective processes of valuation if we first classify capital goods into three general classes:

(*a*) The good which the entrepreneur contemplates purchasing or producing to add to his quantum of capital to be carried from the current to the succeeding Week may be of such a character that it will be destroyed by a single use. So far as the individual entrepreneur's calculations are concerned, this will be a characteristic of units of both working and liquid capital.

(*b*) The good to be produced may offer continuous services in production over a period of Weeks.

(*c*) The good may have a definite *technical* life, but this technical life may be differently distributed over chronological time.

The Valuation Process for Goods which Perish with One Use. If the capital good has one use only,[6] the problem of arriving at its present value is fairly simple. Its present value will be the greatest of the anticipated, discounted forward yields, net of anticipated costs of carrying the good to that point of time. In making these comparisons, the appropriate r' rates and correction coefficients will be used as developed through the formulae of Chapter III above. Because of the heavier and heavier discounts

[5]*General Theory*, pp. 222-34 for Mr. Keynes' method of combining outcomes.
[6]*Ibid.*, pp. 70-1.

on expected proceeds as Weeks recede into the future, and because of costs for storage, chances of deterioration, opportunity costs of making loans with the money invested or sacrifice of liquidity involved in disposition of the cash-balance by the entrepreneur or person from whom he borrows, the single use is likely to be restricted to some date in the relatively near future. The value problem is a comparatively simple one.

Nevertheless, even here the subjective aspects which we summate under the term "expectations" are the determining factors. If additions to stocks of working or liquid capital are to be produced this Week instead of next Week, the choice can be made only on the bases of estimates of technical and other cost advantages to be derived which outweigh the costs of carrying the stock from this Week to next Week by at least as much as could be gained by lending the money involved for the same period.

Entrepreneurs, for example, may produce working and liquid capital units this Week in anticipation of seasonal swings in the propensity to consume. By this means they may economize in their uses of factors and of fixed capital when their plans are considered over long periods of time. For example, the automobile industry may manufacture cars for stock in advance of orders with the purpose of reducing the quantum of fixed equipment required and of avoiding the increase in unit costs connected with over-utilization of plant and over-time for labour supply.

Entrepreneurs may also produce in advance of orders when expectations of rising prices of output give an expectation of an increase of value with the passage of time. That is, cyclical optimism may raise the rate of investment in the types of goods whose demands and prices are affected to the advantage of entrepreneurs by the expansion phases of the cycle.

Valuation Process for Goods of Longer Life but Continuous Use. If the capital good is one which affords services continuously, the value problem has some differences of aspect. The life of the instrument produced may be relatively long, relatively short, or the instrument may be practically immortal so far as the expectations of living men are concerned. The length of the life of the instrument may bring complicating factors into the process of valuation.

If the instrument has an expected life which is relatively long, the problem of deciding whether to produce it this Week or next Week is again relatively simple, once the decision to produce it at all is brought into the longer plan. To find the present value of such an instrument, we use formula (4) of Chapter III.[7] As we look to the end of the *a* series of the formula, the yield to be added by deferring production one Week would be added at the end of a long series of terms while the yield to be sacrificed would be the first yield of the series. Owing to the dispersion of expectations and the operation of the correction coefficients set out in Chapter III, the present value of the end-term of such a series would be practically insignificant and probably insufficient to affect the rate of production this Week. Once the decision to produce the instrument is fitted into the longer plan, the decision whether it will be produced this Week or next must be made upon estimates of the more immediate factors respecting comparative costs of production in the two Weeks and upon the *net* price and other advantages to be gained by having the good ready for use or sale at a nearer or a later date.

If, however, the series of uses afforded by the instrument is relatively short, the postponement of the last term of the series to a later Week may enter the calculation as a factor which bears some weight.

If the capital good has a practically immortal life, the problem of value is essentially the same as that for a good with a relatively long life. This is true because the calculations of living men relate to finite terms of years.[8] Only those terms of the immortal life which affected the expectations of producers or purchasers would be relevant to the problem of the value of the good. Moreover, even though the physical life of the instrument might be estimated to be as lengthy as that of the Pyramids, yet the value of the instrument as reckoned from any given Week would be affected by the dispersion of expectations in forward Weeks because of the chance of obsolescence or changes in the supply of the instrument which would affect its yield in terms of value. Growing uncertainty as futurity grew would also increase the influence of the correction coefficient *s* placed on each forward term of the *a* series.

Valuation Process for Goods whose Uses May Have More than One Possible Distribution over Chronological Time. The third type of capital good in the list which we have presented involves a problem of valuation which more nearly concerns the decisions of entrepreneurs in their establishment and maintenance of modern industrial plants. Such plants normally have reserves of equipment and only very rarely do they utilize their entire equipment even

[7] *Supra*, p. 34.
[8] S. S. Slichter, *Modern Economic Society* (New York, 1931), pp. 685-6 n.

where the basis of organization of an industry is fairly competitive. The instruments they use have commonly a limited technical life and to the problem of technical dis-investment involved in their use is added the problem of the distribution of the technical life of the instrument over chronological time. When such instruments are valued with respect to their series of future uses, the possibility of this variation in distribution of uses must enter into the calculations either subjectively or objectively. We can no longer apply without adjustment the rather simple formula (4) of Chapter III.

The Supply Price of Instruments and the Concept of User Cost: Illustration. Let us illustrate this condition by means of an example and say that we have a plant manufacturing printing presses. We shall divide the analysis into supply and demand aspects. With respect to the supply aspects, let us say that the equipment used to manufacture these presses has a technical life, on the average, of ten years if used continuously, but that these uses may be spread over fifteen, twenty, thirty, or even more years of chronological time if the entrepreneurs find such distributions to their advantage.

When decisions are made respecting the supply price at which printing presses will be offered, the postponement of the first year's use of a given machine to some period beyond the end of the ten years representing the maximum technical life will have an outcome so lost in the mists of unpredictability, so affected by the dispersions of expectations, that a comparison between the two can have but little effect upon the actions of entrepreneurs. But as the term of its life shortens and the date of replacement comes closer, the dispersion of expectations grows less and the costs of replacement grow more imminent. It comes to be a matter of calculation whether or not it is worth while to add to output this year or this Week and thus bring the replacement date a year or a Week closer. To any technical dis-investment involved in the use of the equipment to produce the printing presses must be added a cost to represent the expected disadvantage to be incurred by bringing the date of replacement that much closer. This combined charge represents the "sacrifice which [the entrepreneur] incurs by employing the equipment instead of leaving it idle."[9] This charge we call *user cost.*[10]

Some qualifications must be made with respect to this definition. In the first place, the gross amount of user cost must, of course,

[9]*General Theory*, p. 23.

[10]*Ibid.*, pp. 53-5, 58, 66-73.

be reduced by the irreducible costs of maintaining the machine in good condition during the periods of idleness.[11] If these costs are very high or the physical deterioration and obsolescence "normal" for the machine with the passage of time are very great, postponement of use is not likely to pay and there will be no user cost item in the marginal price for extending output. But where equipment is durable, the replacement date near enough to make expectations active, the services postponable, and current maintenance costs low, there is likely to be such a charge made in the mind of the entrepreneur in calculating the extent to which he will furnish output under current price conditions.

In the second place, it is to be pointed out that before we can apply the concept of user cost to price formation, we must distinguish between *average* and *marginal* user cost.[12] It is marginal user cost which is an element of supply price though we must consider marginal user cost in relation to marginal factor cost. An entrepreneur will tend to bring into operation first those portions of his equipment on which the *sum* of factor cost and user cost is lowest. Other equipment will be brought into use progressively as the current situation makes it appear profitable. This is the principle which dictates the rate of operation of the individual plant. And thus expectations enter into the supply price of new investment goods.

The supply price of instruments and of other additions to the quantum of capital determined in the way outlined forms a minimum which the demand price must meet if the good is to be produced. The fundamental relation in determining whether or not a given item of capital will be produced will be the rate of return over cost, and the preceding analysis is basic for the determination of this cost. But demand valuations must be known also and we turn in the next section to the processes of analysis on this side of the market.

(3) THE PROCESS OF VALUATION ON THE DEMAND SIDE OF THE INVESTMENT-GOODS MARKET

The Demand Price of Instruments. In order to analyse the processes which determine the demand for a capital good, let us extend the example which we have been discussing under the problems of supply. We have discussed the calculations of a plant supplying printing presses with respect to the entrepreneur's

[11] *Ibid.*, pp. 66-9.

[12] *Ibid.*, pp. 54, 67, 72.

marginal costs and have pointed out the subjective elements which enter to condition these estimates. Let us now direct our attention to the demand for printing presses to see the character of the estimates made in such cases. The supplier of printing presses already *has* his instruments to produce these and his judgments relate normally only to the scale of utilization of his instruments which appears to be most profitable for the current Week. Short-term expectations will be prominent in his calculations. But the demander, unless he is also his own supplier, will be in a better position to decide whether or not he is willing to pay the price at which the supplier will offer these presses on the market. Long-term expectations will have more influence upon his actions.

The offers of the demander of printing presses will be based upon his estimates of the present value of the future yields of the printing press, discounted in some fashion to the present date, and qualified further by reference to the entrepreneur's judgment respecting the "liquidity" of his investment. In other words, his methods of valuation will be similar to those which we set out in Section 4 of Chapter III. Week by Week as he looks forward his expectations of yield will be subject to certain dispersions and to different degrees of satisfaction with reference to the mean values arrived at for these dispersions. In these calculations he must consider, for example, future possibilities of changes (*a*) in the prices of the output of the printing press; (*b*) in the prices of factors which must be allied with the instrument in obtaining output from it; and (*c*) in the prices of other factors and in the rates of interest which would affect the future supply prices of printing presses, and which must be considered in planning purchases. In addition, since this instrument is of the third type of capital previously listed in this chapter, some allowance must be made for the possibility that the instrument may be out of use for portions of its life because of the fact that its technical uses may be distributed over chronological time in a number of different ways.

If, in spite of all these complicating factors, the entrepreneur is able, theoretically at least, to set out an *a* series of net yields which he may expect from this printing press, he is then in position to make a calculation as to whether or not it will pay him to buy the printing press. He will reach his decision by comparing the rate of return over cost afforded by this series of yields during its currency with the rates of return he could secure by holding debts or existing equities for the same period or with the estimated advantages of adding to his cash-balances for the Week or reducing his borrowing, or undertaking some other form of new investment.

Let us say that a printing press costs $1000 to produce or to buy, the cost calculations having been based upon the elements set out in our preceding section. The entrepreneur will theoretically consider the terms in his *a* series as annuities and will find the rate of return which this series of terms makes over the present cost of the instrument, due allowance being made, of course, for possible variations in the time-distribution of the services of the printing press. Let us say that when he has performed this calculation, he finds that the investment of $1000 promises an average yield of 9 per cent per Week during its life over the allowances made for risk and other factors influencing net yields. This rate we shall call the *marginal efficiency rate* for this investment. In the next chapter we shall build this rate into the *marginal efficiency schedule.*

Elements of the Decision to Produce during a Current Week. We may, however, examine briefly in this chapter the conditions which determine whether or not the entrepreneur will buy (or make) this printing press. With reference to the entrepreneur's longer plan, it will be worth his while to undertake investment in this instrument if the return upon $1000 to be gained by purchasing an existing debt or equity of the same duration is anything less than 9 per cent. Such a decision does not necessarily involve the decision to produce the instrument this Week. The decision to produce it this Week rather than next Week means that there is an expected advantage in this action at least equal to the i_0 rate for this Week. If the i rates for forward Weeks form a falling or a rising series, it is not enough to know what the marginal efficiency rate for a given instrument is. We must recognize also the possibility of the substitution of investment over time. In the next chapter we shall take cognizance of this possibility in building the Investment Functions.

The tenuity of the bases of the estimates of the value of a capital-asset is plainly evidenced by the importance of expectations in the valuation series and is connected with some of the most important and difficult problems of modern economic organization. To this aspect we shall return briefly after we have in the following chapter analysed the concept of the marginal efficiency of capital further and from it constructed the Investment Functions.

CHAPTER XI

THE MARGINAL EFFICIENCY OF CAPITAL AND THE INVESTMENT FUNCTIONS

(1) THE MARGINAL EFFICIENCY OF CAPITAL

IN terms of the process of valuation of a capital instrument, we shall define the marginal efficiency of a unit of capital as "that rate of discount which would make the present value of the series of annuities given by the returns expected from the capital-asset during its life just equal to its supply price."[1] In setting up a schedule of the marginal efficiency of capital for all possible outlets for investment for a given Week upon the above definition we must take the level of consumption as given. This is sensible, since, as already stated in the preceding chapter, it is evident that expectations of yield from the same physical instruments will vary directly with the level of consumption.

Description of the General Assumptions and Conditions of the Marginal Efficiency Function. We set up on Figure XIX[2] a single function for the marginal efficiency schedule, related to the assumed level of consumption. In setting up this figure we make a special assumption respecting the rate of interest in order to simplify our first approach to the problem of the Investment Functions. We assume that the i rates of valuation series are always equal to each other so that the i_0 rate and the r' rates are always equal

[1]*General Theory*, p. 135. For Mr. Keynes' general discussion of the concept of the marginal efficiency of capital, see chap. XI, pp. 135-46. The main difference between Mr. Keynes' treatment and that of the current volume arises out of the use of the short-term margin of substitution rather than the long-term rate of interest. The use of the short-term margin and the inclusion of the effects of the substitution of investment over time make it necessary to differentiate in this study between the function showing the marginal efficiency schedule for capital and the Investment Functions themselves. Because I am working from my own model system, detailed references are very seldom given lest they should impute identity of reasoning where it actually does not exist.

[2]Mathematical convention requires that I be placed on the vertical axis of Figure XIX since it is the dependent variable of the equation $I=F(i,C)$. Since, however, it is the custom of economists to use the vertical axis for rates and prices, that procedure has been followed.

to each other also, whether the rates be high or low. In this way we are able to use a single interest-rate for the system.[3] The assumption will be abated when we come to modify the function for the marginal efficiency of capital into the Investment Functions.

Before we set this single function up, however, we must consider the problems involved in dis-investment and in conditions where the interest-rate, theoretically at least, may be negative.

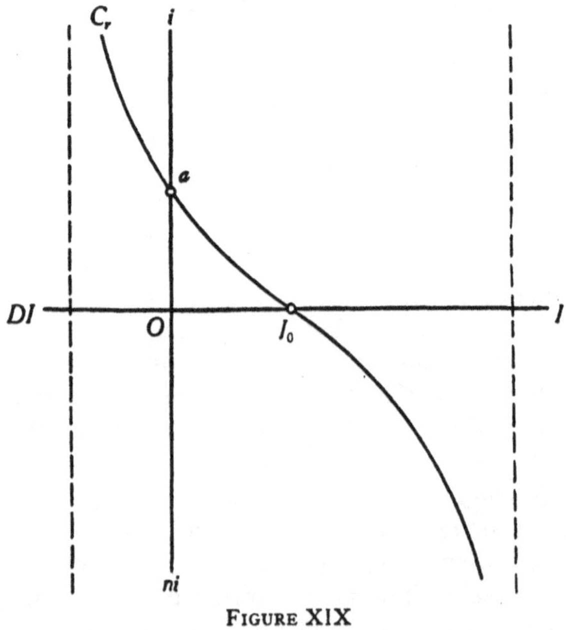

FIGURE XIX

Right-hand Broken Line: Absolute limit on investment for Week at Consumption C_r.
Left-hand Broken Line: Absolute limit on possible dis-investment for Week.

With reference to the first, the potentiality always exists that maintenance funds may be diverted from maintenance and replace-

[3]While Mr. Keynes' function for the marginal efficiency of capital is related to "the" rate of interest (see *General Theory*, pp. 136-7), it must be pointed out here, as has been done several times before, that Mr. Keynes well recognizes the complex character of the interest-rate structure and makes allowance for it in his general analysis even though the technical nature of his apparatus slides over this aspect of economic relations. See once again the foot-note on page 167 and the qualifications, pp. 201-4. Since this chapter was put into final form there has come to my hand an article in which these qualifications of the Keynesian analysis are clearly set forth. See D. W. Lusher, "The Structure of Interest Rates and the Keynesian Theory of Interest," *Journal of Political Economy*, L (1942), pp. 272-9.

ment to the L_2 balances over some "Week-end." A net diversion will result in dis-investment for the community for the Week in question, or in a higher rate of dis-investment than characterized the preceding Week. If the structure of our marginal efficiency function is to be complete, therefore, we must extend the horizontal axis to the left of the vertical axis showing zero net investment in order to show the possibilities of dis-investment for the Week.

The possibilities of dis-investment for a single Week are limited. Even if there were zero employment in industry, in default of the operation of autonomous factors such as war, earthquake, or some other destructive force, a large part of the capital equipment of a modern community would survive the passage of a considerable period of time. The only possible measure which we have for the dis-investment which may occur in one Week will be given by the wage-units which will be devoted to net maintenance at each rate of interest and for each level of consumption.[4] Upon the same basis of reasoning on which we set out our assumptions for the Multiplier Functions, we must select some point to the left of zero investment upon our graph and call this zero employment. When employment is zero, dis-investment for the Week has been carried to its maximum. Some rate of interest would be at least theoretically high enough to cause the quantum of dis-investment possible for a Week to be carried to this maximum. There will be some rate also at which dis-investment and investment will be just equal to each other so that there is no *net* investment. Both these conditions must show upon the structure of our individual function.

With reference to the second problem, at a theoretical negative rate of interest, as we set out in Chapter VII, entrepreneurs will be subsidized by savers, who under such conditions would have a net preference at the margin for future incomes over present incomes. As pointed out also in Chapter VII, entrepreneurs under such conditions would be under incentive to expand production

[4]In note 1, chap. VIII, p. 102, it was set out that the degree of dis-investment for the system under the assumptions made (where consumption exceeds income) would be the higher of two terms: the one term would be given by the wages-bill of the units of labour transferred from maintenance to enlarging the output of goods for current consumption; the other term would be given by the expectation of proceeds in future Weeks which has the highest net value in the present. Above we say that the measure of dis-investment will be the number of wage-units devoted to maintenance. The statements are brought together by the fact that when the expected net proceeds exceed the wages-bill, the value set on the dis-invested goods contains income items for other factors besides labour.

further than would be the case at any positive rate. For that reason, therefore, we must extend the investment function below the horizontal axis to show the quanta of investment per Week which would be undertaken at various negative rates.

It must be pointed out, however, that, in spite of the negative character of the rate of interest, the function cannot be continued indefinitely toward the right but will first lose elasticity and finally become completely inelastic. At a *given* level of consumption, the facilities available for use by the investment-goods industries have definite physical limitations. In order to induce *increased* investment activity, the rate of interest must fall faster than other costs rise. As the absolute limit upon the services of factors available for use in the investment industries is approached, the function for the marginal efficiency of capital must grow increasingly inelastic until finally it becomes completely inelastic.

Graphical Representation of the Marginal Efficiency Function. We are now in position to describe the individual function of Figure XIX more explicitly. Upon this figure, C_r stands for a given potential level of consumption under the conditions of expectation which apply to one Week. The function shows growing inelasticity at both extremes. Some kinds of capital will be so valuable that even if *very* high rates of interest were to be earned on the transference of maintenance funds to the debts market, still some expenditure of funds upon maintenance and replacement will be worth while. But as the rate rises, the justification for the expenditure of such funds grows less and less. Some rate will give an absolute limit at which all maintenance funds would be diverted to other uses and *gross* investment be *nil.* This limit is shown at the left extreme of the function. As set out in the preceding paragraphs, it is also true that at the right extreme of the function, no matter how high the premium offered upon *future* income in comparison to present income, the operation of the law of diminishing returns will finally make the inclusion of further wage-units in investment expenditure unprofitable. For this reason we show the function approaching another absolute limit, this time on the quantum of investment for the Week, as interest-rates fall farther into the negative range.

The relation of the function to the vertical axis shows that at interest rate *Oa* the level of activity in the investment-goods industries and the amount of employment devoted to maintenance in individual plants would be such that the quantum of capital which is passed on from this Week to the succeeding one will be unaltered. Similarly, the function shows that at zero rate of interest under the conditions assumed, the level of new investment activity in the system for the Week would be I_0.

(2) THE STRUCTURE OF THE INVESTMENT FUNCTIONS

Two modifications of the foregoing analysis are required in order to translate the function showing the marginal efficiency rates of capital into the full structure of the Investment Functions. The first requires that we dispense with the assumption that the system contains only a single rate of interest. The second calls for the arrangement of the individual functions in accordance with their relation to the levels of consumption potential for the system for a given Week.

The Effects of Possible Substitution over Time on the Elasticity of the Investment Functions. When we substitute the rate i_0 and the rates connected with it under a given state of expectations for the single rate of interest used above, we have conditions similar to those already analysed in connection with the Liquidity Functions.[5] There will be a series of interest-rates considered "normal" for the system under the state of expectations which applies. For this "normal" range, the i rates of valuation series will tend to be equal to each other and hence the r' rates will be equal to each other and to i_0.[6] For the range of rates considered "normal" therefore, the individual Investment Function based upon a given level of consumption will agree with the function showing the marginal efficiencies of capital. The differences will occur (as with the Liquidity Functions) at the two extremes of the individual functions.

Where the complex of interest-rates is felt to lie higher than the normal range, the i series will constitute a falling series, the r' rates will lie below rate i_0 in accordance with the rate of fall in the i rates during their expected duration, and the *expected* r' rates, as already explained in connection with the Liquidity Func-

[5]See chap. VI, sec. III, pp. 76-9.

[6]Differences in quoted market yields under these conditions will be related to differences in the correction coefficients, d, s, and l. These may result from actual differences between expectations of marginal holders with reference to specific assets or alternatively from larger corrections made on assets having longer currencies. Since these correction coefficients are accounted for under costs of production, the rates of the marginal efficiency schedules are "pure" rates also and may be compared directly with the "pure" rates of the valuation series for market prices.

tions,[7] will lie under the current r' rates. Under such conditions there will be some items of investment otherwise profitable which will be justifiably postponed to await the fall in the complex of the rates of interest. For example, a given capital-asset may promise to earn over its life the r' rate appropriate to its duration, but the a series may have such a character that it does not earn the higher r' rates connected with the shorter terms of a falling series of i rates. Postponement of investment in such assets and temporary investment of funds at the full marginal short-term rates will appear more profitable. Under such circumstances there will be substitution over time, some items of investment on the marginal efficiency schedule will be transferred to the future, and the left section of the individual Investment Function will be more elastic than we have shown the marginal efficiency schedule to be in Figure XIX.

Toward the other end of the function, the opposite conditions will obtain. Where the i_0 rate is under the normal rate and there is an expectation of a rise in the complex of interest-rates, there may be some premium to be earned by transferring investment otherwise planned for the future to the current Week. Substitution over time works in the opposite direction but the effect here also is to increase the elasticity of the individual function. Since the minimum institutional rate is not likely to lie under zero, the function will show growing elasticity at positive rates as the complex falls below the normal range.

The Arrangement and Dispersion of the Investment Functions in Relation to the Levels of Consumption. With reference to the arrangement of the individual functions in relation to the levels of consumption potential to the system for a given Week, it is evident that higher levels of consumption carry higher yields from existing units of capital and that the existence of higher yields in the present will tend to carry with it the expectation of higher a series in the future. Hence such yields will have a tendency to stimulate higher investment demands. We therefore arrange the functions to show direct variation with the level of consumption. In Figure XX[8] below, it is assumed that C_r, C_s, and C_t give potential levels of consumption, measured in wage-units, for a given Week. Since investment is presumed to vary directly with consumption, C_s represents a higher level of consumption than C_r and C_t than C_s.

[7] *Supra*, pp. 71-2.

[8] In Figure XX, the functions are not carried to their left and right extremes, since these extremes will ordinarily be irrelevant to the problems of the real world.

The dispersion of the Investment Functions will be affected by the same conditions which give the single function growing inelasticity at the right extreme (exclusive of the effects of the substitution of investment over time). As the level of consumption rises, the quantum of physical factors available for the investment industries decreases and we may expect the operation of the principle of diminishing returns to show itself sooner in the investment industries. By definition, the marginal efficiency rate is the rate which makes the present value of the series of annuities promised by an instrument ***equal to its supply price.*** The rise of

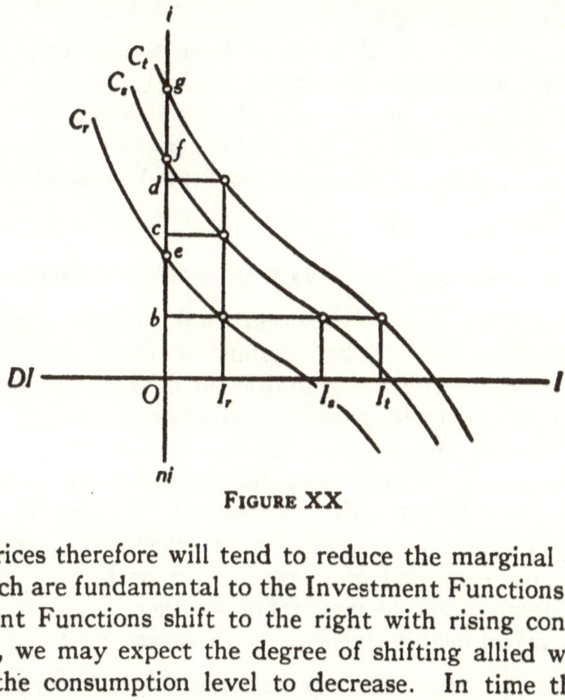

FIGURE XX

supply prices therefore will tend to reduce the marginal efficiency rates which are fundamental to the Investment Functions. As the Investment Functions shift to the right with rising consumption therefore, we may expect the degree of shifting allied with given rises in the consumption level to decrease. In time the effects of rising costs will overtake the effects of rising expectations of yield and shifting will cease entirely.

The Investment Functions themselves as shown do not give a basis for finding which level of consumption will actually emerge for the Week. We need the complete set of structures for the equations of the shifting equilibrium in order to establish this solution. But under the functions as given in Figure XX, if the i_0 rate is b, that rate allied with consumption C_r would give investment level I_r; with C_s it would give I_s; and with C_t it would give I_t. If, on the other hand, we take the level of investment as given rather than the i_0 rate of interest, investment level I_r will be associated with consumption level C_r only if the interest rate is *b*, with C_s only if the rate is *c*, and with C_t only if the rate is *d*.

With respect to the possibilities of dis-investment connected with these functions, if the interest-rate were higher than *e*, there would be no *net* investment connected with consumption level C_r but instead a net diversion of maintenance and replacement funds to the L_2 balances "over the Week-end" between the current and preceding Week.[9] A similar condition would be potential respecting consumption level C_s if the rate of interest were higher than *f* and for C_t if it were higher than *g*.

We may defer further discussion of the nature of our construction until we assemble the structures for the three equations in the next chapter. Only one more task remains for this chapter, namely a consideration of the factors causing changes in the position of the sheaf of functions between Weeks or over series of Weeks.

(3) THE INSTABILITY OF THE INVESTMENT FUNCTIONS

The Instability of the Investment Functions and the Organized Market for Securities. "The outstanding fact" with respect to the calculations of investors as to the outcomes of their investments "is the extreme precariousness of the basis of knowledge on which our estimates of prospective yield have to be made."[10] Under former, simpler conditions, when decisions to invest were "largely irrevocable, not only for the community, but also for the individual,"[11] optimism rather than "cold calculation" was likely to be behind the extension of investment in particular fields. But under modern economic organization another element has entered to bolster investment activity, since the presence of the organized

[9]We recall that for the Fundamental Model all transfers to hoards will be made by entrepreneurs between Weeks.

[10]*General Theory*, p. 149. For Mr. Keynes' general discussion of the problems set out in this section, see *General Theory*, chap. XII, pp. 147-64. The problem of population changes which is discussed in this section receives only passing attention by Mr. Keynes (see p. 318). Yet Professor Hicks holds that this is Mr. Keynes' "strongest card" and "alone establishes the high significance of Mr. Keynes' theory of long-period unemployment," since Professor Hicks feels that there is "little doubt that we are heading for these dangers." See "Mr. Keynes' Theory of Employment," *Economic Journal*, XXVI (1936), p. 252. See also A. H. Hansen, "Progress and Declining Population," *American Economic Review*, XXIX (1939), pp. 1-15.

[11]*General Theory*, p. 150.

security market gives to the investor the hope that if he sees cause to revise his judgments adversely with respect to the particular prospects of a specific investment, he may be able to unload his equities upon the market before others discover the changes in prospects which he himself finds disquieting. Thus "Investments which are 'fixed' for the community are . . . made 'liquid' for the individual."[12]

But the presence of the organized market which bolsters the level of investment by giving equities greater liquidity has an adverse effect upon the stability of expectations. The valuations set on specific capital-assets become subject not only to expectations respecting their own particular demand and supply prospects but they become open also to the effects of the warm and cold gales of opinion which typically sweep across organized markets for more general reasons. "Since there will be no strong roots of conviction to hold it steady,"[13] the valuation placed upon a particular investment may be blown about just because of general pessimism or optimism in the debts-equities markets.

If this instability in the values of existing securities were a factor which affected only the current markets, it would not be a matter of high importance. It would affect the distribution of income but not its size. But since windfall profits upon the existing quantum of securities are factors influencing the propensity to consume[14] and since, as an even more important factor, the entrepreneurs making new investment for the Week depend upon the valuations of existing securities as guides to their expectations of values to be placed upon investment output for the current Week, these values of the market become matters of supreme importance in determining the character of the demand for investment for the Week. Even the degree to which maintenance funds will be expended will be affected by these valuations.

For these reasons the sheaf of functions which we have shown upon Figure XX may be subject to wide shifting between Weeks and over series of Weeks in a society where industry is organized predominantly upon a corporate basis. This instability will have a reflection in instability of the levels of output and employment. One of the prime objects of social policy in such a society may therefore be the stabilizing of the state of expectations.

There are other types of expectation also which have an adverse

[12]*Ibid.*, p. 153.
[13]*Ibid.*, p. 154.
[14]*Supra*, p. 105.

effect upon the positions of the Investment Functions. These will be longer-term in nature and the most important of them will be connected with the expected trend of population changes.

The Investment Functions and the Expected Trend of Population Changes. In order to analyse the probable effects upon the Investment Functions of expectations respecting population trends, let us consider the reported decline by two million in the number of children in the United States between the fall of 1930 and the fall of 1939. Such a condition, if true, must have tremendous significance in the minds of entrepreneurs directing large-scale enterprises engaged in producing durable consumers' goods, residence and other buildings, and the equipment for the production of these. It is not implied that entrepreneurs use the figures for the birth-rate as a barometer in deciding upon long-term plans for output! Rather is it true that changes in this rate will bring with it a train of changes in the demands for specific types of goods and that entrepreneurs will extrapolate these changes into the future.

In an expanding society in which there is an assurance of a comparatively steady yearly addition to the number of family units, there will be a steady backlog of demand for necessities in establishing these new homes which will be a part of the expectations supporting investment demand. But if the number of children is growing smaller year by year, the marriage rate in time will grow less also, unless there is an offsetting trend toward earlier marriages. Fewer families with fewer children will require less house-room and less of many other types of goods.

Under such conditions, the quantum of capital can be continuously expanded only if there is a constantly rising standard of living. The demand for investment must under such conditions be supported by an expansion of the demand for "luxury" goods,—goods whose demands are typically elastic. The dependence upon such demands will bring tendencies to lower the positions of the Investment Functions for two reasons.

In the first place, the dependence of the demand for new investment upon a possibility of a constantly increasing standard of living for a stable or declining population will be accompanied by an anticipation of a tapering off of demands for many different kinds of goods if the population had formerly been expanding (or even declining at a lower rate). Everything else being equal, entrepreneurs will prefer investments which bring results in the relatively near future. Where long-term commitments are made, these will tend to be where circumstances are estimated to be particularly favourable or where some type of monopolistic control gives the expectation that during the nearest years, returns made under the monopoly will be large enough to offset adverse, long-term expectations.

In the second place the dependence of the demand for investment upon the development of new techniques and the new wants will bring a wider dispersion of expectations and hence lower mean values ordinarily. The bases of demands are more aleatory than under conditions where population is expanding, and the chances of "prizes" in the outcomes will be lower. Moreover, if there is to be a net increment of capital in any Week, outlets in these directions must be so promising that investment in them will exceed dis-investment in the enterprises whose capital instruments may be in excess from a market standpoint.

If investment opportunity is genuinely deficient under the incentives connected with organization of enterprise upon a purely private basis, so that the level of employment is not only subject to great fluctuations but is chronically depressed below the optimum level, the problem of the support of the Investment Functions through some long-term programme of public investment may become a matter for discussion and decision. We defer these considerations and others relating to the longer-period prospects for the maintenance of the level of full employment, however, until we have in the succeeding chapter assembled our whole system of structures and demonstrated its operation.

CHAPTER XII

THE SYSTEM OF THE SHIFTING EQUILIBRIUM

THE tasks for this chapter are to assemble the structural elements of the shifting equilibrium, to demonstrate the interdependence of the system by showing the way in which it responds to changes in the quantity of money, and to indicate the nature of repercussions upon the system through effects of changes upon the psychological-institutional complex.

(1) THE SOLUTION OF THE SYSTEM

The set of equations is shown again below for purposes of reference and in Figure XXI we give a complete set of constructions for this set of equations, based upon a hypothetical group of mathematical formulae for L, ϕ, and F:

$$i = L(M, Y) \qquad (1)$$
$$C = \phi(Y, i) \qquad (2)$$
$$I = F(i, C) \qquad (3)$$
$$Y = C + I \equiv C + S \qquad (4)$$

The forms of the equations indicated in Figure XXI are assumed to hold good for a Week. In the first instance all contracts for factors and for consumption goods and securities are assumed to be made on Monday under the conditions indicated for the Fundamental Model.

With the equations for L, ϕ, and F given, in order to solve the set of relations we need know only the quantity of money given in wage-units. Once the size of the wage-unit and the quantity of money-units are known, the four unknowns, namely the levels of income, consumption, investment, and the i_0 rate of interest will be given by the functions shown for the Week. Since I and S are by definition equal to each other, the level of saving for the Week is also given. If the i_0 rate of interest is far enough within the normal range, so that the "pure" rates for all durations will be equal to each other, these rates will follow from the i_0 rate. But if the i_0 rate is near or outside the normal range of rates, we must take the r' rates connected with the i_0 rate as among the "given" factors of the situation. We cannot deduce them from the system as it stands. A simpler model which ignored the fact that interest-rates of the future may be expected to differ from

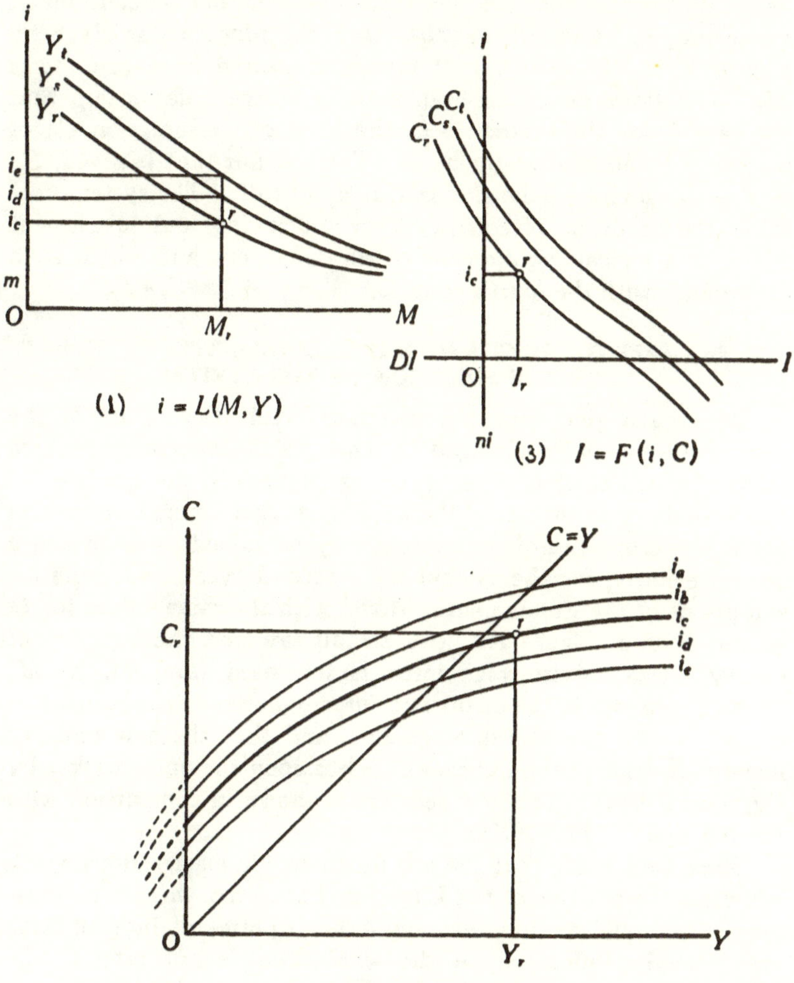

(1) $i = L(M, Y)$

(3) $I = F(i, C)$

(2) $C = \phi(Y, i)$

FIGURE XXI

those of the present will give us more facts *about the model* but it would be farther away from the world in which we live.

With the size of the wage-unit and the quantity of money-units given (or alternatively with the wage-unit and the quantity of money-units varying with each other in such a way that the quantity of money measured in wage-units is always the same) there can be only one consistent solution for one set of equations. While all the functions are held stable, the solution is determinate. For example, let us assume that with the functions as given by Figure XXI, the quantity of money measured in wage-units is M_r. It follows as an inevitable mathematical relationship that the rate i_0 for the system is i_c, the level of consumption C_r, of income Y_r, and of investment I_r. The amount that is saved, S_r, is $Y_r - C_r$ which by definition is also equal to I_r. The system thus fulfils the condition of equality between saving and investment which is a logical requirement of its definitions and which is in accordance with the fourth equation, $Y_r = C_r + I_r \equiv C_r + S_r$.

(2) THE EFFECTS OF CHANGES IN THE QUANTITY OF MONEY UPON THE SOLUTION OF THE SYSTEM

Between a given and a succeeding Week, the nature of the relationships may be changed by changes in expectations which affect the values of L, ϕ, or F or by changes in the quantity of money-units or in the size of the wage-unit. Some more information about the properties of the system may be gained by analysing a second solution for the system for a second Week under the assumptions of the Fundamental Model with the same values for L, ϕ, and F as in Figure XXI. We shall say that the quantity of money, measured in wage-units, is increased from M_r to M_s through a change in the quantity of money-units with no correlative change in the size of the wage-unit, and that the new units of money are added by purchases of debts upon the open market by the central bank. The new solution is shown in comparison with the old upon Figure XXII.

Since we assume that there is no change in expectations which will alter the position of the Liquidity Functions, this action must lower the liquidity premium and other i_0 rates of interest with accompanying effects upon the whole complex of rates. The reduction of the supply of debts by the central bank will push their prices upward and marginal holders must therefore be satisfied with a lower rate of return on them. Substitution of one maturity for another will tend to spread the effects over the whole debts market. Parallel with this effect, the supply of cash-balances will have been increased and marginal holders of cash-balances must be satisfied with a lower liquidity premium than before, since we have assumed no change in L which will alter the *willingness* to hold cash-balances. Thus the rate will be pushed down upon two of the multiple margins.

But the tendency to make substitutions at the margin will not end with substitution in the debts and money markets. Lower

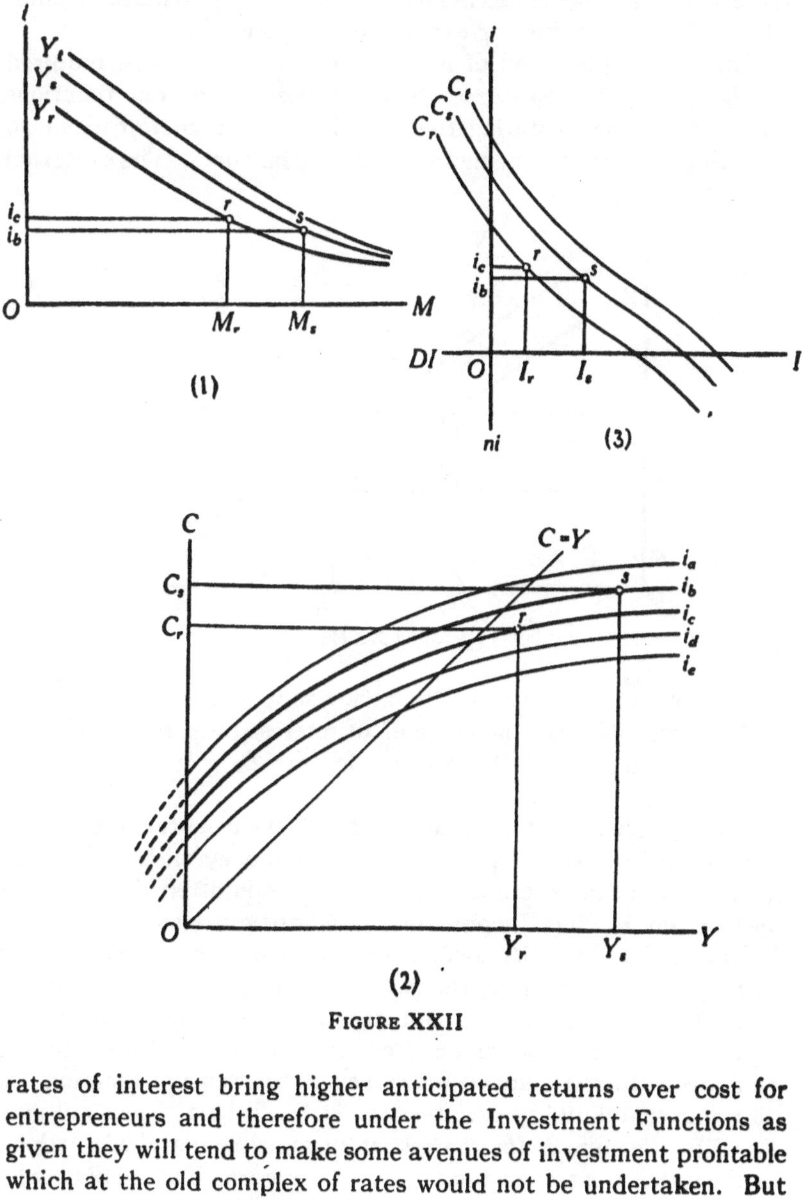

FIGURE XXII

rates of interest bring higher anticipated returns over cost for entrepreneurs and therefore under the Investment Functions as given they will tend to make some avenues of investment profitable which at the old complex of rates would not be undertaken. But the higher rate of investment brings the Multiplier into operation. The level of consumption as well as the level of investment will be raised, and if this extension of consumption finds equipment for any types of consumption goods relatively deficient in supply, there may be new inducements to invest along particular lines which will cause a further expansion of Y and C.

But at a higher level of income, more money will be required by the active (L_1) balances. Since by assumption our functions remain the same as during the preceding Week, there can be no offsetting shift in the demand for the L_2 balances. The diversion

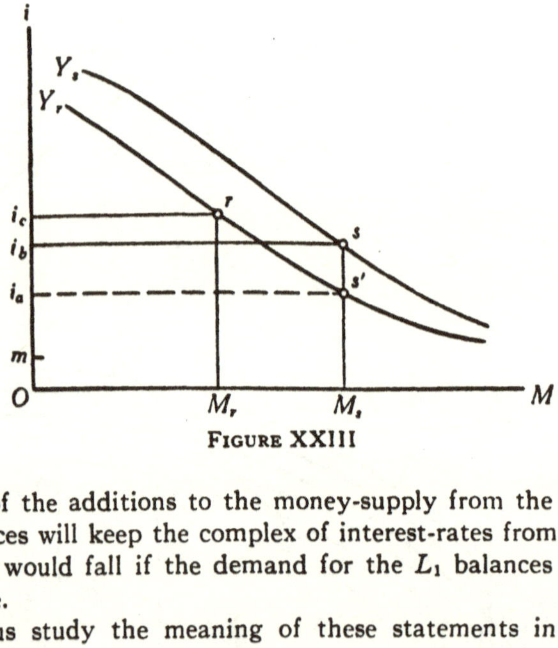

FIGURE XXIII

of part of the additions to the money-supply from the L_2 to the L_1 balances will keep the complex of interest-rates from falling as far as it would fall if the demand for the L_1 balances had been the same.

Let us study the meaning of these statements in terms of Figure XXIII. If the demand curve for money with the change in the level of income had not shifted, it would remain as shown on function Y_r. The increase in the quantity of money, measured in wage-units, from M_r to M_s, with the schedule of demands for cash-balances remaining the same, must have reduced the i_0 interest-rate to $i_a = M_s s'$. But the increase of investment and consumption activity which increases the demand for the L_1 balances shifts the demand for money to the demand function Y_s. The marginal liquidity preferences which will be satisfied will give liquidity premium i_b for the system of multiple margins. As long as the current set of relations given by Figure XXIII holds true, the complex of interest-rates connected with this i_0 rate will form the bases of capitalization in the debts and equities markets. In the production market, this complex of rates will be the system of i_0 and connected r' rates for which investors must make allowances before they reckon their own net returns over cost upon expenditures of funds for maintenance or new investment.

At the new temporary equilibrium, the levels of income and consumption will therefore be Y_s and C_s, and the level of investment for the new Week will be I_s, all as shown on Figure XXII.

We must make some qualifications of our reasoning for the Supplementary Models. Under the conditions of the Fundamental Model, the system will proceed smoothly to the new solution because of the degree of market perfection assumed. But under the conditions of the Supplementary Models there may be an interval of adjustment due to incorrect expectations of entrepreneurs. It may take a series of Weeks to reach the adjustment. Over that series of Weeks the price- and income-distribution effects of the errors in judgment may somewhat disturb the shapes of the functions L, ϕ, and F which would be associated with "correct" expectations. It is also probable that the errors themselves will become the bases of revisions in expectations which will bring cyclical changes into operation. In the case we set out here of an increase in the quantity of money, a cyclical expansion may be set off, which must, of course, be supported by further expansions of the supply of money if price-expectations and the size of the wage-unit are not to be changed.

It is evident that while a change in the quantity of money *may* raise the level of income and employment, the effects of such a change cannot be exactly predicted even under situations so highly simplified as are those of our model systems. Moreover, when we consider the effects of changes in the quantity of money measured in money-units, we must not lose sight of the limits set upon the effects by the existence of a minimum conventional i_0 rate of interest and by the possibilities of revision in the size of the wage-unit. The structure of our analysis applies, as we have used it, essentially to the world of under-equilibrium in the orthodox sense of equilibrium analysis. Its precise relationship to conditions of full equilibrium we have not undertaken to develop in this study. Before we leave the nature of the structure as a whole, we should, however, devote some space to an analysis of the nature of repercussions within the system.

(3) REPERCUSSIONS

We shall take up first in our discussion of repercussions the effects of an increase in the quantity of money, measured in wage-units, upon the part of the psychological-institutional complex which we have called the "state of expectations." The effects upon expectations in terms of the functions L, ϕ, and F may serve either to increase or to decrease the effects of monetary action as these have been set out in terms of the change in the supply of money from M_r to M_s in the preceding section. We shall examine the effects first under conditions where the outcome is to reinforce the effects of an increase in the quantity of money.

An increase in the quantity of money through open-market operations of the central monetary system, if it comes at certain periods of the business cycle, may cause the Liquidity Functions associated with the various potential levels of income to shift downward. To have such an effect, the action of the monetary authorities must increase the optimism of the community with respect to one or more of the future levels of economic activity, prices or interest-rates. Because of this optimism, "bears" may become "bulls" at lower average rates of interest than formerly. This means that there will be a tendency to release money from the L_2 balances for the purchase of debts at lower rates of interest. Release of money from the L_2 balances will help to provide new funds for the L_1 balances and the downward shift of L_2 will thus act as a deterrent on the rise in the function L and in the rates of interest otherwise accompanying the rising level of activity. The interest-rate complex would fall to a lower point than would be possible if the original functions held their position. The effect of the initial increase in the quantity of money upon the level of economic activity will be intensified. Alternatively, if changes in the other functions would, even with the increased quantity of money, bring a tendency to raise interest-rates, the change in the position of the Liquidity Functions will offset part if not all of this potential rise in rates.

Similarly, if the initial increase in the quantity of money and the resultant fall in the interest-rate complex actually start an upward expansion in the system, as the expansion gathers force, better prospects for employment may shift upward the sheaf of functions representing the propensity to consume. Cyclical plans for expenditure may be revised. The new car may be bought this year rather than next. The Multiplier associated with given i_0

rates of interest and levels of output may be raised and this will intensify the operation of the increase in the quantity of money.

On the Investment Functions, the initiation of an expansion may change the nature of expectations with respect to the future yields of existing capital goods and hence support larger expenditures of funds for maintenance and replacement and new investment activity for a given level of consumption in the present. Thus the Investment Functions will shift to the right. If the process of expansion starts an expectation of rising prices, that factor also may raise the Investment Functions. These shifts of expectations in turn will tend to increase the effects of the original increase in the quantity of money.

What we get in effect is a new set of functions. Let us take our structure for the shifting equilibrium as shown on Figure XXII, and on Figure XXIV show a shift in the positions of the functions arising out of more optimistic expectations. The effects of the shift are obvious. Rising expectations have prevented the rate of interest from falling but have supported an increase in the levels of employment and output. We get interest-rate i_c *in this case* as we did for Figure XXI with the original amount of money M_r, but we get income Y_t, consumption C_t, and investment I_t instead of Y_s, C_s, and I_s, the levels formerly connected with quantity of money M_s. If the impulses toward expansion in the system had been strong enough, we should have had the rise in the interest-rate which is so characteristic of the expansion phases of the cycle as to have been given a name of its own, namely the "Gibson Paradox."[1]

If the central bank should endeavour to bring about a deflation by reducing the quantity of money, the effects may be reversed. We might in such a case regard a reduction of the quantity of money from M_s to M_r as bringing the level of income from Y_t to Y_r because of an upward shifting of the function L and downward shiftings of ϕ and F.

Effects of changes in the quantity of money may not cause an actual movement of the functions of the system but they may arrest or slow down a movement which exists for other reasons. Thus active central bank operations may provide funds which keep the "secondary" recessions of a cycle from developing because of support given member banks in extending loans at relatively

[1]On pages 198-208 of volume II of the *Treatise on Money*, Mr. Keynes gave a description of the Gibson Paradox and an explanation in terms of the "stickiness" of the "market rate of interest." The explanation given above in terms of the structure of the *General Theory*, appears to be more logical.

low rates. But whatever the nature of the changes, for any definite values for the functions there will again be a determinate solution for the equations of the system.

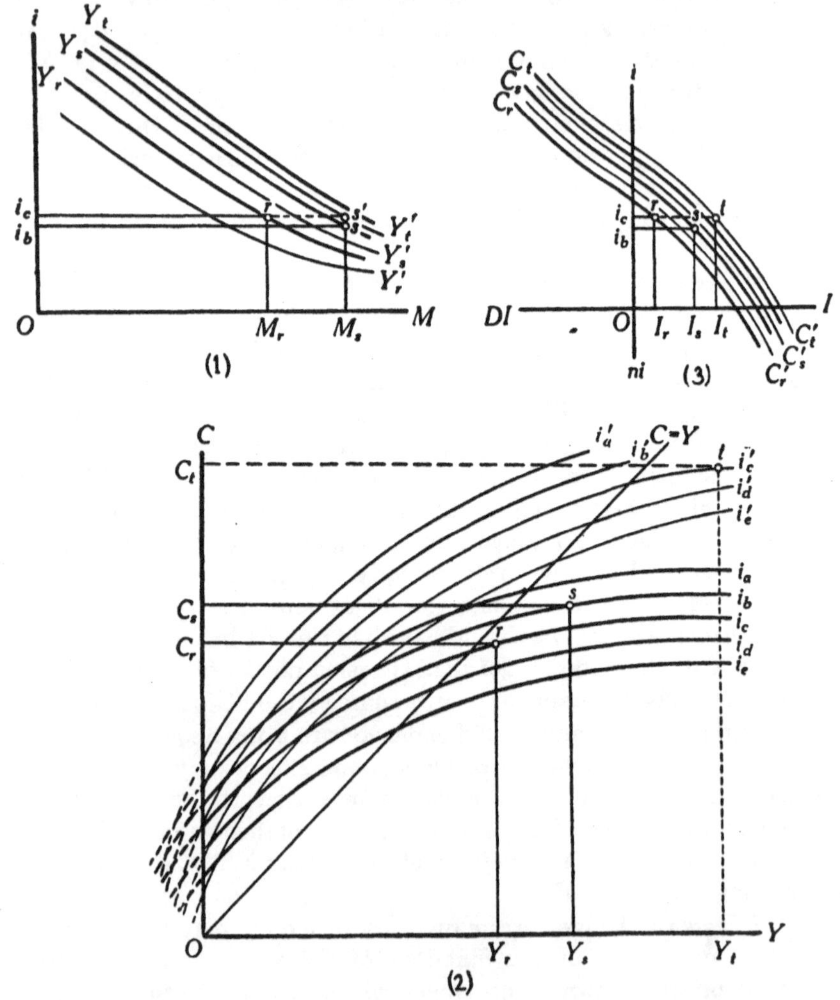

FIGURE XXIV

We have not exhausted the subject of repercussions in the system when we have considered changes in the effective quantity of money. Whatever the nature of the change, autonomous or otherwise, if it is interpreted optimistically, the effects will be to lower the Liquidity Functions, or to raise the Multiplier or Investment Functions, or some combination of these effects. If a change is interpreted pessimistically, the effects upon the positions of the functions will be reversed. An impact upon one set of functions which does not affect the other initially may be transmitted to them over a series of Weeks as the favourable or unfavourable solutions of the system become part of its history. Brief consideration will be given in the last chapter of this study to some of these implications in a number of fields of social policy. In the meantime, we turn in the following chapter to some of the relations between the structure we have set out and general orthodox equilibrium theory.

CHAPTER XIII

THE FIELD OF THE SHIFTING EQUILIBRIUM

IN the foregoing twelve chapters we have completed the main structure of the analysis which it was intended to present. The one remaining task is to indicate somewhat more clearly than we have yet done the connection of the functional relationships with orthodox equilibrium analysis and in particular with the theoretical level of employment. In performing this task, we must go back to the analysis of Chapter IV. In the first section of the current chapter we shall consider the determinants of the level of employment in a society which has reached full stationary equilibrium under the conditions of Figure I.[1] In the succeeding section we shall discuss the determinants of the level of employment in an economic society which has reached stationariness under conditions where there is a long-period inconsistency between the marginal propensity to save and the inducements to invest at the level of full employment. We return here, therefore, to the conditions analysed in connection with Figures III and V.[2] In the third and last section we shall attempt to move through the conditions of the First Supplementary Model to a place from which we may get a glimpse of the conditions of the real world.

(1) EMPLOYMENT IN THE STATIONARY STATE (FIRST TYPE)

The Description of Full Equilibrium in the Stationary State (*First Type*). We begin the definition of the relations of the shifting equilibrium to the level of employment under the conditions of the stationary state with a positive rate of interest by reviewing the conditions of such an equilibrium as expressed or implied in Chapter IV. The stock of capital is assumed to be *ON*, as shown on Figure I. "The" interest-rate is *NN'* as shown on the same figure; that is to say, all rates of interest in the interest structure will be equal to each other and to *NN'*. The level of saving per Week is zero. The quantum of property titles is adjusted to the demand for these

[1]*Supra*, p. 39.
[2]*Supra*, pp. 45, 49.

in such a way that the saving by new savers per Week is equal to the dis-saving by old savers or their heirs. Activity in the investment-goods industries is only sufficient to maintain the quantum of capital in the system intact. Activity in the consumption-goods industries is equal to consumption for the Week. If goods of some kinds are withdrawn from hoards of liquid capital for the Week, equivalent amounts of consumption goods are added to other hoards of liquid capital. There are no hoards of money as such. The stationary state is assumed to have lasted long enough for the L_2 balances to have been absorbed into the L_1 balances and the only demands for money are those of the types analysed in Chapter V. All enterprises are operating under conditions where marginal costs are equal to marginal revenues with no unemployed factors of production. If a single enterprise attempts to push output beyond the level associated with conditions of equilibrium or if the attempt is made to establish more than the equilibrium number of enterprises, factors can be secured for such activities only by bidding them away from other enterprises, a proceeding which will not be worth while because it will increase costs more than it will increase revenues.

On Figure XXV we establish these relationships. On the vertical axis of this figure we measure the real wage-rate. On the horizontal axis we measure units of employment in labour-units. The supply curve for labour for a Week under the conditions of the stationary state we set out upon the basis of Figure I on page 166 of Mrs. Robinson's *Essays in the Theory of Employment*. This curve assumes that at very low wage-rates, labour supply will increase as real wages are raised but that at some level of the real wage-rate the supply of labour will be at a maximum and that at higher real wage-rates there will be a disposition to prefer increased leisure so that as the real wage-rate rises, the function shows negative elasticity. The function is related to responses of labour to real wage-rates under conditions of full employment.

The demand curve, DqD', is the curve which represents the demand for labour which will be associated with capital stock ON of Figure I, with all forms of capital presumed instantaneously adjustable to the supply of labour. Changes in the rates of interest which will be associated with each level of employment are subsumed in the form of the function. The point q gives the level of effective demand for the system when the interest-rate is NN' (Figure I) and all firms have adjusted output to "correct" expectations in such a way that for each Week's operations marginal costs are equal to marginal revenues and both prime and supplementary costs are covered for all firms. Because we are assuming "correct" expectations, we may also assume that the form of the demand curve will be dominated by the operation of the principle of diminishing returns in such fashion that "in general, an increase in employment can only occur to the accompaniment of a decline in the rate of real wages."[3] At a later place in this chapter we shall set forth some reasons for thinking that the reasoning of the

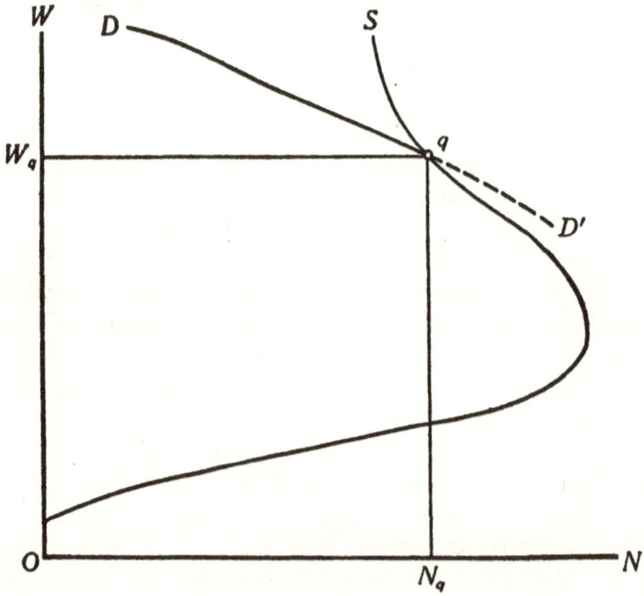

FIGURE XXV

Keynesian system itself gives ground for challenging the complete validity of this generalization except under stationary conditions.

The pertinent demand for labour in this system under these assumptions is therefore *Dq*. The functions of the shifting equi-

[3]*General Theory*, p. 17. Dr. Jacob Viner challenged this position in his review article which was included in the symposium upon the *General Theory* in vol. LI of the *Quarterly Journal of Economics*. See "Mr. Keynes on the Causes of Unemployment," pp. 149-51. A considerable volume of critical literature has grown up about the problem of the relation of money wages to economic fluctuations. A list of some of the main articles, other than the article by Dr. Viner named above, is given below:

R. B. Bangs, "Wage Reductions and Employment," *Journal of Political Economy*, L (1942), pp. 251-71; J. T. Dunlop, "The Movement of Real and Money Wages," *Economic Journal*, XLVIII (1938), pp. 413-34, "Trends in the

librium will find a solution which will bring this demand into being under the conditions outlined. The values established by the solution will agree with the values of a set of general equilibrium equations of the Walrasian type. The equilibrium achieved will be one built upon a balance of opposing forces and it will be a stable equilibrium only as long as these opposing forces are in perfect balance with each other.

The Movement toward Full Equilibrium under Conditions of Full Employment. We have described the situation only after full equilibrium has been reached. We must take a brief look at the changes involved as such a system moves toward a point of rest. If we go back in the system to where the quantum of capital is, say, *OA* as shown on Figure I, and hold to all other assumptions made, the demand curve *DqD′* will lie much lower down. In the movement toward capital level *ON* (Figure I), with the interest structure perfectly malleable, we may expect the price- and wage-rate structures to accommodate themselves to the changing situation in such a way that employment is always full. The point *q* will travel the path shown by the supply curve *SS′* (by assumption supposed to remain in the same position) as the system moves over time and the quantum of capital grows. For each Week of the period it takes to increase capital to *ON*, there will be certain values for the structure of the shifting equilibrium. The values of this system will determine how *fast* the system moves toward the

'Rigidity' of English Wage Rates," *Review of Economic Studies*, VI (1938-9), pp. 189-99; N. Kaldor, "Professor Pigou on Money Wages in Relation to Unemployment," *Economic Journal*, XLVII (1937), pp. 745-53, "Stability and Full Employment," *Economic Journal*, XLVIII (1938), pp. 642-57, "Money Wage Cuts in Relation to Unemployment: A Reply to Mr. Somers," *Review of Economic Studies*, VI (1938-9), pp. 232-5; M. Kalecki, "The Determinants of Distribution of the National Income," *Econometrica*, VI (1938), pp. 97-112; J. M. Keynes, "Professor Pigou on Money Wages in Relation to Unemployment" (Note), *Economic Journal*, XLVII (1937), pp. 743-5, "Relative Movements of Real Wages and Output," *Economic Journal*, XLIX (1939), pp. 34-51; A. P. Lerner, "Ex-Ante Analysis and Wage Theory," *Economica*, VI n.s. (1939), pp. 436-49, "The Relation of Wage Policies and Price Policies," *American Economic Review*, XXIX (1939), Supplement, pp. 158-69; A. C. Pigou, "Real and Money Wages in Relation to Unemployment," *Economic Journal*, XLVII (1937), pp. 405-22, "Real and Money Wages in Relation to Unemployment" (Note), *Economic Journal*, XLVIII (1938), pp. 134-8; J. H. Richardson, "Real Wage Movements," *Economic Journal*, XLIX (1939), pp. 425-41; H. M. Somers, "Money Wage Cuts in Relation to Unemployment," *Review of Economic Studies*, VI (1938-9), pp. 161-3; L. Tarshis, "Changes in Real and Money Wages" (Note), *Economic Journal*, XLIX (1939), pp. 150-4; J. Tobin, "A Note on the Money Wage Problem," *Quarterly Journal of Economics*, LV (1940-1), pp. 508-16.

stationary state. The influences of time-preference elements will show themselves in the position, arrangement, and dispersion of the Multiplier Functions. The influences of the laws of cost as the consumption and investment industries come into competition with each other will show themselves in the shape, arrangement, and dispersion of the Investment Functions. The requirements of the system for quantities of money, measured in wage-units, will show themselves in the Liquidity Functions.

The successive solutions which emerge from the functions of the shifting equilibrium Week by Week will tend to make the i_0 rate of interest agree with the current marginal product of capital, but the related r' rates will fall below that rate in accordance with the expected falls in the marginal product over the life of the securities. But under the assumptions made, the whole complex of rates will drift downward and there will be a connected upward trend in real wages, relatively accelerated when the supply function of labour begins to show negative elasticity toward increases in rates. Progress toward the ideal quantity of capital for the system will, however, tend to be slower than it would be if the supply curve were still positively inclined.

If we postulate certain minimum frictions connected with the adjustment of capital to new forms as the quantity of capital to be allied with the labour supply increases, and connected also with moving labour from job to job or retraining it for new forms of capital made available, the values of the system will depart somewhat from those described above. Employment may be always a little below the ideal; the rates of interest may always be a little higher than the ideal rates because of an artificial scarcity of capital due to lack of adjustment to its ideal forms. But the character of the relationship will be substantially the same and the system will move toward a set of relationships of the character of those shown in Figure I.

In terms of the shifting equilibrium, in such a system the Investment Functions will be falling as the channels of investment available under the existing state of technical knowledge and supplies of physical factors are progressively filled up to the level justified by the equilibrium margin of substitution, NN' (Figure I). In terms of the Multiplier Functions, increases in real income will be bringing a tendency for the marginal propensity to consume to fall, offset to some degree by the fall in the i_0 rate of interest. In terms of Figure I, when the system has reached the place where the maintenance rate is equal to the current marginal product of capital, or i_0 rate, it will come to the full point of rest. Since no further fall is expected in the marginal product, all interest-rates will be equal to the i_0 rate and equal to NN' of Figure I. All of the multiple margins of substitution throughout the system will be in equilibrium.

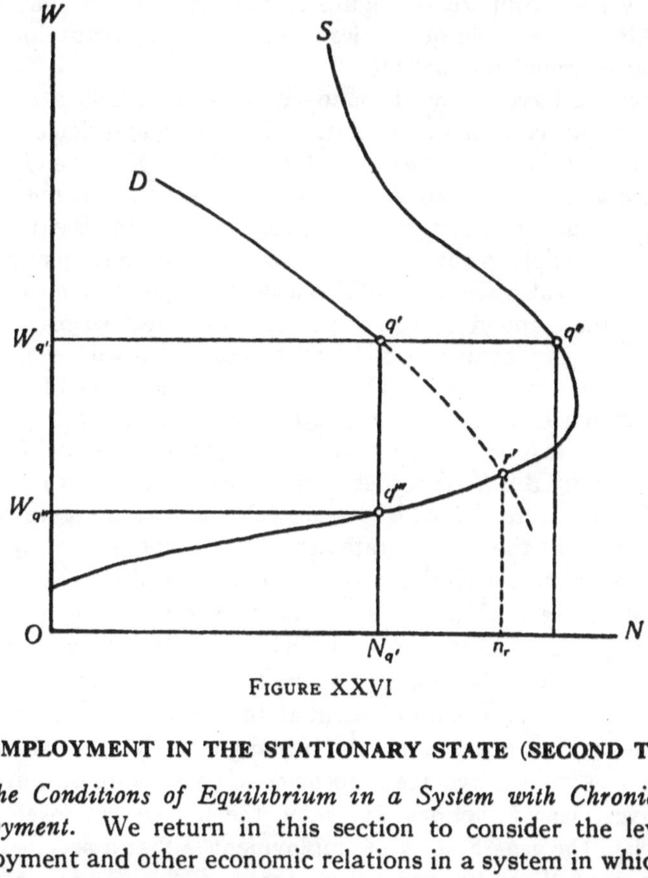

FIGURE XXVI

(2) EMPLOYMENT IN THE STATIONARY STATE (SECOND TYPE)

The Conditions of Equilibrium in a System with Chronic Unemployment. We return in this section to consider the level of employment and other economic relations in a system in which the i_0 rate is too inflexible to permit the economic community to come to full stationary equilibrium at the level of full employment. We go back, therefore, to the conditions of Figures III and V. We shall in what follows use Figure V and its symbols for points of reference and we show in Figure XXVI the character of the relationships which will apply. The supply curve for labour of this figure is set up under the same conditions as the supply curve of Figure XXV. It is in connection with the demand curve for labour that we must analyse the differences in the situation.

As before, the demand curve $Dq'r'D'$ illustrates the demand for labour under conditions where changes in the rate of interest are subsumed under the functional forms. The demand curve is shown lower down than the demand curve in Figure XXV upon the hypothesis that with the lower quantity of capital (*OM* of Figure V instead of *ON* of Figure I) demand prices in real wages will be lower for given quantities of labour-units because of lower physical marginal productivity.

What we have in the demand curve is essentially a series of partial equilibria, based upon certain definite assumptions. If the real wage-rate and the amount of capital are given, and if the system operates under conditions where it must reach temporary equilibrium under expectations of stability each Monday, then the amount of employment to be associated with that quantity of capital and real wage-rate will be a definite quantity also. Any point on the demand curve shows the rate of real wages and the quantity of employment which will be associated with each other under these assumptions. The complex of the rates of interest to be associated with each wage-rate and each associated quantity of employment is as before subsumed under the functional form.

The essential difference between the case illustrated in Figure XXVI and that illustrated by Figure XXV is that in Figure XXVI we assume that the interest-rate actually does lose flexibility when employment strikes level $N_{q'}$, associated with q' on the demand curve of Figure XXVI. This will mean in terms of Figure V that the i_0 rate has reached the level *Om*. Since the stock of capital is assumed to have become stationary at *OM*, not only the current marginal product is equal to *Om* but all the future marginal products are expected to equal *Om*. At interest-rate *Om* the Multiplier Functions show the average propensity to consume to be unity and the Investment Functions will show the investment level to be zero when the general level of employment is that associated with employment $N_{q'}$ and the real wage-rate is $OW_{q'}$. In terms of the graphic systems shown in Chapter XII, as employment rises above $N_{q'}$ and the associated level of *Y*, the propensities to save increase faster than the inducements to invest; as employment falls below $N_{q'}$, the propensities to save fall off faster than the inducements to invest.

The Equilibrium Rate of Real Wages. We have yet to show that this solution gives stability under the conditions of the Fundamental Model and that the situation requires that the real wage-rate be

$OW_{q'}$ if equilibrium is to be reached *and held*. This situation appears to be true for the following reasons:

(1) At any higher level of employment with capital stock OM and wage-rate $OW_{q'}$, operation of the principle of diminishing returns will push the physical marginal productivity of the existing stock of capital below the rate Om while the increase in real income will increase the marginal propensity to save. For such a situation S would exceed I. For the reverse situation I would exceed S. By the definitions of S and I such inequalities are impossible.

(2) At any lower quantum of capital stock for the same level of employment and real wage-rate, the physical marginal productivity of capital will be above Om and the marginal propensity to save will be lowered by the fall in real income. I will exceed S. In the reverse situation, S will exceed I. The situations are again impossible.

(3) At any lower real wage-rate than $OW_{q'}$ with capital OM and employment $N_{q'}$ there will be a degree of inequality in the distribution of income which will lower the Multiplier Functions and destroy the equality between S and I in such a manner that S would exceed I. In the reverse situation I would exceed S. The situations are again impossible.

We have still to inquire whether or not any combination of changes can bring another solution which may be permanently maintained. This really means, can equilibrium be established with any lower wage-rate than $OW_{q'}$? Lower wage-rates may be combined with (1) the same amount of capital and level of employment as above, (2) less employment and less capital, (3) more employment and more capital, (4) less employment and more capital, or (5) more employment and less capital. No. (1) is covered by case (3) above. No. (5) is the relevant case, for it is the case where entrepreneurs under the spur of lower money wages attempt to substitute labour for capital in their operations. This is the case most favourable to the establishment of another equilibrium for the system. If another level of equilibrium for the system does not appear probable here, the probability is that stable equilibrium can be achieved for the system only with the wage-rate $OW_{q'}$.

The effects of a substitution of labour for capital under the spur of a lower real wage-rate achieved through a lower money wage-rate may be divided into an income effect and a distribution effect. The distribution effect is clearly to raise the marginal propensity to save by throwing real income to the higher income classes and thus increasing inequality. The income effects are uncertain.

The decrease in capital stock and increase in employment which accompanies the substitution may result in a total real income in goods and services per Week which is (*a*) equal, (*b*) more, or (*c*) less than with stock *OM* and employment $N_{q'}$. If income is equal to, or more than, income at stock *OM* and employment $N_{q'}$, distribution effects will tend to make $S > I$ and no solution can be reached under the conditions of the Fundamental Model for the system of the shifting equilibrium. If dis-investment of capital is carried to the point where real income is lowered, it must be lowered enough to make the effects of the fall in income exactly absorb the effects of the greater inequality in distribution.

Nevertheless, this situation will not give a new equilibrium. Capital is created also by labour. The dis-investment of capital will throw the marginal returns on capital instruments over the rate *Om*, the lower real wage-rate in itself being a factor in the situation lowering costs of production for capital instruments as well as for direct output. Labour will be used for the production of capital goods again until there is no difference at the margin between the rewards for applying labour directly and indirectly. If, as real income increases with the increase in capital, some of the real income increases do not fall to wage-workers, distribution effects again will disrupt temporary equilibrium.

It does not appear therefore that any other wage-rate than $OW_{q'}$ will give a definitive equilibrium under the conditions given. If entrepreneurs do not realize this, the system is subject to error and may wander back and forth between investment and dis-investment, with the real wage-rate varying between the limits given. We have, however, exhausted the capacities of the Fundamental Model, which cannot afford us information respecting such a situation. We shall gain more information regarding the probable behaviour of employment, real wage-rates, interest-rates, and prices, if we leave this Model and go over to the conditions of the First Supplementary Model.

(3) EMPLOYMENT, REAL WAGES, AND THE SHIFTING EQUILIBRIUM

The First Supplementary Model and the Nature of Entrepreneur Errors. We shall still be dealing with the conditions implied in Figure XXVI and shall follow through certain processes of change connected with it in a world of imperfect foresight built upon the plan of the First Supplementary Model. In the course of that inquiry we shall come to much closer terms with the nature of that Model than we have hitherto done. In addition we shall assume within the Model the degree of separation between the retail and other markets and the time-lags in the movements of prices which are customarily present in the real world.

Since we are working from the conditions of Figure XXVI, we assume that the quantity of capital to start with is OM and that the interest-rate is at its institutional minimum of Om. We also assume to simplify exposition that the quantity of money measured in money-units is a datum. These assumptions mean that if entrepreneurs were to offer employment $N_{q'}$ at real wage-rate $OW_{q'}$ with no expectations present of changes in prices, money wages, or interest-rates, the situation would be stable. $S = I = 0$ as long as changes in tastes or technical knowledge, autonomous changes in the physical supplies of factors, changes in population factors, or changes in the aversion to work do not upset the conditions for equilibrium.

Our first inquiry leads us to ask what types of error can occur in the Model and how these conditions may affect the equilibrium relationship. Investigation will show that there will be four basic types of error with two cases to be listed under each:

I. Employment is at the equilibrium level ($N_{q'}$) but the real wage-rate is (1) more or (2) less than the equilibrium rate ($OW_{q'}$).

II. The real wage-rate is at the equilibrium level ($OW_{q'}$) but employment is (1) more or (2) less than $N_{q'}$.

III. Employment is greater than $N_{q'}$ and the real wage-rate is (1) more or (2) less than $OW_{q'}$.

IV. Employment is less than $N_{q'}$ and the real wage-rate is (1) more or (2) less than $OW_{q'}$.

Inspection of the relationships above will show that in cases I (1), II (1), and III (1), there is an apparent condition where marginal costs exceed marginal revenues if we reason that under the influence of the principle of diminishing returns, the marginal product of labour will have a value equal to $OW_{q'}$ for each labour-unit expended when employment is $N_{q'}$, and for all levels of employment beyond that will have a lower marginal product. By similar reasoning there is an appearance in cases I (2) and II(2) that marginal costs will be less than marginal revenues and that in cases III (2) and IV (1) and (2) the effects cannot be generalized because there are offsetting influences present.

These appearances rest upon the possibility of hoards of liquid capital in the system which may be subjected to dis-investment or further investment and upon the degree of separation between the wage-goods (retail) market, and the tendency for pricing in the latter market to exhibit lags with the wholesale and other production markets. It will be shown by analysis that we should fall into errors in reasoning if we should think that the appearance that marginal costs are exceeding marginal revenues which is present in type cases I (1), II (1), and III (1) above means necessarily that there are influences present tending toward immediate contraction of output, as is the ordinary reasoning with respect to the individual business enterprise showing such an inequality.

In order to investigate the sequences of error under the technical apparatus we have developed in the past twelve chapters, we shall cut in on the First Supplementary Model under an assumption that entrepreneurs on Monday make an error of type I (1) in making contracts with the factors of production. We shall not inquire as to the circumstances which lead to the error here. We must start somewhere and we shall find as we go on that the course of errors appears to lead nowhere to a clear-cut establishment of an equilibrium position even in the simple case laid down here.

If with employment $N_{q'}$ wage-workers take the money given them on Monday by entrepreneurs into the retail market on Tuesday and are able there to buy wage-goods (in Professor Pigou's phrase, meaning types of goods that wage-workers buy) on terms which make their *real* wages exceed those that entrepreneurs thought they were handing to them on Monday, there will be two possible types of adjustment to this situation. The first adjustment is that entrepreneurs in manufacturing and wholesaling should *raise the prices of wage-goods* furnished to entrepreneurs in the retail market until the demand for these goods comes into equilibrium with the marginal costs of production, that is, until wage-workers can get in the market a real wage equal to the current value of the marginal product. If that could be done at one sudden *coup* under conditions where there were no further expectations of price rises, the equilibrium levels of employment and wage-rates would be established.

The second type of adjustment would be that *money wages would be lowered* and prices left as they were. In view of the price-mindedness of entrepreneurs and the money-mindedness of workers, we are going to say that in the present case, the adjustment is made by price rises rather than by cuts in money wages. Since the original error will have resulted in a dis-investment in liquid capital hoards, it will influence entrepreneurs optimistically. It will be interpreted as meaning that the demand for wage-goods is getting "stronger."

Since individual entrepreneurs really do not know very much about the general situation, it is unlikely that the price adjustments will be made by a sudden *coup*. Rather where the errors are of the type I (1), entrepreneurs in the retail market will tend to make gradual price adjustments, experimenting to see how much demand has increased and how much of a price rise in the various lines will give the relationship between price and quantity sold which will be most advantageous from the retailers' point of view.

But a gradual adjustment is likely to affect the psychological-institutional complex in a world of imperfect foresight and in so doing it will affect the functional forms of the shifting equilibrium. Entrepreneurs, aware as individuals only of their own immediate situations, may extrapolate this price rise and the expectation may become a part of the situation determining the functions of the shifting equilibrium in a way which will throw them farther from the position which the situation may from a standpoint closer to the underlying economic realities be able to fulfil. The Liquidity Functions attached to definite levels of activity will fall; the Investment Functions will rise. Some avenues of investment now *promise* to pay more than the rate *Om*, part of the expected yields coming from expectations of price rises. There will be an investment in these and a tendency for expansion in the consumption-goods industries under the Multiplier influence.

Under these conditions we may expect employment to increase beyond the equilibrium level $N_{q'}$ and the system will be thrown from the error of type I (1) to that of type III. In the first instance the enlarging of the wages-bill resulting from investment activities may be paralleled by dis-investment of hoards of liquid capital on a scale and at prices which leave real wage-rates still higher than the equilibrium level. But as the price adjustment catches up, the errors will be those of type III (2).

If the error is of type III (2), it is possible that the effects of the excess employment are counterbalanced by the lower real wage. Under these conditions entrepreneur incomes take on the appearance of being maximized. But here action of the interest-rate will bring disequilibrium again. The rise of the Investment Functions and the fall of the Liquidity Functions had been based upon an expectation developed by the period of rising prices that certain new investments would in fact pay more than the institutional minimum rate *Om*. Sooner or later the increase of these investment goods will culminate in an increase in the quantity of consumption goods placed on the market. When that happens the price rises will decelerate and then level off with the slackening of investment activity, and finally there will be a fall in employment as it becomes evident that the new investments (or some portions of the old ones) are not likely to pay as high even as the rate *Om*.

The fall in employment will tend to cause or to accelerate a price fall in the wage-goods market which will tend to raise the real wage-rate toward the equilibrium rate. Both employment and the wage-rate will be moving toward the equilibrium levels therefore but there will be at least three influences tending to carry the system past the equilibrium relationship of employment, wage-rate, and interest-rates:

(1) By the period of positive investment the quantum of capital has been carried beyond *OM*, or the equilibrium amount for rate *Om*.

(2) During the period of price falls, entrepreneurs may grow to expect further price falls and the L_2 function may rise carrying the L functions up, while the Investment Functions will fall. Employment will tend to be thrown below $N_{q'}$.

(3) If money wage-cuts accompany the price-cuts (as is likely) another element of instability enters, namely entrepreneurs who would otherwise be planning the expenditure of maintenance or replacement funds may find that it looks profitable to postpone expenditures until money wages have fallen further. The quantity of capital will fall not only back to *OM* but below it.

Under these influences, the general situation may pass over from error of type III (2) to type IV (1). This implies again that the real wage-rate is receiving support from the liquidation of stores of liquid capital. That is to say, under these circumstances, entrepreneurs with stores of liquid capital may be attempting to sell them before prices fall farther or may be forced to sell them in "distress" sales. But as the liquidation of inventories comes to an end, real wage-rates will fall. An error of type II (2) may appear but there is no reason inherent in the situation for the wage-rate to stop at the equilibrium level. The situation is likely to carry over into error of type IV (2).

Here again effects on entrepreneur action appear uncertain. If the effects of lower real wage-rates exactly balance the effects of a smaller level of employment, entrepreneurs may feel that since current marginal costs appear equal to the value of the product in the market, the situation is stable.

Once again the interest-rate comes in to change this situation. The period of dis-investment will have brought the marginal productivity of remaining instruments over the level where it agrees with the rate *Om* under conditions of stable (or rising) prices. As the price falls and wage falls level off, this condition becomes apparent. The Liquidity Functions will fall and the Investment Functions will rise. Re-investment begins. If we could jump straight to the equilibrium levels, all might be well. But it is likely that the level of employment $N_{q'}$ may be reached with an error of the type I (2) if expansion of the consumption-goods industries lags behind expansion of the investment industries, waiting for the effects of prices transmitted through the retail market. Under such conditions there will be elements of expansion in the system tending to carry it over into errors of type III (2) and then III (1), as the expansion of consumption goods from the newly produced investment goods begins to flow into the market. But as the newly produced goods begin to flow into the market, the price rise will slacken off, the new investments will prove again to be too optimistically undertaken, and the system is ready for another downward spin.

Many different sequences of error may occur and it is hard to see, once the sequence of error has started, any reason why the equilibrium levels should ever be established. It is to be noted too that the cyclical movements have been supported without an expansion of the supply of money, by transfers to and from the L_2 deposits. It is perhaps advisable at this point to consider the relation of the quantity of money to the process analysed.

The Elasticity of the Supply of Money, the Interest-Rate Structure, and Investment Activity. If the stock of money is a datum, in the rising phases of the cyclical process, the short rates may be driven above *Om* by competition for the available stock. If there is an expectation that *Om* is a "normal" rate, this rise will communicate itself only to a degree determined by the advantages of substitution over time to the longer rates. The r' rates will lie below i_0 and the expected r' rates will be lower than current r' rates in accordance with futurity and the nature of interest-expectations. Such a state of affairs will strengthen the long-term market for investments against the short-term market. In the short-term market, investments of short duration must promise to make returns high enough to cover higher rates and there will be no chances of capital appreciation to give them higher liquidity. To the extent that the situation puts a premium upon long-term investments which are too optimistically undertaken, the problems are probably made more serious, since the dislocations will take longer to liquidate when opinion as to their profitability changes. It is to be noticed, however, that the effects upon long-term investment may be relative only, when the short rates are higher than the long rates. The strength of price-expectations may favour the short-term investments rather than the long-term ones, because of the size of correction coefficients on the *a* series as futurity grows.

In the case under consideration, during the falling phases, changes in interest structures will not have much importance, owing to the importance of the rate *Om* in the interest-rate structure. The fall of interest-rates will have some effect as a cushion against the fall in values of equities and debts from rising correction coefficients and falling *a* series. If the situation *does* arise where the short rates are lower than the long rates, the rate structure will favour short-term investments and longer-term investments will have a drag against them in the form of a probability of a depreciation of capital values. Even when all the rates are back to the *Om* level such a condition may colour the psychology of the investment market. Since at rate *Om* the "only way to go is up," the very nature of interest-uncertainties will tend to make long rates somewhat higher than short rates and lead the market to *act* as though there were an expectation of rising rates. The more pessimistic the current outlook the greater the drag such a state of interest-expectations will exert upon investment activity.

If the monetary authorities make the money-supply perfectly elastic at rate *Om* and it becomes a matter of expectation that they will continue to do so, there seems to be no reason for changes in the interest structure which will complicate the distribution of investment activity over different durations. But if the monetary authorities operate with unequal efficiency in different markets, changes in the interest structure may enter in accordance with the institutional arrangements for making advances in the various markets, with consequences analogous to those already described.

The Money Wage-Rate. This analysis of the First Supplementary Model has been developed in terms of an initial situation where there was a quantum of unemployment at the long-period equilibrium level for the system. We have also implied some lack of flexibility in the money wage-rate due to "money-mindedness" on the part of wage-workers who will oppose decreases in money-wages with some fierceness though they will within limits acquiesce in decreases in the real wage-rate operating through the price system. It is to be inferred, therefore, that during the process we have outlined, money-cuts in wage-rates will be made during the falling phase of activity when money-mindedness decreases under the threat of unemployment and that increases in money wage-rates may be made during the rising phase of activity in spite of existing unemployment because of money-mindedness on the part of employees and the lesser fierceness of entrepreneurs in opposing rises in money wage-rates when they are correlated with price rises. It is to be added, however, that if the quantum of unemployment is very great even in the rising phase, increases in money wages during the rising phase of the cycle may not equal the decreases during the preceding falling phase and in such a case we might have a long wave or downward trend of wages and prices over several cycles.

But we are still left with a system which alternates between investment periods and dis-investment periods, and we must give some consideration to the possibility of cyclical fluctuations of the same type in systems characterized on the whole by continuous investment activity.

Variations in Employment in a System Characterized by Continuous Investment. We return here to a system similar to that typified by Figure XXV. That is to say, there is no inflexibility of the interest-rate structure as such to prevent the system from reaching the level of full employment, and no obstacles against maintaining that level of employment if expectations can be "correct." If such a system is one in which population, tastes, aversion to work, and techniques are stable, this will mean that the short rates of the system will be above the longer rates in accordance with the fall in the size of the marginal product of capital during the life of the equities in question. If the expected falls are very small, the different "pure" rates of interest may be substantially identical with each other. Since correction coefficients under such a stable situation would be at a minimum, this will mean that the *r* rates or market yields will be substantially identical with the "pure" rates too. So far as the long rates *are* under the short rates the factor is one to give buoyancy to the system, since falls in long-term rates will be expected which will tend toward capital appreciation so far as market values are concerned. Such an expectation of capital appreciation serves as an offset to the action of the remaining correction coefficients.

If, on the other hand, there are factors in the situation leading to an expectation of a rise in the marginal productivity of capital, owing, let us say, to population increases, the long rates of the equilibrium structure of rates will be above the short rates and the long rates of interest will be expected to rise. Under such a state of expectations, the structure of the interest-rates may again be a healthy element of the economy, for it will prevent too explosive a readjustment to the expected changes.

If we take this system over into the conditions of the First Supplementary Model and admit the possibility of errors in foresight, we have first to inquire what types of error are possible. It would appear that the same basic types of error are likely as were listed for Figure XXVI but that errors in which the level of employment runs beyond the equilibrium level are likely to be unimportant if not non-existent. They can only occur where the money-mindedness of wage-workers obscures for them for a time the fact that the relations of prices in the wage-goods market to money wages have thrown the real wage-rate outside the one for which marginal units of labour would stipulate under the conditions. In the negative sector of the supply function, this means that the wage-rate is so *high* that employment would be reduced if it were not for money-mindedness.

The great difference between this situation and the one already analysed is that whereas in the former one the economy revolved substantially about *one* interest-rate, namely *Om*, in this case if the complex of interest-rates to be associated with full employment and "correct" expectations is significantly above the minimum rate *Om*, changes in the structure of the interest-rates themselves enter as important de-stabilizing factors. Short rates may vary between *Om* and the highest rate which will be accepted by borrowers under the demand conditions which apply. The long rates, on the other hand, for reasons which have been presented in the foregoing analysis, will tend to vary over a much narrower range. The de-stabilizing effect comes from the fact that when there are errors of pessimism present, the margins of substitution for the system and the nature of interest-expectations, together with the increasing subtractions from valuation series for risk, uncertainty, and illiquidity, will ordinarily act in such a way as to push down the margins of substitution for the system until the "pure" short rates lie below the "pure" long rates. Under the analysis we have presented, this will mean general sluggishness in the system. Fear for future declines in the values of equities from loss of capitalized values resulting from rises in capitalization rates will tend to hold investment even lower than it would otherwise be under the low levels for the Investment Functions which characterize such a period. Even if the "pure" long rates *are* pushed down to practical equality with the short rates, as long as the character of interest uncertainties is such as to favour upward rather than downward movements of the long rates, this influence will be present. The difficulty is increased during the down-swing by the fact that the i_0 interest-rate may relatively soon be pushed to the place where it is *Om*, or the minimum institutional rate. As long as the current interest-rate lies at *Om*, the reward for initiating investment activity this Week rather than some future Week is too insignificant to tempt money from the L_2 balances. Progress of long-term investments initiated in previous Weeks may give some support to investment activity.

In the opposite condition where errors of optimism are present, operation of the multiple margins of substitution will be such as to tend to push the short rates over the long rates. Under such conditions, hopes of appreciation in capitalized values will stimulate investments of the speculative type. So far as these expectations are erroneous, this condition will leave behind a train of ill-conceived investments whose additions to the volume of consumers' goods may impair the profitability of investments otherwise healthily undertaken. The discovery and necessity for liquidation of such errors may be the prime movers in turning the psychology of the community from errors of optimism to errors of pessimism.

The establishment of equilibrium requires that the real wage-rate, the level of employment, and the interest-rate structure should all be those consistent with full employment. Once we introduce error under conditions such as those of the First Supplementary Model, there seems to be no more reason to expect any inherent tendency which will bring all the variables of the situation to their equilibrium magnitudes *at the same time* than was present in the case of an economy showing inflexibility of the interest-rate of the type analysed in connection with Figure XXVI. In the case we are analysing in connection with Figure XXV, the *average* level of employment may be higher, *ceteris paribus*, because there is no real reason for chronic unemployment, but the range of unemployment may be greater because the greater variability of the interest-rate complex and the fact that interest-expectations make changes in the complex of interest-rates de-stabilizing provide the basis for such a width of variation.

Intelligent intervention by the monetary authorities may be used to keep the interest-rate structure from changing in ways which are de-stabilizing to the economy, but the authorities themselves may be unequal under dynamic conditions to the task of deciding just what the interest-rate structure *ought* to be. The ideal levels are those which would characterize the equilibrium situation, but who is to know what these are?

The First and Second Supplementary Models and the Real World. We have followed the foregoing analysis through in terms of the First Supplementary Model. If we followed the same problems through under the conditions of the Second Supplementary Model, we should be likely to find less instability. Since in the Second Supplementary Model, entrepreneurs take orders for goods before they hire the factors to produce them, the lags in the Model are of a type which will tend to eliminate the effects of separation of the wage-goods from other markets. So far as the real world shows the conditions of the Second Supplementary Model or the Fundamental Model, the hope for achieving the combinations of real wage-rates, interest-structures, and price systems which are consistent with full employment or with a lower level of unemployment may be higher. But the description of the First Supplementary Model as given appears to bear a remarkable resemblance to the description of the world in which we live.

CHAPTER XIV

IMPLICATIONS

THIS concluding chapter is of the nature of an epilogue. We set down here very briefly some of the implications to be drawn from the foregoing analysis, disregarding for the most part specific institutional elements.

The first implication of a study of economic theory of the character of the analysis behind us is that there are value judgments and value systems outside economic value systems as such which may prescribe ends to which the economic value systems may be asked, within the limits of possibility, to conform. The *mores* of a community may, for example, refuse to tolerate a condition of chronic unemployment or may object to the degree of inequality in the distribution of real income which the free play of economic forces within the existing institutional framework brings about. If such a community is also one whose *mores* call for maximum freedom for the human personality under the hereditary institutions of liberalism, the problem for the economic theorist is the reconciliation of these various ends.

From the analysis which has been presented in this study, certain inferences may at least tentatively be drawn to assist in this reconciliation. The first is that the structure of the interest-rate complex may be just as important in establishing and maintaining an equilibrium level of employment as the average level of interest-rates. The second is that very low rates of interest as well as very high rates may be damaging to the level of economic activity. The third is that lack of foresight and the variable nature of human psychology and expectations may keep an imperfectly monetized economic system running from low levels of employment to levels more or less high with no inherent tendency to reach the combination of values which gives a stable equilibrium. The fourth is that business cycles may occur even though the quantity of money is a datum because of transfers of money between active and inactive balances. The fifth and last is that the nature of a monetary economy is such that unemployment may be chronic. A corollary of the last three is the theory that both the average levels of interest-rates and the internal arrangements of the structure of rates are the outcome of substitution over a number of margins of substitution of which the substitution of money for other forms of holdings is only one.

The general division of interventionary policies suggested here will be among those which seek to manage the levels of economic activity by manipulating the interest-rate complex through the quantity of money, those that attempt to provide support for the functions of the shifting equilibrium through policies which stabilize the state of expectations, and those which attempt to bring the system nearer to the ends prescribed by the community as good by manipulating the institutional framework to change the shapes and positions of the functions.

With respect to monetary management, the reasoning of the analysis is that the capacity of the monetary authorities for effective management of the level of economic activity lies for the most part within the range of interest-rates which are considered "normal." Only if these "normal" rates are outside the complex of rates at which full employment is possible for the system is it likely that monetary management should attempt to drive the rates of interest outside the normal range. Reasons for this may be briefly reviewed again here.

Control of inflation by rising short-term rates may "feed the fire" if the controls are applied after the inflationary condition has been allowed to start. Owing to the character of interest-expectations, it is possible that rises of the short-term rate, unless they are undertaken on a scale which affects price-expectations, may support speculative activity in the long-term market by creating expectations of rises in the capitalized values of securities based on the probability of falls to come in the longer-term rates of interest. On the other hand, because of the strength and inelasticity of interest-expectations and the separation of the market for industrial bonds from the market for government bonds, it may be a difficult matter for the monetary authorities to operate with equal efficiency in the long-term and short-term markets at the same time. Moreover, if the inflationary condition is allowed to start on its way, control through a drastic rise in short-term rates may cause a collapse of the functional relationships of the shifting equilibrium which will set the system of economic relationships racing in the other direction. Yet the influence of price-minded entrepreneurs and money-minded wage-groups upon political institutions and the general limitations of human foresight may make the proper control of incipient inflation in ordinary times practically impossible.

At the other end of the range of cyclical fluctuations, the effort to control depressions by forcing the complex of rates downward, if it pushes the short rates below the long rates, may result in sluggishness and chronic depression because entrepreneurs contemplating investment will be faced by threatened falls in the capital values of equities through possible rises of interest-rates. As we have seen, if interest-rates are very low, the expectation of an extraordinarily small rise in longer-term rates may be sufficient entirely to destroy the running yield.

If the monetary authorities seek to control either a cyclical or a secular condition of unemployment by driving the whole complex of interest-rates to levels near the institutional minimum on the rate of interest in a monetary economy, the situation is not likely to be saved from sluggishness by the fact that the "pure" long rates are very close to the "pure" short rates. Since "the only way to go is up" the very character of interest-uncertainties will make the market act as though there were a net expectation of rising rates.

If the authorities attempt to unite stabilization of expectations with a more conservative monetary policy as methods of controlling cyclical unemployment, the methods indicated are public works programmes, various types of social insurance, manipulation through the tax system, or widening of the area of public goods. The implication here is that these programmes should be managed in such a way that effects of public action on the Multiplier and Investment Functions are not offset to a significant degree by declines of private investment and diversions of private funds to the inactive bank deposits, originating in pessimism among entrepreneurs caused by unbalanced budgets and prospects of rising taxes.

If unemployment is of the secular type and existing institutions would make equilibrium rates of interest lower than are practical for a monetary economy, the implication of the analysis is that the situation may be modified by a redistribution of income through the tax system, insurance and pension policies, or through some other modification of the institutional framework. The problem for the economic theorist here is to find a way which can afford support to the Multiplier Functions without creating offsetting effects through the Liquidity and Investment Functions.

An alternative to the means suggested for the control of the level of investment is the passing over of large-scale investment completely into the hands of the state and the restriction of private investment to fields in which variation is limited, or relatively insignificant in the determination of the levels of employment and output. Judgments with respect to the desirability of such changes in the institutional framework belong to the broader value systems rather than to economic value systems as such. But the economist must have it on his conscience to see to it that in prescribing palliatives or cures directed to more limited ends he does not bring about changes in the institutional framework which the political community would not approve if the change were to be proposed by direct methods.

For both cyclical and secular maladjustment the analysis suggests that the spreading of information about business conditions and the elimination of time-lags are in the interest of a higher level of employment and output. That is to say, the more the economy can be brought from conditions like those described in the First Supplementary Model toward those of the Second Supplementary and Fundamental Models, the more the problem of controlling the range of variations of employment may be eased.

If it be given that the character of population and other changes leave the underlying conditions such that the establishment of full employment at real wage-rates recognized as socially desirable is possible under the existing framework of institutions, the paramount problem for the managing authority is the establishment of a complex of interest-rates which is neither higher nor lower than, nor different in internal relationships of long and short rates from, the structure to be allied with equilibrium conditions. Because of the lack of human foresight, the only way to reach such an end would appear to be by a policy of trial and error, directed in the first instance to diminishing the range of fluctuations in the levels of output and employment and to bringing them down to those prescribed as socially tolerable.

INDEX

D

E

M

Q

R

S

V

W

Z

www.ingramcontent.com/pod-product-compliance
Lightning Source LLC
LaVergne TN
LVHW100310210926
848480LV00003B/1078